SECOND EDITION

Interpersonal Process in Psychotherapy

A GUIDE FOR CLINICAL TRAINING

SECOND EDITION

Interpersonal Process in Psychotherapy

A GUIDE FOR CLINICAL TRAINING

Edward Teyber

CALIFORNIA STATE UNIVERSITY, SAN BERNARDINO

BROOKS/COLE PUBLISHING COMPANY
PACIFIC GROVE, CALIFORNIA

Brooks/Cole Publishing Company
A Division of Wadsworth, Inc.

Printed in the United States of America

10 9 8 7 6 5 4 3 2 1

Library of Congress Cataloging-in-Publication Data

Teyber, Edward.
    Interpersonal process in psychotherapy : a guide for clinical training / Edward Teyber.—2nd ed.
    p. cm.
    Includes bibliographical references and indexes.
    ISBN 0-534-16920-1
    1. Psychotherapist and patient. 2. Psychotherapy. I. Title.
RC480.8.T38 1991
616.89′14—dc20   91-21952
                                                                              CIP

Sponsoring Editor: Claire Verduin
Editorial Assistant: Gay C. Bond
Production Editor: Ben Greensfelder, Nancy Shammas
Manuscript Editor: Evelyn Mercer Ward
Interior Design: Lisa Berman
Cover Design: Vernon T. Boes
Art Coordinator: Cloyce Wall
Typesetting: Shepard Poorman Communications Corp.
Cover Printing: Lehigh Press Lithographers/Autoscreen
Printing and Binding: Arcata Graphics/Fairfield

Dedicated to those

who are struggling

to change.

ABOUT THE AUTHOR

Edward Teyber, Ph.D., a clinical psychologist, is Professor of Psychology and Director of the Community Counseling Center at California State University, San Bernardino. He is also the author of *Children and Divorce: A Practical Guide for Parents*. He has published numerous research articles on the effects of marital and family relations on child adjustment, and he regularly contributes articles on parenting and postdivorce family relations to newspapers and magazines. Dr. Teyber is also in private practice.

PREFACE

The relationship between therapist and client is the foundation of all counseling theories and is the key to client change. However, specific guidelines for understanding and using the therapeutic relationship are seldom provided, leaving therapists in training uncertain as to how to proceed with their clients. The purpose of this text is to teach beginning therapists how to conceptualize what is occurring between the therapist and the client and how to use this understanding of the therapeutic process dimension to guide their interventions. This book is intended as an applied clinical text for practicum, internship, field placement, and other direct service courses in which graduate students are seeing clients and receiving supervision.

In preparation for actual clinical work, graduate students take courses on counseling theories, interpersonal skills, and introductory counseling methods. Although this preparation is useful, it is too general to provide students who are seeing clients, the in-depth understanding needed for such clinical practice. Fully cognizant of their limited experience and knowledge, practicum students are often painfully aware that they do not really know what to do or how to help their clients. Many feel inadequate and are afraid of "making mistakes" and doing something wrong that would "hurt" their clients. As a result, beginning therapists are eager for practical instruction that will provide specific guidelines for helping them understand and respond to their clients' problems. This text meets this need, replacing the nebulous ideas students often have about treatment with a well-developed framework for the change process and the role of the therapist-client relationship in that process. The following section highlights the specific features of the text.

FEATURES OF THE TEXT

It is difficult for clinical instructors to find readings that effectively demonstrate how theory guides clinical practice. The principal strength of this book is that it provides a well-developed theoretical framework for understanding clients' problems as well as specific intervention guidelines that are conceptually based. In Chapter 1, for example, the interpersonal process approach is firmly based in a theoretical context. Clearly articulated interventions, with specific "how to's" for beginning therapists, are then programmatically developed in each successive chapter. In this way, the text enables trainees to bridge the gap between client conceptualization and direct therapeutic interventions.

Therapists in training need concrete examples of how broad therapeutic principles apply with clients, as well as case studies that specifically illustrate how theory guides clinical practice. This text meets this need by providing therapist-client dialogues, clinical vignettes, and extended case studies in each chapter. These illustrations reveal the real experiences of practicing therapists. The authenticity of these illustrations, which link theory to practice, make the clinical process "come alive" for beginning therapists.

Beginning therapists bring a great deal of enthusiasm to their clinical training, and their initial work with clients is often one of the most important experiences of their lives. This text strongly emphasizes a student/learner perspective, capturing the intensity of the subjective experience of becoming a therapist and articulating the questions, concerns, and aspirations of beginning therapists. Case examples throughout the text capture the complexities of clinical training, as, for example, in the case example in Chapter 5 in which a practicum student is told to manage her case in two different ways by her practicum instructor and her supervisor. The student, a child of embattled divorced parents who was always trying to please "both sides," was temporarily immobilized in working with her client by this conflict. Students will resonate to these and other issues presented and will learn how to manage such real-life dilemmas. Understanding the process dimension and how the therapist-client relationship can be a vehicle for change requires an understanding of how the therapist participates in the relationship. To this point, this text examines how the therapist's own personality, developmental history, and current life situation are key elements in the therapeutic relationship and how they influence the course of treatment.

The text has ten chapters and is organized into four parts: (1) theoretical context and basic premises of the interpersonal process approach, (2) responding to clients' concerns, (3) conceptualizing client dynamics, and (4) resolving problems. Rather than being composed of discrete chapters on free-standing topics, the text has been organized so that each successive chapter progressively builds on the preceding chapters and leads directly to the clinical issues in the next chapter. This structure creates an integrated, unbroken progression that helps beginning therapists experience the natural course and development of therapeutic relationships. In line with this, the text has been organized to parallel the course of treatment from initial client contact to termination. Further continuity is provided by a focus on the process characteristics of the therapist-client relationship throughout, which is also related to therapeutic goals and intervention strategies at each successive stage of treatment.

In sum, this text helps beginning therapists conceptualize what is occurring in their real-life relationships with clients and use this understanding of the therapeutic process to guide their clinical interventions. It teaches trainees how to use themselves and the relationships they provide their clients to help clients change.

CHANGES IN THE SECOND EDITION

The purpose of the second edition was to elaborate and clarify the interpersonal process approach, not to change the basic message of the first edition. Although the second edition has been expanded in length by one-third, care has been taken to preserve the original thrust of the successful conceptual approach and organizational structure of the first edition. However, in expanding and refining the text, many significant changes have occurred, several of which are discussed below.

One of the principal strengths of the first edition was the clarity and immediacy of its approach to the actual clinical process, and the revision has built on this approach. In every chapter, new case examples, clinical vignettes, and therapist-client dialogues have been added that further illustrate the interpersonal process approach.

The text provides clinical trainees with a theoretical framework for understanding clients' problems and with specific conceptually based intervention guidelines. Because the practice component was stronger than the theory component in the first edition, the conceptual basis for the interpersonal process approach has been expanded in this revision. New discussions of interpersonal and family systems theories are provided in Chapter 1 and elaborated throughout the text. This text has been unique in integrating family systems theory with the practice of individual therapy, and this integration has been further developed in this second edition. A great deal of new information on structual family relationships, family-of-origin work, intergenerational family relations, and other family systems concepts has been added. Finally, object relations theory and attachment literature have been integrated into the second edition.

The strong student/learner emphasis of the first edition has been expanded in this revision. The second edition further addresses the complexities and ambiguities of becoming a therapist and highlights pivotal points in the therapeutic process that can be problematic or anxiety arousing for beginning therapists. For example, many trainees struggle to use process comments and make overt how the client's conflicts are expressed in the therapeutic relationship (for example, Therapist: "Does the control battle you have been describing with your wife go on between us? Where do you see the control issue in our relationship?"). Although most beginning therapists readily see how powerful it is when the therapist can address and resolve the client's conflicts in their real-life relationship, responding in these direct ways is often threatening. Guidelines are provided to help trainees learn to recognize and feel comfortable using the process dimension in interventions within the therapeutic relationship.

Finally, the second edition includes sections on working with client diversity, applying the process model to short-term therapy, and showing how therapists of differing theoretical orientations can adapt this model to their own work. Many of these changes were facilitated by helpful comments from four Brooks/Cole reviewers: Nancy Abramson, University of Minnesota; Dr. Betty Campbell, Texas Woman's University; Dr. Neal King, Sonoma State University; Dr. Helen Moore, James Madison University. I would especially like to thank my wife, Dr. Kathy Pezdek, and my friends, Dr. Sam Plyler and Dr. Keith Valone, for their continuing support and substantial contributions to the second edition.

Edward Teyber

CONTENTS

CHAPTER THREE

HONORING THE CLIENT'S RESISTANCE   45

CHAPTER FOUR

AN INTERNAL FOCUS FOR CHANGE   68

CHAPTER FIVE
RESPONDING TO CONFLICTED EMOTIONS   89

PART THREE
CONCEPTUALIZING CLIENT DYNAMICS   121

CHAPTER SIX
FAMILIAL AND DEVELOPMENTAL FACTORS   123

CHAPTER SEVEN

A MODEL FOR CONCEPTUALIZING CLIENT DYNAMICS 148

CHAPTER EIGHT

CURRENT INTERPERSONAL FACTORS 166

PART FOUR

RESOLUTION AND CHANGE　　197

CHAPTER NINE

AN INTERPERSONAL SOLUTION 199

CHAPTER TEN

WORKING THROUGH AND TERMINATION 229

PART ONE

AN INTERPERSONAL PROCESS APPROACH

CHAPTER ONE

INTRODUCTION AND OVERVIEW

INTRODUCTION AND OVERVIEW

P aul is a first-year practicum student about to see his first client. He has long and eagerly awaited this event. Like many of his classmates, Paul decided to become a therapist while working on his undergraduate degree. Psychotherapy was always intrinsically interesting to him, which is why this career choice held so much promise. Being a therapist meant far more than just a "good job" for Paul; it was the fulfillment of a dream. How exciting, he thought, to make a living by talking to people about the most important concerns in their lives. The potential for such meaningful human involvement filled Paul with anticipation as he began his clinical training.

At this moment, though, Paul felt the real test was at hand: his first client would be arriving in a few minutes. Worries raced through his mind: What will we do for fifty minutes? How should I start? What if she doesn't show up? What if she doesn't come back next time? Needless to say, it was extremely important to Paul that he find a way to help this client with her problems. He had learned something about therapy in his undergraduate psychology classes, and a good deal more from his volunteer experience with callers on the local crisis hotline. But even with these experiences and a supervisor to guide him, Paul was painfully aware of his novice status and of the fact that he didn't know very much about actually doing therapy.

Although some of Paul's classmates thought he was a little too idealistic, they did share his excitement about becoming a therapist. Many of them were older than Paul and far more experienced in life. Some had raised children; others had already had careers as teachers, nurses, and businesspeople. For these more seasoned classmates as well, a counseling career held new hopes. With the successive steps of completing undergraduate requirements, being accepted into a graduate program, and now starting their first practicum, their goals were becoming reality. Like Paul, however, realizing their dreams of new and rewarding careers also depended on their ability to help others. And the test of that ability, or so it seemed, was about to be met with the arrival of their first clients.

THE NEED FOR A CONCEPTUAL FRAMEWORK

Beginning therapists' anxieties about their ability to help are not necessarily neurotic insecurity or obsessive worrying. It is realistic to be concerned about one's performance in a new, complex, and ambiguous arena. Paul and his classmates, however, like most students who enter graduate training in clinical work, already bring many strengths to their new profession. Most students who are selected for clinical training already possess sensitivity, intelligence, and a genuine concern for others. Such personal assets, as well as their own life experiences, will prove enormously helpful to their future clients.

Although personal experience, common sense, and intuition are useful, they alone do not prepare one to negotiate an affect-laden therapeutic relationship. In order for a therapist to be effective with a wide range of people and problems, these valuable human qualities must be wed to a conceptual framework. Therapists must understand very specifically what they are trying to do in therapy—where they are going and why—in order to be consistently helpful to clients. Every therapist needs a conceptual framework as a guide, and this is especially true for the beginning therapist. Without this framework, decisions about intervention strategies and case management are too arbitrary to be trustworthy, and the therapist's confidence in the therapeutic enterprise lessens as a result.

Many therapists become exceedingly anxious in their early counseling work because of their conceptual uncertainty. Ambiguity over how to conceptualize client problems and proceed in the therapy session heightens their insecurity and preoccupation with their counseling performance. These performance anxieties arise because their strong needs to be helpful clash with ambiguous guidelines for how to proceed. When this occurs, the inherent abilities of novice counselors to help are diminished by their anxieties, and their effectiveness with clients actually declines.

Finally, the lack of a conceptual framework hinders novice therapists as they try to find their own identities as professionals. An important part of seeing oneself as a competent therapist is having a theoretical framework that is applicable across clients yet congruent with one's own values and life experiences. The purpose of this book is to provide one such conceptual framework for understanding the therapist-client relationship and the developmental course of therapy. Students will be able to refine this framework to fit their own personalities and preferred therapeutic styles as they continue to develop professionally.

THE INTERPERSONAL PROCESS APPROACH
Theoretical and Historical Context

The therapeutic model presented here will be referred to as the *interpersonal process approach*. This is not a new theory of psychotherapy but a synthesis of ideas from three clinical theories: interpersonal theory, object relations theory and the attachment literature that has developed from it, and family systems theory. Although focusing on interpersonal, intrapsychic, and intrafamilial domains, these concepts are closely related. This text links these ideas together and applies them to the practice of individual psychotherapy. These theories are introduced here to provide a context for the clinical approach explored later.

Interpersonal Theory. Harry Stack Sullivan (1968) first brought the interpersonal focus to psychotherapy. He remains an enormously influential but insufficiently recognized figure who radically broke with Freud's biologically based libido theory. Sullivan was a maverick and one of the first major theorists to argue that the basic premises of Freud's psychoanalytic drive theory were inaccurate in regard to human motivation, the nature of experience, and clinical technique. Emphasizing instead interpersonal relations and the child's actual experience with parents, Sullivan argued that every major tenet of Freud's theory could be understood better through interpersonal and social processes. Sullivan developed an elaborate developmental theory of psychopathology that emphasized what people do to avoid or manage anxiety in interpersonal relations, viewing anxiety as the central motivating force in human behavior. He described a painful and pervasive core anxiety rooted in dreaded expectations of derogation and rejection by parents and others, and later by oneself. Following from this, Sullivan conceptualized personality as the collection of interpersonal strategies one employs to avoid or minimize anxiety, ward off disapproval, and maintain self-esteem.

According to Sullivan, the child develops this personality, or "self-system," through repetitive interactions with his or her parents. More specifically, the child organizes a self around certain basic relational configurations that characterize important patterns of parent-child interaction. These repetitive interactions with parents, which may be painful or anxiety arousing, are structured into the child's personality through a collection of complementary self-other relational patterns. For example, children may develop internal images of themselves as helpless yet deserving and expectations of parents and others as tyrannical. Alternatively, children may evolve images of themselves as special and expectations of others as admiring.

Based on these self-other relational patterns, people behave in ways that systematically elicit responses from others that avoid or minimize the experience of anxiety. For example, suppose that a particular aspect of the child, such as sadness or crying, consistently results in parental rejection or ridicule. The child learns that these more vulnerable parts of oneself represent a "bad self," and these anxiety-arousing aspects of the self are split off or disowned. The child also develops interpersonal coping styles (for example, a macho manner) that preclude being subjected to anxiety-arousing rejection again. These coping styles, or "security operations," are interpersonal defenses that originally were necessary to protect the self in the early parent-child relationships. Unfortunately, these interpersonal defenses are overgeneralized to other relationships in adulthood and become "characterological" as the child now grown to an adult anticipates that new experiences with others will repeat the relational patterns of the past.

Sullivan developed his rich but sometimes elusive interpersonal theory through his clinical work with schizophrenic patients. He was a gifted therapist and had great respect for the personal dignity of his very disturbed patients. His sensitivity to patients, compassion, and genius for understanding the intricate workings of anxiety inspired a new direction in American psychiatry. Sullivan worked with and influenced Erich Fromm (1982), Karen Horney (1970), Frieda Fromm-Reichmann (1960), and other seminal thinkers in the interpersonal field. Although a single integrated theory was never developed, these theorists shared basic concepts and values and have been variously called neo-Freudians, culturalists, interpersonal theorists, or Sullivanians.

Sullivan has also influenced many other clinical theorists, such as Erik Erikson (1986) and Carl Rogers (1951), and has even prefigured family therapy theory in his study of close relational systems. In fact, two of the founding fathers in the family therapy field, Don Jackson and Murray Bowen, trained under Sullivan. Many of the basic concepts of the interpersonal process approach can be traced back in some form to Sullivan and the other interpersonal theorists.

Object Relations Theory. Since "objects" refers to people or, more precisely, internal representations of them, object relations theory is about interpersonal relationships—especially those between parents and young children. In particular, object relations theorists try to account for the meaning of attachment and the emotional need for relationships with others in the development of a self. Sullivan's theory centers on relationships, but the question that drove his work was very pragmatic: "What do people do to avoid anxiety in interpersonal relations?" In contrast, the question for object relations theorists is more abstract and inferential, namely: "How are early parental relations internalized, and how do these mental schemas provide the structure for developing a sense of self and templates of self-other relational units that shape subsequent relationships?"

Object relations theorists believe that the primary motive of human development is to establish and maintain emotional ties to parental caregivers (object relatedness). The greatest conflicts in life are threats to or disruptions of these basic ties (separation anxieties and abandonment terrors). In this regard, anxiety is a *signal* that emotional ties are being threatened. If parents are dependably available and emotionally responsive to a child's attachment needs, the child is secure in his or her ties. Through the course of development, such children can gradually internalize their parents' availability and come to hold the same constant loving affect toward themselves that their parents originally demonstrated. As these children progress toward maturity, they become increasingly able to comfort and soothe themselves, function for increasingly longer periods without emotional refueling, and effectively elicit support when necessary. "Object constancy" develops as their ability to comfort and nurture themselves becomes the source of their own self-esteem and secure identity as capable, love-worthy persons. Further, they possess the internal objects, or self-other relational templates, necessary to establish new relationships with others who possess this same affirming affective valence.

But what if the child cannot establish and maintain emotional ties to the primary caregivers? In some families, parents are preoccupied, depressed, rejecting, or even abusive. Children of such parents are biologically organized to have attachment longings fulfilled, but they are frustrated by arbitrary or unresponsive parents. These children are trapped in an unsolvable dilemma: they cannot succeed in influencing a reliable response to them from their parents, nor can they escape or forsake their need for attachment. In a word, they feel anguish. What do they do? Object relations theory tries to account for the different solutions and adaptations the child must make to this poignant and all-too-human dilemma.

Object relations theorists propose complex (and competing) developmental theories to account for the intrapsychic and interpersonal mechanisms children employ to protect against the painful separation anxieties aroused when they cannot maintain secure emotional ties. These theorists propose that all children mature through different stages of development that progressively allow for a more integrated, stable view of self and others. However, if development is problematic, children remain "stuck" or regress under stress to less integrated, immature stages of development. In particular, when parents are excessively inconsistent or unresponsive, the child must resort to "splitting defenses" to maintain ties to an idealized loving parent. When this occurs, the child separates and internalizes the "bad" (threatening or rejecting) aspects of the parent from the "good" (loving or responsive) aspects of the parent. In healthier parent-child interactions, the young child can tolerate some frustration and gradually integrate ambivalence into a stable self-other relational unit. Under greater attachment threats, however, the child cannot do this without resorting to splitting defenses. These splitting defenses preserve the necessary image of an idealized "all good," responsive parent with whom the child is internally connected. But the price is high: reality is distorted, the self is fragmented, and the child becomes the one who is "bad." The frustrating parent is no longer "bad," and the external world feels safe; the price, however, is inner conflict: the child believes that if only he or she were different, parental love would be forthcoming. This situation is illustrated most poignantly by the bruised and battered child who nevertheless continues to idealize and defend the abusive parent, maintaining that he or she is bad and deserves the punishment.

Why is this complex and abstract theory relevant to interpersonally oriented therapists? Realizing that the child must find some way to maintain ties with a good, loving parent helps us as therapists understand why clients persist in maladaptive behavior and self-defeating relationships. When clients relinquish symptoms, succeed, or become healthier, they often feel anxious, guilty, or depressed. Loyalty and allegiance to symptoms, and the bad objects they represent, are not maladaptive to insecurely attached children because such loyalty preserves the ties to the "good" or loving, parent—that is, clients maintain their childhood fear that if they disengage from these internal objects (or the symptoms that represent them), they will find themselves again helpless, alone, and frightened. The interpersonal process approach is well suited to resolving these irrational beliefs and painful interpersonal conflicts.

Certain ideas in this book are drawn from the relational school of object relations, especially the writings of R. D. Fairbairn, W. D. Winnicott, and John Bowlby (see Greenberg and Mitchell, 1983). These theorists have also influenced contemporary clinicians, such as J. Masterson's (1976) important contributions on treating borderline personality disorders and H. Kohut's (1977) work in self-psychology and narcissistic conditions. Unfortunately, it is exasperating to many beginning therapists to find that much object relations theory is presented in obtuse, inaccessible jargon. It is paradoxical that object relations theorists address the most sensitive and personal dimensions of human experience in impersonal, distancing terms. However, we will be able to use certain aspects of this theory to understand clients better, relate more empathically to them, and guide our therapeutic interventions.

Family Systems Theory. Not only must children adapt to their attachment figures, they also must adapt to their familial and cultural systems. Beginning therapists can glean a wealth of information about their adult clients' dynamics from family systems theory. This is true even for therapists who have no interest in ever working with children or families. We become who we are in our families of origin, and family process researchers have learned much about the workings of multigenerational family relations.

In the late 1950s, Gregory Bateson, Virginia Satir, Jay Haley, and others began studying communication patterns in families (see Goldenberg and Goldenberg, 1991). They found that intrafamilial communication followed definitive but unspoken rules that determined who spoke to whom, about what, and when. Adult clients are usually continuing faulty communication patterns learned in their families of origin (for example, addressing conflicts through a third party rather than speaking directly to someone, allowing others to speak for them and say what they are thinking or feeling, and/or never making "I" statements or saying directly what they want).

Early family researchers also learned that children are often scripted into roles—such as the "responsible" child, the "outsider," or the "invisible" member—within the family. According to object relations theory, most common is the "good child"/"bad child" role split that occurs in so many families. Most adult clients are still performing these childhood roles, which distort and deny many important aspects of who they really are. In the process of adapting in their families, these children placed their families' demands and expectations on themselves. Many clients who have played the "good child" role in their families are still perfectionistically demanding of themselves, guilty about doing anything for themselves, worried about the needs of others, afraid of their anger, and confused by their sad and empty feelings. Whereas the "bad" child usually acts out his conflicts externally (substance abuse, promiscuity), the "good" child often seeks treatment and enters therapy, presenting with anxiety or depression.

Families also have unspoken rules about how in late adolescence children can leave home and emancipate. For example, the oldest daughter may not be allowed to grow up and leave home successfully on her own. Often, she may try to emancipate through pregnancy, only to find herself even more dependent on her parents than before and forced to live at home again. Or the brother may only be able to leave home through rejecting confrontations with parents, and then may live in another part of the country and have little or no continuing contact with the parents. Family rules, faulty communication patterns, and roles all serve to maintain family myths that, in turn, function to avoid anxiety-arousing conflicts. For example, some common family myths are: Dad doesn't have a drinking problem; Nobody is sad in our family; Mom and Dad never fight and are very happily married. In sum, family myths and all of these other family characteristics are rule-bound, "homeostatic mechanisms" that govern family relations and establish repetitive, predictable patterns of family interaction.

Salvadore Minuchin (1974) and other family researchers have also explored the alliances, coalitions, and subgroups that make up the structure of family relations. In some families, for example, the maternal grandmother, mother, and eldest daughter go together, and the father is the "outsider." This structural road map for reading family relations becomes even more illuminating when these family dynamics are examined in a three-generational perspective (Bowen, 1966; Ivan Boszormenyi-Nagy and Spark, 1973). It is fascinating, and sometimes disturbing, to see how these same family rules, roles, myths, and structural family relationships can be reenacted across three or four generations in a highly patterned, rule-governed system.

This book draws on all of these important family systems concepts, as well as something else the family therapy movement has contributed—the effects of parental relations and familial experience on clients' problems. Therapists need to help clients make realistic assessments of the strengths and problems that actually existed in clients' families of origin. However, in our culture it is taboo to speak critically of parents, which, as Alice Miller (1984) observes, breaks the Fourth Commandment to "Honor thy parents." Herein, though, is one of the great strengths of family systems theory. The family systems therapist is trying to change hurtful familial interactions, not to place blame. The family therapist is also concerned about the well-being of *every* family member, parents as well as children. As clients realize that the therapist wants to understand, not blame and take away, the internalized parent, clients are able to explore highly threatening material and make significant gains in therapy.

In line with object relations theory, there are some good things in every family, even in very troubled or abusive families. There are also limitations and conflicts in the healthiest families. Clients are complying with binding family rules and protecting their parents at their own expense when they continue to idealize parents and deny real problems that existed. However, clients cannot simply reject hurtful parents and emotionally cut them off or they will tend to reenact these same problematic relations with others. This means that clients must find a way to keep parents (or healthier aspects of them) alive inside as partial identifications. How can clients accomplish this?

In order to get better, clients must be able to come to terms with "the good news and the bad news" in their families. Clients cannot achieve this integration and resolution if the therapist also employs his or her own splitting defenses, however. In other words, the therapist does not want to identify with and idealize the wounded child that exists within some clients and reject the hurtful parent. Neither does the therapist want to support clients' continuing denial of familial problems and idealization of parents. Instead, the therapist's appropriate role is to try to understand what actually occurred in clients' development and help them come to terms with the good and the bad in their experience. These and other family systems concepts inform and guide the interpersonal process approach.

Basic Premises

What are people's problems about? Where do they come from and how can they be resolved? Every beginning therapist grapples with questions such as

these and will continue to do so throughout his or her life. One of the enduring satisfactions of a counseling career is in continuing to evolve one's own
ideas about the nature of people and their problems.

This section introduces some ideas and assumptions that are central to
the interpersonal process approach: (1) Problems are interpersonal in nature.
(2) Familial experience is the most important source of learning about ourselves and others. (3) The therapist-client relationship can be used to resolve
problems. In other words, this overview examines how problems are expressed, how they have developed, and how they can be resolved.

The Nature of Problems: A Separateness-Relatedness Dialectic. Most client conflicts arise in close relationships, and clients often enter therapy when they
are beginning or ending a primary relationship. One useful way to conceptualize many of these interpersonal problems is along a continuum of separateness and relatedness. This is examined below from a family systems
perspective.

Most family systems theorists agree that the basic dimension of family life
is a developmental continuum of separateness-relatedness. Families must
nurture young children and provide them with a secure sense of acceptance
and belonging (relatedness). As children grow older, the developmental task
of the family shifts from nurturing children to training them for independence
and preparing them for emancipation (separateness). The family must have
flexibility and a range of interpersonal responses in order to meet offspring's
needs for both closeness in early childhood and autonomy in later years.

If there are problems in forming an attachment bond in infancy or in
meeting the strong dependency needs of young children, family members will
be disconnected from one another. Children will develop neither a shared
sense of family identity nor loyalty to each other. Most important, children
will not be motivated to comply with parents' socialization demands unless an
affectional bond exists. Young children fail to relinquish their own wishes and
adopt more mature and responsible behavior if they are not concerned about
maintaining parental approval. As a result, children from such disengaged
families do not internalize social rules and self-controls adequately. They do
not feel responsibility toward others or the culture at large and are likely to
develop acting-out symptoms and to externalize blame. These offspring are
more likely to come in contact with police and judges than with mental health
professionals.

Problems also arise at the other end of the continuum. When there is too
much closeness and family members are enmeshed, parents cannot tolerate
the individuation or emancipation of their offspring. An example of this can
be seen when enmeshed families stifle individuation by making anger an
unacceptable feeling and by avoiding conflict rather than addressing and resolving it. Individuation is also blurred by ineffective communication patterns,

such as when family members express what another is thinking or feeling or speak to each other through a third person rather than directly.

Enmeshed families also inhibit emancipation by discouraging developmentally appropriate steps toward independence and autonomy. For example, these families do not give offspring in late adolescence permission to leave home psychologically and succeed on their own. Such offspring often feel a binding guilt as they try to become independent adults and make commitments to love relationships and career choices (Teyber, 1983).

In contrast to offspring in disengaged and enmeshed families, offspring in families that function well integrate the relatedness and separateness dimensions. These offspring develop a sense of self that allows them to feel emotionally connected to others while still remaining separate or individuated from them (Stierlin, 1972; Mahler, Pine, and Bergman, 1975; Boszormenyi-Nagy and Spark, 1973).

The same dialectic of separateness and relatedness continues into adulthood. Here again, the challenge of successful relationships is one of balancing intimacy and autonomy. On the one hand, we need to have a sense of belonging and being cared about. It is important that others acknowledge our experience and respond to us in caring and confirming ways. At the same time, however, we must also be separate and independent. All of us have the right to our own feelings and perceptions, even if they differ from those of significant others. We need to be able to express our own preferences and beliefs and to pursue our own interests and goals. Healthy individuals can accommodate the polarities of separateness and relatedness at the same time.

The problems that most clients present reflect an inability to achieve an integrated sense of self as both an independent and competent person and an emotionally available and committed person. Thus, several unifying themes encompass many of the varied problems clients present. Client conflicts will often embody *separateness* issues of autonomy, initiative, and power on the one hand, or *relatedness* issues of intimacy, trust, and commitment on the other.

The Source of Problems: Affective Learning in the Family of Origin. Social learning in the family of origin is the most important source of long-standing personality strengths and conflicts. Family homeostasis requires that many patterns of interaction and communication become repetitive and rule-bound. These transactional patterns are strongly maintained in the family of origin and can be highly resistant to change in adulthood.

There are two reasons why familial experience has such a powerful, long-term impact on the individual. The first factor is the sheer repetition of family transactional patterns. The same types of affect-laden interchanges are re-enacted thousands of times in daily family life. Suppose, for example, that a parent has difficulty responding positively to a child's successes. When the young child enthusiastically seeks the parent's approval for an accomplishment, the parent might ignore the child and change the topic, compare the child unfavorably with a sibling's greater accomplishment, turn away and look vaguely sad or hurt, or take the success away from the child by making it his or her own.

The same type of parental response usually occurs when the child shows the parent a favorite drawing, makes a new friend, wins a race at school, or earns a star from his or her teacher. This transactional pattern becomes a powerful source of learning when it continues over a period of years and even decades. As an adult, the child is likely to feel conflicted about completing his or her educational degree or about taking pleasure in a promotion earned at work. Thus, the most important problems in people's lives are the generic conflicts that develop from these characterological or habitual response patterns. Long-standing personality problems are shaped more by repetitive family transactional patterns (strain trauma) than by isolated traumatic events or time-limited stressors (shock trauma) (Wenar, 1990).

Second, the learning from these repetitive transactions is even more significant because of the intensity of the affect involved. Parents are the pillars of the child's universe, and children depend on them with a life-and-death intensity. Thus, these repetitive transactional patterns are even more influential because they have been reenacted in highly charged affective relationships with the most important people in one's life. The child in the example above may well feel a desperate need somehow to win the parent's approval, yet simultaneously feel increasing anxiety about trying to succeed or about approaching the rejecting parent. Thus, our sense of self in relation to others is learned in the family of origin and, in many ways, will carry over to adulthood.

In summary, family interaction patterns may be hurtful and frustrating for the individual, or they may be validating and encouraging. For better or worse, these repetitive patterns of family interaction, roles, and relationships are internalized and become the foundation of our sense of self and the social world. Of course, other factors are influential as well, and familial experience will not be relevant to many situational problems that clients present. Familial experience, however, does provide our first and most long-lasting model for what goes on in close relationships. It will figure significantly in one's choice of marital partner and career, in how adult offspring will, in turn, parent their own children, and in many of the other most enduring problems and satisfactions found in adult life.

Although such important learning as this has taken place in the family of origin, ineffective and painful transactional patterns can be relearned. Change is indeed possible and, as we will see below, occurs in part through a relational process of affective relearning.

Resolving Problems: It Is the Relationship That Heals. The relationship between the therapist and the client is the foundation of the therapeutic enterprise. The nature of this relationship is the therapist's most important means
of effecting client change, and it determines the success or failure of the
therapy. In order to utilize the therapeutic relationship systematically as a
vehicle for change, however, therapists must understand very specifically the
meaning of their dynamic interactions with their clients. Thus, the interpersonal process approach focuses on understanding what goes on between the
therapist and client in terms of their interaction or *process.*

The therapist-client relationship is complex and multifaceted, as different
levels of communication occur simultaneously. For example, one subtle but
important distinction is between the overtly spoken *content* of what is discussed, and the *process* dimension of how the therapist and client interact. In
order to work with the process dimension, the therapist must make a percep-
tual shift away from the overt content of what is discussed and begin to track
the relational process of how two people are interacting as well. This means
that at times therapists must be able to step beyond the usual social norms
with clients and take the risk of describing their current interaction and talking about what is occurring between them. This will be challenging for many
beginning therapists, because most of us have been taught that it is improper
to be so forthright. In this text, however, we will see how powerful it can be
when therapists can talk directly with clients about what is going on between
them. Further, we will also see how therapists can use this "metacommunica-
tion" in a sensitive and respectful way that does not threaten the client.
Although the process dimension cannot be explained so briefly, the following
vignette further introduces the concept.

Suppose that during their first session the client tells the therapist that he
resents his wife because she is always telling him what to do. He explains that
he has always had trouble making decisions on his own, and as a result his
wife has often simply told him what to do. Even though he felt that she was
just trying to help him with his indecisiveness, he resented her "bossiness"
and "know-it-all attitude." After describing the presenting problem in this
way, the client asked what the therapist thought he should do.

Let us look at the process dimension of their interaction. Suppose the
therapist complied with the client's request and said: "I think that the next
time your wife tells you what to do you should . . . " If therapy continues in
this didactic vein, the therapist and client will begin to reenact in their relationship the same conflict that led the client to seek treatment. That is, the
therapist will be telling the client what to do, just as his wife has done. The
client has certainly invited this response, and will probably welcome the therapist's suggestions at first. In the long run, however, he will probably come to
resent the therapist's directives just as much as he resents his wife's, and will
ultimately find the therapist's suggestions to be of just as little help as hers.

Alternatively, the therapist might respond to the other side of the client's conflict and say: "I don't think I would really be helping you if I just told you what to do. I believe that clients need to find their own solutions to their problems." Frustrated, the client responds: "But I told you I don't know what to do! It's hard for me to make decisions. Aren't you the expert who is supposed to know what to do about these things?"

This response throws the client back on the other side of his conflict and leaves him stuck in his own inability to make decisions. If this mode of interaction continues and comes to characterize their relationship, their process will recapitulate the other side of the problem that initially brought the client to therapy. That is, the client's inability to initiate, make his own decisions, and be responsible for his own actions will immobilize him in therapy, just as it has in other areas of his life.

The key point is that clients do not just talk with therapists about their problems in an abstract manner; rather they actually recreate and act out in their relationship with the therapist the same conflicts that have led them to seek treatment. *This recapitulation of the client's problem in the therapeutic relationship is a regular and predictable phenomenon that will occur in most therapeutic relationships.*

In order to resolve problems, clients must experience in their real-life relationship with the therapist a new and more satisfying solution to their problems. When clients terminate prematurely or therapy reaches an impasse, the therapist and client are usually reenacting in their relationship the same conflict that the client has been struggling with in other relationships. For example, clients may feel that they are being controlled by the therapist and have to do everything the therapist's way, or that they have to take care of the therapist and meet his or her needs, or that they must please the therapist and win his or her approval, or that they have to compete with the therapist . . . just as they are doing with others in their lives. When this occurs, the therapeutic process has metaphorically repeated the same type of conflicted interaction that clients have not been able to resolve in other relationships, and that they have often experienced in earlier formative relationships in the family of origin.

Thus, clients will begin to play out with the therapist the problem that brought them to therapy. The issue is whether they will elicit the same problematic response from the therapist that they have received from others, or whether the therapist can respond in a new and more effective way that enables clients to resolve the conflict within their relationship. It is easier to understand this conceptually, however, than it is to carry this out in affect-laden relationships with clients.

In successful therapy, clients experience a different kind of relationship than they have had in the past. They participate in a relationship in which their old conflicts are intensely aroused, but this time the therapist does not respond in the same problematic way that others have in the past. Even though the client tries to elicit or reenact the same conflict with the therapist, the therapist is able to offer a different and more satisfying response than the client has had before. If the therapist and client are able to address and resolve the conflicts that emerge in their relationship, the client can generalize from this new experience and successfully adopt more adaptive responses with others. *This is the fundamental premise of interpersonal process psychotherapy.*

This has also been the cornerstone of other dynamic and interpersonally oriented therapies. For example, Alexander and French (1980) originally developed this conceptualization. They used this more active, direct approach to provide clients with a "corrective emotional experience" in the here-and-now relationship with the therapist. Similarly, Weiss and Sampson (1986) elucidate how the therapist must "pass transference tests" and respond to conflicted developmental needs in a different and more helpful way than parents did originally. If therapists do this consistently, they will disconfirm the client's "grim, unconscious pathogenic beliefs" that developed in problematic parent-child interactions (for example, "If I get stronger and do what I want, I will hurt my parent.").

Focusing more specifically on the process dimension, Mueller and Kell (1966) illuminate how the client's central conflicts are metaphorically reenacted with the therapist. These conflicts can then be either resolved or recapitulated, depending on the nature of the relationship that the therapist provides the client. These and other clinical theorists use different terms to emphasize the same direct, immediate experience of change in the real-life relationship between the therapist and client. Perhaps Frieda Fromm-Reichman (1960) has captured this best by saying that the therapist must provide the client with an *experience* rather than an *explanation*.

In order to provide this corrective emotional experience, the therapist must be able to work with the process dimension. In the previous illustration, when the client asked his therapist what he should do, one option would have been for the therapist to make a *process comment* that described their current interaction, making it an overt topic for discussion. For example, the therapist might have said: "It seems to me that you are asking me to tell you what to do, which will bring up the same problem for us in therapy that you are having at home with your wife. Let's see if you and I can do something different in our relationship. Rather than having me tell you what to do, let's try and work together to understand what is going on for you when you are feeling indecisive. Where do you think is the best place to begin?"

In this instance, the therapist is being supportive by offering the client a new and different *collaborative* relationship in which they can work together on the client's problems. If this collaborative effort continues to develop over the course of treatment, their working relationship will provide the facilitative context necessary for change to occur. Of course, the therapist's initial attempt to offer the client a corrective response to his conflict will need to be repeated in many different ways for change to occur. If the therapist can establish this type of collaborative relationship, however, it will facilitate other types of therapeutic interventions as well. Educational inputs, behavioral alternatives, dynamic interpretations, and interpersonal feedback will all be more effective when they occur in this type of interpersonal context.

As stated earlier, the guiding principle in the interpersonal process approach is to provide a corrective emotional experience in which clients experience a new and more satisfying response to their conflicts than they have received in the past. This requires a great deal of personal risk and involvement on behalf of the therapist and is therefore difficult to do. For this type of corrective emotional experience to occur, the therapist must be personally engaged and emotionally available to the client. The relationship must hold real personal meaning for both participants in order to have the emotional impact necessary to effect change. If the therapist is psychologically removed or safely distant from the client, the relationship will be too insignificant to be utilized as a vehicle for change. Again, the client needs an experience, not an explanation, for this type of emotional relearning to occur. In this simple human way, it is the relationship that heals.

The dialectic of separateness-relatedness similarly applies to the client/ therapist relationship. Just as the extent of change is limited if the therapist is distant and merely serves as an objective technician, so therapy will also falter if the therapist becomes inappropriately close. If therapists overidentify with the client or invest in the client's changing in order to shore up their own feelings of adequacy, therapy will not progress. When this occurs, therapists stop seeing the process they are enacting with the client and begin to respond in problematic ways that recapitulate the client's generic conflict.

In this regard, the most common problem beginning therapists have is experiencing the client's situation or concerns as identical to their own. The solution is a supervisory relationship that helps therapists see the ways in which their own experience differs from that of the client's. Once able to differentiate their own issues from those of the client, therapists will often be able to see how the therapeutic process has been reenacting the client's generic conflict. This understanding usually enables therapists to return to the therapeutic relationship and provide the client with the interpersonal experiences needed for change.

While learning to attend to this process dimension, beginning therapists should expect to make many mistakes with their clients. All therapists are going to become overinvolved or underinvolved with some clients, recapitulate the client's conflict in the therapeutic relationship at times, and make many other "mistakes." Few clients are fragile, however, and therapeutic relationships are often remarkably resilient. Unfortunately, most beginning therapists do not know this, so concern about making mistakes remains one of their biggest anxieties. Beginning therapists will do better therapy, and enjoy it more, once they find that *mistakes can be undone.* In fact, when therapists are willing to work with the process dimension, they will often find that mistakes can turn into opportunities. As their performance anxiety declines, beginning therapists will find that they are better able to identify and work with the process dimension. In turn, this focus on process will usually be the most effective way to undo mistakes and realign the therapeutic relationship when it has gone awry.

Client Diversity and Response Specificity

We have already seen that beginning therapists need a theoretical framework to guide their therapeutic interventions. But what are the requirements of this theory? What must the theory provide if it is to be of help to therapists and their clients?

One feature of an effective clinical theory is that it must have the flexibility and breadth to encompass the diversity of clients who now seek treatment. Although unifying patterns in personality certainly exist, every client is different. Each client has been genetically endowed with a unique set of features, and each has been raised differently in their families. Women have been socialized differently than men, minorities have different experiences than members of the dominant culture, and economic class shapes opportunity and expectations. To be helpful, a clinical theory must be able to help therapists work effectively with all of these highly diverse clients.

Adding to this complexity, each therapist also is a different person. Like clients, therapists differ in age, gender, ethnicity, sexual orientation, and developmental background. Therapists also bring diverse training, theoretical orientations, and personal styles to their clinical work. How can any theory help such a diversity of therapists respond to the extraordinary range of human experience that clients present? "Client response specificity" will be one of our best tools.

Interpersonal process psychotherapy is a highly idiographic approach. In the chapters that follow, we will be emphasizing the personal, subjective experience of each individual client more than diagnostic categories and personality typologies. Therapists will be encouraged repeatedly to try to find the subjective meaning that the particular experience at hand holds for the particular client. We will be trying to achieve this goal even when the meaning the experience holds for the client differs greatly from the meaning the same experience holds for the therapist. In this regard, we will also be trying to assess how each individual client's developmental history and current life circumstances guide the therapist's choice of interventions. Therapists must be able to respond to the unique circumstances of each client and provide the specific interpersonal experiences the client needs to change.

To illustrate, consider the often-raised question "Should therapists self-disclose to their clients?" Client response specificity emphasizes that self-disclosure (or any other response) will hold very different meanings for different clients. In fact, based on their developmental histories, the same response will often have exactly the opposite effect on two different clients. For example, if a client's parent was distant or aloof, the therapist's judicious, well-timed self-disclosure may be very enabling for the client. In contrast, the same type of response early in treatment may be anxiety arousing and counterproductive for a female client who had a seductive stepfather or a mother who was depressed, "needy," and used her as a confidant.

With the first client, greater intimacy and sharing with the therapist may help the client learn that he or she does matter and is of interest to other people. For the second client, the same response from the therapist may have the opposite impact. For her, greater "intimacy" may imply that she is again supposed to meet the unwanted, threatening, or burdensome needs of others. Either response may work fine with a particular client. However, therapists will be most effective if they first consider how the client's developmental history may shape the impact of their interventions.

To illustrate further, we will examine the question "Should therapists give opinions when clients ask for advice?" As before, the therapist's response is also informed by the client's current life circumstances. For example, offering advice may be counterproductive for a compliant, female client who is trying to assert herself with a dominating, dependency-fostering husband. For such a client, it may be better for the therapist to ask "What do you think would be best to do?" In contrast, giving advice and directives may work well with clients whose parents were incapable of or uninterested in preparing them for aspects of adult life. To withhold information, advice, and opinions from these clients may only re-enact their developmental conflict with the therapist and impede progress.

In these ways, the same intervention or response from the therapist will have very different effects on different clients. Taking client response specificity one step further, the therapist can assess how the client utilizes the particular response. For example, if the therapist observes that the client gets anxious and distant, or alternatively more engaged and available, in response to the therapist's self-disclosure, the therapist can further learn how to respond most effectively to the particular client. Working in this idiographic way adds complexity to the therapeutic process and places more demands on the therapist. However, such an approach gives therapists the flexibility to respond to the specific needs and unique experiences of the diversity of clients that seek help.

Model of Therapy

Some concepts in this chapter will be drawn upon to provide a brief overview of the therapeutic model. It is often the case that certain basic developmental tasks were left unfinished in the client's family of origin, usually resulting in conflicts along the separateness-relatedness continuum. The purpose of therapy is to complete these developmental tasks by providing a corrective emotional experience within the therapeutic relationship. The therapist does this by providing a relationship that enacts a resolution of the client's conflict rather than a repetition of it. Since clients are often adept at eliciting and engaging therapists in their conflicts, providing such corrective experiences is much easier to say than to do.

The client simultaneously seeks to avoid reexperiencing painful conflicts and also to find a new and more satisfying response to them. The client does this, partly by trying to assess safety and/or danger in the therapeutic relationship. The client's conflicts are activated with the therapist and are especially likely to be played out along the process dimension. Throughout the course of treatment, the client continues to assess at different degrees of awareness whether the therapist responds in new safer way than others in the past or whether the therapist responds in the same problematic way experienced in the past. For example, if the client risks becoming stronger and begins successfully pursuing goals, will the therapist take pleasure in the client's strength and success or feel threatened and competitive as the client's parent used to feel? Or if the client reveals vulnerabilities and has emotional needs of the therapist, will the therapist respond by offering comfort or will the therapist instead feel overwhelmed and responsible for this sadness as the client's parent used to?

Clients resolve their conflicts when the therapist's response repeatedly disconfirms their pathogenic developmental experiences. Through this corrective emotional experience, clients find that it is safe to act in new and more adaptive ways with some people. Clients can then begin exploring new aspects of themselves and the social world and can begin to generalize their experience of change to other relationships beyond the therapeutic one.

Therapists cannot simply tell clients that relationships can be different than they have been in the past; they must show the client that this is so. Meaningful relearning of embedded transactional patterns only occurs if the therapist and client confront, struggle with, and jointly work through in their real-life relationship a resolution of the client's conflict. *Finding this interpersonal solution commonly entails conflict and anxiety for the therapist as well as for the client.* Thus, the power to effect enduring change does not come from reassurances, explanations, or directives but rather from the client's having lived out with the therapist the actual conflict and discovering that relationships can exist "another way." This experiential relearning is the basis of interpersonal process psychotherapy. This process places real demands on the personhood of the therapist but holds the great reward of helping people change.

Limitations and Aims

Limitations. This text introduces beginning therapists to the practice of interpersonally oriented psychotherapy with individual adult clients. This therapeutic approach is best suited for clients with long-standing problems in close interpersonal relations. These problems include issues of dependency, trust, control, and commitment in interpersonal relations. This approach is also directed toward resolving developmental ego conflicts that may include identity and self-esteem problems; concerns over initiative and adequacy; and accompanying emotions of anxiety, depression, guilt, and shame.

Other types of therapeutic approaches are better suited for many clients. For example, many clients who function well need short-term supportive therapy. These clients need help coping with situational crises that do not reflect broader problems in living or with problems that do not tap into other enduring personality conflicts. Behavioral approaches are the treatment of choice for clients who have circumscribed problems such as an isolated phobia or who are seeking only symptomatic relief from their problems. Some clients will not be suited for the more intensive, interpersonal process approach because they are too impulsive or are psychotically disorganized. These clients will not be able to tolerate the anxiety aroused by this affectively uncovering approach. Finally, many clients require educational and skill development approaches. Sex education, time management, assertion training, or parent training is the treatment of choice for many clients.

This text focuses on the process dimension in psychotherapy and on how the therapist-client relationship can be used as a vehicle for change. This applied focus prevents us from addressing other important aspects of clinical training. Basic information about ethics, confidentiality, report writing, record keeping, informed consent, legal reporting, and other practical concerns is beyond the scope of this text. Similarly, clinical interventions in many important situations are not addressed, such as responding to client emergencies, managing suicidal crises, or mandated reporting of abuse. Further, this text does not address other therapeutic modalities such as child, marital, or family therapy or treatment complications when clients are referred by a court. Although the information presented here may be relevant to some of these treatment concerns, the subjects themselves are beyond the scope of this presentation.

It is important for beginning therapists to learn how to work in different modalities and in varying treatment lengths. The therapeutic model presented here is designed for an intermediate treatment length of six to eighteen months. This treatment length is not necessary for many clients and is not possible in many clinic settings. However, the treatment fundamentals presented here comprise the basic clinical skills necessary for other modalities, such as initial intakes, crisis intervention, and short-term therapy, as well as group and family work. The interpersonal process approach presented here provides trainees with many of the clinical skills they need to work in these other essential modalities.

In particular, the interpersonal process approach can be readily adapted to short-term and time-limited treatment modalities of 10 to 12 sessions (see

Mann, 1973; Mann and Goldman, 1982; Malan, 1976; Davanloo, 1980; Sifneos, 1979). However, beginning therapists must first acquire certain basic clinical skills and gain more experience working with the interpersonal model. For example, short-term work with this model requires therapists to "bring the conflict into the relationship" and make overt how the therapeutic process may be reenacting the client's conflict. Most beginning therapists are not ready to do this or, as we will see later, to be as forthright and direct as is necessary in this approach. Short-term work also requires therapists to conceptualize clients' developmental conflicts and interpersonal dynamics more quickly and more accurately than most beginning therapists are able to do. Thus, it is beyond the scope of this book to apply this model to short-term therapy, but beginning therapists will acquire the basic clinical skills necessary to extend the interpersonal process approach to short-term and other treatment modalities. In addition to the references above, interested readers are encouraged to examine excellent short-term, interpersonal treatment approaches to depression (Klerman et al., 1984), personality disorders (Horowitz et al., 1984), and psychotherapy (Strupp and Binder, 1984).

Finally, medical interventions will be an important aspect of treatment with some clients. Temperamental and biological factors do play a causative role in some disorders, and medications will be necessary at times. However, the purpose of this text is only to present the essential elements of interpersonal psychotherapy to clinical trainees.

Aims. The interpersonal process approach presented here emphasizes three broad aims that are essential to helping clients change. First, therapists must try to establish a significant emotional relationship with their clients. In addition to the relationship issues discussed earlier, this means that therapists must maintain their own internal commitment to helping clients change. It is especially important, but challenging, for therapists to do this during periods of intense client resistance, ambivalence, and negative transference toward the therapist. Conceptions of therapeutic change often vary on a continuum from the application of discrete, problem-solving techniques on the one hand, to some vague allusion to "the relationship" on the other. Somehow, the relationship is supposed to produce change, but it is not clear how or why change occurs. The interpersonal process approach presented here offers a middle ground between these two extremes. Change *is* predicated on the nature of the therapist-client relationship, but specific guidelines are provided to show how the therapeutic relationship can be utilized to effect change.

Second, in order to effect change, therapists must also be able to respond effectively to the client's emotions and inner life. Therapy is a private and intimate sharing in which therapists respond to clients' pain and help them understand their conflicted emotions. Making contact with clients in these very personal ways is a critical aspect of therapy, yet it is the dimension along which therapists are most likely to stumble. Most therapists, like other people reared in our culture, have been socialized to avoid rather than approach strong feelings, such as anger, despair, fear, and shame. In addition, it is often difficult for therapists to respond to their clients' emotions because they arouse the therapist's own conflicted feelings as well. The most effective way for therapists to facilitate change, however, is to help clients integrate emotional reactions that they have not been able to resolve on their own. Thus, specific guidelines will also be provided to help beginning therapists understand and respond to their clients' conflicted emotions.

The third component of effective therapy is to conceptualize the client's personality and problems and formulate what experiences the client needs to undergo in therapy in order to change. This conceptualization should enable the therapist to identify the client's central conflict, understand the resistance and defenses that have kept the client from changing, and provide direction for the ongoing course of treatment. Typically, the least developed skill for beginning therapists is their ability to formulate a useful conceptualization of the client's personality and problems. However, the most effective therapists are equally adept in the conceptual as well as the affective and relational domains. Thus, this text aims to facilitate the therapist's effectiveness in all three areas.

Another aim of this text is to provide an overview of the nature and course of a therapeutic relationship. Therapeutic relationships usually have a coherent life course and follow a predictable developmental pattern from beginning to end. Although variations and exceptions occur with every client, therapists can often identify an ordered sequence of successively unfolding stages. At each successive stage of therapy, the therapist must negotiate certain therapeutic tasks with the client. If the therapist achieves this, the next set of issues and concerns will often emerge from the client. This epigenetic unfolding provides an integrating structure for conceptualizing the temporal course of therapy and suggests intervention goals and strategies for each successive stage. The chapters that follow are organized to reflect this developmental schema and to parallel the course of therapy from beginning to end.

Finally, beginning therapists reading this book must have realistic expectations for learning the interpersonal process approach. Beginning therapists who are seeing their first clients will find much to help them in their initial work with clients. However, more information is presented here than a novice clinician can integrate and apply fully. The attempt here is to present the interpersonal process approach as simply and clearly as possible while still trying to do justice to the complexity and emotional depth of the work. It is unrealistic for beginning therapists to expect to readily master this complex, conceptual material or to use with clients all of the challenging interpersonal processes that are presented here. A more realistic goal is for beginning therapists simply to try to understand the concepts presented and gradually try them out *at the therapist's own pace*. Some beginning therapists may begin to feel that the more they learn, the less they know. With more experience, however, second-year students will be able to employ many of these concepts successfully. Typically, it takes about three years before clinical trainees have the confidence to employ routinely these concepts and to respond to the powerful effects the interventions generate. Since it will take some time to learn how to work in this way, the best approach is to be patient and enjoy the learning.

With these general considerations in mind, we can now examine more specifically how to begin a therapeutic relationship. We turn now to the first stage of therapy: establishing a collaborative relationship.

SUGGESTIONS FOR FURTHER READING

1. The reader is encouraged to examine the book by William Mueller and Bill Kell entitled *Impact and Change: A Study of Counseling Relationships* (Englewood Cliffs, N.J.: Prentice-Hall, 1966). Chapters 1 through 4 provide a rich conceptualization of the therapist-client relationship and how it can be used to help clients change. This is an illuminating book that deserves to be read and reread by beginning and experienced therapists alike.

2. The reader may also wish to examine Salvadore Minuchin's book, *Families and Family Therapy* (Cambridge, Mass.: Harvard University Press, 1974). Chapters 3 and 5 provide a succinct presentation of structural family relations and family developmental processes. This discussion will help individual therapists understand the genesis and familial context of their clients' problems.

3. A highly readable application of object relations and attachment theory to psychotherapy can be found in Chapters 6 through 9 of John Bowlby's book "A Secure Base" (New York: Basic Books, 1988). An excellent conceptual overview of object relations theory may be found in *Object Relations in Psychoanalysis* by J. Greenberg and S. Mitchell (New York: Basic Books, 1984).

4. Readers interested in the large body of empirical research on interpersonal theory and a history of seminal ideas in the field should examine *Handbook of Interpersonal Psychotherapy* by J. Anchin and D. Kiesler, eds. (New York: Pergamon, 1982). See especially Chapters 1 (pp. 14–20), 2, and 15.

5. The great novelists best bring to life the profound impact of childhood and familial experience on adult personality. John Steinbeck's *East of Eden* (New York: Viking, 1952) and Franz Kafka's *Letter to His Father* (New York: Shocken, 1966) put flesh and blood to the conceptual skeleton of familial influences on personality development.

RESPONDING TO CLIENTS

CHAPTER TWO

ESTABLISHING A COLLABORATIVE RELATIONSHIP

CONCEPTUAL OVERVIEW

Psychotherapy is a profession of trust. Clients enter therapy with a need—they are in pain, asking for help with something they have not been able to alleviate on their own. A trustworthy response is to honor the dependency in clients' requests for help and to respond compassionately to their pain. Yet to be most effective, the therapist must also respond in a way that helps clients gain a greater sense of their own capabilities. Thus, the goal is not only to resolve specific situational problems, but to do so in a way that leaves clients with a greater sense of their own competence and mastery. In this way, the interpersonal process approach to psychotherapy fosters independence as it aims for broader personality growth and maturation.

Clients cannot resolve problems and achieve a greater sense of their own personal power in a hierarchical or one-up/one-down therapeutic relationship. This means that clients need a *collaborative relationship* in order to grow beyond their situational dependency. Clients must be active participants when working with the therapist, rather than being passively "cured" or told what to do. This chapter presents a model for a collaborative relationship that accepts the client's need for comfort, understanding, and guidance, yet does so in a way that equally encourages the client's independence.

CHAPTER ORGANIZATION

This chapter presents issues that are fundamental to a successful initial therapist-client interview. The first section elaborates the concept of a collaborative relationship in terms of a balance of directiveness/nondirectiveness in the therapeutic relationship. Sample therapist-client dialogues will be used to illustrate how the therapist can establish a collaborative working alliance in the initial session.

The second section presents ways to foster the therapeutic relationship and further engage the client in treatment. Principally, these goals are achieved by listening carefully and understanding the subjective meaning in what the client is saying. The therapist can better understand the client's experience by (1) clarifying the repetitive themes that recur in the different stories and vignettes the client presents, (2) identifying the central conflicts that link the client's problems and concerns, and (3) approaching the client's central affect in a direct but caring way. Following the central theme of this book, both sections will focus on interpersonal process characteristics of the therapist-client relationship, and how they can be used to facilitate change.

A COLLABORATIVE RELATIONSHIP

At each successive stage of treatment therapists have a different overarching goal to guide their interventions. At the beginning stage of therapy, the therapist's goal is *to establish a collaborative relationship or working alliance* with the client (Greenson, 1967). In the initial sessions the therapist must "join" with the client, set expectations for how they are going to work together, and behaviorally enact these spoken expectations by giving the client the *experience* of working together on his or her problems. If a collaborative relationship is established early in the course of treatment, it will facilitate change later in therapy and ultimately help clients to achieve a greater sense of their own mastery and competence.

A Directive/Nondirective Balance

At the outset, the therapist should explore the client's expectations for how they are going to work together and how change is going to occur. For example, does the client believe that the therapist is the authority or healer who is the agent for change—perhaps via advice, explanations, interpretations, information giving, modeling, reinforcing, encouraging, confronting, challenging irrational thinking . . . ? That is, will the process of therapy be a hierarchical doctor-patient or teacher-student relationship in which the powerful therapist leads and the dependent client follows? Many clients believe the process of therapy is primarily having the therapist tell them what to do. When this one-up/one-down relationship occurs, it fosters the client's continuing dependency on the therapist. Although few therapists overtly subscribe to this type of therapeutic process, it is commonly enacted without the therapist realizing it.

Many clients enter therapy expecting the therapist to be the "doctor" who is going to prescribe their route to mental health. This doctor-patient role will work well with many clients in the *short run*. The client's expectations will be fulfilled if the therapist takes the role of leader or healer, but little client change will occur in the long run from this teacher-student mode of interaction. Clients will not be able to gain a greater sense of their own personal power as long as they believe that the source of potency resides in the therapist rather than in themselves.

Whereas a directive stance may work in the short run, a purely nondirective approach will often sputter right from the start. Typically, clients feel frustrated if their requests for help or direction are continuously reflected back upon them. A negative cycle may ensue in which the client becomes increasingly angry and demands direction from the therapist, who further eschews this role and talks about inner direction and finding one's own answers. This, in turn, further frustrates the client who does not feel he has the answer to anything at that moment.

The client often sees the therapist's attempts to be strictly nondirective and avoid the leader role as manipulative and evasive. Clients do need advice and direction from an expert. They need suggestions and guidance for how to proceed, and the therapist should provide it. However, the therapist must provide this structure and direction without falling back into the other extreme of a counterproductive authoritarian role.

How can such a structured but nonauthoritarian relationship be achieved? In the initial interview, the therapist must make *an overt bid to establish a collaborative relationship in which the therapist and client work together to resolve the client's problems*. For example, this attitude may be conveyed in the following type of message:*

Therapist:

I would like for you and I to become partners. I cannot figure out what is wrong and tell you what to do on my own, and you have not been able to solve your problems by yourself, so let's work together on them. You are the world's foremost expert on you, and I have skills and knowledge about problems such as yours to contribute. By working together we have the best chance of succeeding. How does that sound to you?

This type of message communicates that the therapist is going to be an active participant and respond to the client's need for help. However, the

---

*Throughout this book sample dialogues are provided to illustrate the concepts that are discussed. Beginning therapists should not use these words (or try to say what a supervisor might say in a similar situation) but should find their own ways to express these concepts. Beginning therapists will lose their creativity with their clients if they try to imitate someone else.

client is not going to be a passive recipient who is being cured by the therapist, but an active participant who is sharing the driver's seat with the therapist. Clients must be given the expectation that they share responsibility for the direction and outcome of therapy. The therapist thus is taken off the pedestal, and the client becomes an equal participant, with valuable information, abilities, and resources to contribute. Whether the therapist and client can continue this process of mutual collaboration will largely determine the eventual outcome of therapy. Let us look now at some specific ways to establish a collaborative relationship in the initial therapy session.

Beginning the Initial Interview

Therapists must begin to establish a collaborative relationship in their initial contact with the client. The therapist structures the session by providing the client with guidelines and direction for what is going to occur in the interview. This can be done simply and briefly by offering clients an open-ended bid to talk about what brings them to therapy. For example:

Therapist:
> I'd like to begin by learning more about the concerns that have brought you to therapy. What has been the difficulty?

This type of message communicates several important things to the client. At the simplest level, it ends the opening phase of social interaction that occurs as the therapist and client are introduced and walk to the interview room. More important, it tells clients that the therapist is someone who is willing to talk directly about their personal problems, and is ready to respond to their need for help by listening. However, it does this in a way that still gives clients the freedom to choose where they want to start and leaves them in charge of how much they want to disclose. From the outset, clients are sharing control of the interview by choosing what they want to talk about, yet the therapist is an active participant who has offered some direction for where they are heading. This type of constructive collaboration does not occur if the therapist gives the client a more specific cue such as:

> When we talked on the telephone you said you were having trouble with your boss. What is the problem there?

Although the difference between these two openings may seem insignificant at first, it is important to communicate that clients should talk about what they want to talk about and not feel that they have to follow the therapist's agenda. Why? From the start, we want the client to take an *active role* in

directing the course of therapy, while still feeling that the therapist is participating as a supportive ally. *Enacting this process dimension in the initial
session is more important than the content of what is discussed.*

In most cases, clients will readily accept the therapist's open-ended bid
and begin to share their concerns with the therapist. The therapist can then
follow the client's lead and begin to learn more about this person and his or
her problems. Therapy is underway when this occurs. Before we go on to the
next step, however, we must examine two exceptions in which the client does
not accept the therapist's offer to begin.

Previous Screening Interview. If another therapist has previously conducted an
intake interview, the client may not be so ready to begin. For example:

Client: [impatiently]
　　I've already been through all of this in the intake with Dr. Smith. Do I
　　have to go over it all again just for you?
　　　　　　　　　　　　　　　　OR
　　[hesitantly] I don't know how much you already know about me. What
　　has Dr. Smith told you about me?

Our initial goal is to develop a working alliance between the therapist and
the client. In the two hypothetical responses above, the previous intake therapist is a third party who is psychologically still in the room with them. This is
especially problematic for many clients who have come from families in which
a third person was triangulated into every two-person relationship (Bowen,
1966). That is, whenever two people were close, or in conflict, a third family
member would be drawn in and would disrupt the dyad (Haley, 1967). To
keep therapy from recapitulating this transactional pattern, the therapist and
client must begin their own relationship as a stable dyad. It is important to
maintain a dyadic therapeutic relationship that does not allow others to disrupt the therapeutic alliance, especially as so many clients have a strong
propensity to bring a third person into every relationship. For example:

Therapist:
　　I know that you have already spoken with Dr. Smith, and I have learned a
　　little bit about you from his intake notes. But just you and I are going to
　　work together from now on, and I'd like to hear about you in your own
　　words. It may be a little repetitious for you, but this way we can begin
　　together at the same point.

Most clients appreciate this offer for a dyadic relationship and will begin
to share their concerns with the therapist.

Conflicts over Initiating. There is another common circumstance in which the client does not respond to the therapist's initial request to begin. The central conflict for some clients involves issues of leading, initiating, or accepting responsibility. This type of client cannot begin at the therapist's request. By asking the client to begin, the therapist has inadvertently presented the client with her central conflict. Asking these clients to initiate in the therapy session is precisely what they cannot do in their lives. It is difficult for this type of client to decide what to talk about or to assume any responsibility for the course of therapy. Thus, an impossible demand is placed on this client when a therapist nondirectively sits and waits for the client to lead.

On the other hand, it merely reenacts the client's conflict when a directive therapist begins the session by telling the client what to talk about. Thus, therapy stalls right from the start if the client has problems with initiative and the therapist responds in either a directive or non-directive manner. What can the therapist do in this case? One way to find a more effective middle ground is to make a process comment, as discussed in Chapter 1. An effective intervention is simply to describe, ask about, or make overt what is occurring between the therapist and client at that moment. For example:

Therapist:
> It seems to be hard for you to get started. Maybe we can begin right there. Is it often hard for you to begin, or is there something about this situation in particular that is difficult for you?

By first identifying this as a problem and then encouraging the client to explore it, the therapist has offered the client a focus and helped the client move forward. However, the therapist has provided this focus without taking over and telling the client what to do, which would only recapitulate the client's conflict with the therapist. The therapist's open-ended inquiry is supportive by responding to the client's immediate concern. Yet the client can take this issue of initiating where he or she wants, and can share responsibility for the course of treatment. This type of response provides a new opportunity for clients to explore their problems in a supportive environment. Our first goal is met as the client *experiences* a collaborative interaction with the therapist, rather than merely having a conversation about "the need to work together." Such a collaborative experience sets important expectations for the future course of therapy.

UNDERSTANDING THE CLIENT

The therapist has begun the session by giving the client an open-ended bid to talk about whatever is most important to the client. Now imagine that the client has begun to share his or her concerns with the therapist and is clarifying the background and context of his or her problems. The therapist must find the subjective meaning that each successive story or vignette holds for the client. It is critical for the therapist to see what is most significant to the client *from the client's point of view* (Kelly, 1963). The client will feel *understood* by the therapist when the therapist can find a common meaning that links together the client's concerns or distills the central feeling in his or her experience. When this occurs, clients become more interested in exploring their problems and more engaged with the therapist. They are encouraged to reveal even more about themselves and their problems.

The section that follows examines what it means to understand the clients' experience. We will see why it is important to acknowledge clients' experiences, explore what therapists can do to better understand what their clients are saying, and see how beginning therapists' own performance anxieties make it difficult for them to listen effectively to clients. Finally, therapists will be encouraged to share their understanding with clients in a caring and compassionate way.

Clients Do Not Feel Understood

Most clients are concerned that others do not really listen to them, take them seriously, or understand what they are saying. Clients often describe themselves as feeling invisible, alone, strange, or unimportant. Many clients feel this way because their subjective experience was not validated or responded to in their family of origin. For example, while growing up, others often responded to the client by saying:

Why would a silly thing like that make you mad?
You can't possibly be hungry now.
I'm cold, put your sweater on.
How can you be tired, you've hardly done anything?
You shouldn't be upset at your mother, she loves you very much.
You don't really want to do that.

Most clients repeatedly received messages like these that deny their feelings and invalidate their experience. Further, family members often changed the topic or simply did not respond when the client expressed a feeling, concern, or interest. One of the most effective ways therapists can help their clients change is to validate and confirm their subjective experience. R. D. Laing goes so far as to suggest that people stop feeling "crazy" when their subjective experience is validated (Laing and Esterson, 1970).

Consistent invalidation, disconfirmation, or mystification in the client's family of origin has profound, long-lasting consequences. In its extreme forms, some authors describe it as "soul murder" because clients lose themselves when they lose the validity of their own experience (Schatzman, 1973). Whereas invalidation has occurred to some extent in most clients' families, it has usually been a pervasive experience for victims of physical and sexual abuse. Disempowerment is one of the most serious consequences of such systematic invalidation. When feelings and perceptions are denied repeatedly throughout development, clients are incapable of setting firm limits with others, saying no, and not going along with what does not feel right to them.

What engenders this victim-prone status? Consistent denial of their experience leaves clients unsure of what has actually happened to them and of the subjective meaning that events hold. They no longer trust their own perceptions of what may be making them uncomfortable. They often cannot find words to communicate their experience and, even if they could, do not expect others to respect or understand what they say.

When their subjective experience has been denied repeatedly, such as commonly occurs in alcoholic families, clients do not know what they are feeling, what they like or value, or what they want to do. In place of clear feelings and confident perceptions, a vague, painful feeling of internal dissonance results. Fortunately, this undifferentiated, dissonant feeling state can be replaced with emotional clarity and an accompanying sense of greater personal power. This change can occur readily if the therapist consistently listens to, accepts, and validates clients' experience. We will now look more specifically at what therapists can do to confirm clients and empower them in their own personhood.

Therapists can respond effectively by listening intently to the client, taking seriously whatever matters to the client, and communicating understanding and acceptance of what the client has said. Although this type of empathy and validation may sound like a simple and common human response, it is not. As we have seen, many clients have not had their feelings and perceptions acknowledged in current and past relationships. Thus, therapists must validate the client's experience by identifying and articulating the central meaning that this particular experience seems to hold for the client. For example, in the phrases below the therapist is trying to capture the central meaning or issue in what the client has just said:

It didn't seem fair to you.
You were frightened when he did that.
Here again, you have to take care of everyone else.
It's been too much for you, more than you can stand.
It felt great to be so effective and in charge.
It was disappointing; you wanted more than that.

It is profoundly reassuring and empowering to clients when therapists can consistently and accurately offer such validation. In fact, a primary working goal for the therapist is to provide validation throughout each session. To appreciate how important validation is, beginning therapists may reflect back on what others have done to help them during their own crisis periods. Almost universally, helpful responses included an empathic understanding and validation of one's feelings and perceptions.

This discussion becomes even more relevant for clients from culturally diverse backgrounds. We have seen that therapists must work affirmingly with minorities, same-sex couples, economically disadvantaged clients, and others. These clients will bring issues of oppression, prejudice, self-hate, and injustice into the therapeutic process, and their personal experiences will have routinely been invalidated by the culture at large. These clients, in particular, will not expect to be heard or understood by the therapist. The first step in working with all people is to listen empathically and hear what is important to them. Therapists respect the personal meaning that experiences hold for different people when they enter into and confirm the client's subjective experience. Observing exceptionally effective therapists of any theoretical orientation, one learns that the best therapists offer these basic human responses profoundly well.

Therapists Must Demonstrate Their Understanding

To engage a client in a working relationship, the therapist must listen to the client's experience, find the feeling and meaning the stories hold for the client, and accurately reflect what is most significant in the client's experience. An accurately empathic reflection that *captures the meaning of the client's experience* is a complex and significant intervention. It is never just a rote parroting of what the client has said. An effective reflection is more akin to an interpretation that goes *beyond* what the client has said and communicates that the therapist understands what is most important in the client's experience (Rogers, 1951). Therapists become credible to their clients when they *demonstrate* their understanding in this tangible way.

It is easy to trivialize the response I am suggesting and allow it to become a cliché. The simplistic, inauthentic stereotype of the therapist is someone who readily says: "I hear you," "I know just what you mean," "I understand completely." This type of global, undifferentiated response is not effective and, paradoxically, often furthers the client's sense of never being seen, heard, or understood. It is not just a matter of saying "I understand" but of demonstrating that understanding by articulating the central meaning or issue in what the client has said. Therapists show the client that they can be helpful when they capture and express the specific meaning in the client's experience, rather than offering well-intended but vague reassurances.

The therapist does not have to be an exceptionally insightful or perceptive person to understand the client's experience. Therapists can check out their perceptions with the client and invite the client to clarify them. For example, the therapist replies: "As I listen to you, it seems as if you feel so hopeless that you just want to give up. Is that how it is for you?" This dialogue takes the pressure of having to be right off the therapist and furthers the collaborative alliance. And, even though the therapist's perceptions will be inaccurate at times, clients often feel cared for by the therapist's sincere efforts to understand their experience.

Although it is easy to read about "hearing the client's experience" and "demonstrating understanding," things get a little more ambiguous as the beginning therapist tries to put all of this into practice. To illustrate these concepts more concretely, we now examine a brief case study of a client who initially had the experience of not being heard by her therapist but later felt understood with a second therapist.*

While growing up, Marsha did not feel heard or understood by her parents. Her father was a distant, "old school" man. He was not comfortable talking with his adolescent daughter and believed his wife should "handle" the children. Her mother was critical, demanding, and intrusive. Whenever her mother felt or believed something, she demanded that her children see it the same way. For example, if Marsha felt something that her mother did not, her mother would angrily charge, "What's wrong with you?" As an adolescent, Marsha felt sad, lonely, and afraid. She had no idea why she felt this way, however, and often thought, "There's just something wrong with me." Marsha frequently cried alone in her room.

Marsha had always thought that everything would get better when she went away to college. To her great dismay, though, she found herself depressed during her first semester away. She could not stop crying and started losing weight. More confused about herself than ever, Marsha began seeing a counselor at the Student Counseling Center. Although she did not really have words for what was wrong, Marsha tried to help her counselor understand her problems:

Marsha:
I feel empty—kind of lonely.
Therapist:
Do you have any friends in your life? What are your peers like?
Marsha:
I guess I have friends. I have a roommate in the dorm.
Therapist:
What do you do with your friends—go to the movies, shopping?
Marsha:
Yeah, I do those things. I belong to the swim team, too.

---

*The clinical examples in this text are actual cases, but identifying information, including gender of the client or therapist, has been altered at times to ensure confidentiality.

Therapist:

Do you like your friends? You're new to the university; maybe you need some new friends here at school.

Marsha:

Well I've had friends, but I just feel empty.

Therapist:

But you've just left your family and come to college. You must miss your family and feel lonely. It's natural to feel lonely when you move away from home. Most of the other kids in the dorm feel that way, too. I know I sure did when I moved away to college.

Marsha:

Oh.

Therapist:

This is not unusual at all. You're going to be just fine.

Marsha:

I hope so. Maybe my family is different though. In high school, I always thought that my family had more problems than my friends' did.

Therapist:

Yeah, but like I said, it's real natural for you to be kind of emotional at this time in your life.

Marsha:

It is? But I still feel different than everybody else.

Therapist:

Sure, it's real natural for you to feel different than everybody else. Late adolescence, moving away to college—it's a tough time in life. You're going to be just fine. Do you have a boyfriend?

Marsha:

Yes, I try to tell him what's wrong, but it doesn't work. And then he gets angry at me because nothing helps. I just don't know why I get depressed a lot. My mother used to yell at me a lot, though.

Therapist:

Do you have trouble eating or sleeping?

Marsha:

I've lost five pounds, and I wake up at night crying sometimes.

Therapist:

Are you eating alone? Maybe you should be eating with friends.

Marsha: [with resignation]

Maybe that would help.

Marsha could not say exactly why, but she did not like seeing the counselor and she did not go back. She became even more depressed as the semester went on, wondered what was "wrong" with her, and struggled in her classes. During advising for second semester, a concerned professor saw her distress and talked her into going back and trying another counselor. Reluctantly, Marsha agreed.

Therapy began much more slowly this time. Marsha found herself angry at the therapist and reluctant to share much. She alternately acted blasé and then distressed, but would never allow the therapist to stay with her experience for very long. The therapist was not frustrated, however, and was effective at communicating his continuing interest and concern for her. After about six weeks, Marsha sensed that this relationship might be safe enough to risk disclosing her feelings again:

Marsha:
I feel empty.
Therapist:
What's it like to feel empty?
Marsha:
I just feel empty.
Therapist:
Can you show me in some way what that emptiness feels like?
Marsha:
[long pause; nothing is said]
Therapist:
Can you use just adjectives, or make a sound, or a gesture?
Marsha:
There's just an emptiness inside. The wind blows right through me. I'm always hungry—it never gets filled up.
Therapist:
That's right—you just feel empty inside. Sex, alcohol, food—nothing fills it up. The hole just stays there.
Marsha:
[doesn't speak; nods and becomes teary; looks at therapist]
Therapist:
[holding her gaze kindly] I feel for you. I can see how much you are hurting. It's very sad that things have happened to make you feel this empty and alone.
Marsha:
[cries and nods again] There's something wrong with me.
Therapist:
Tell me about it.

This time, Marsha was heard and felt understood. She was not crying alone in her room unanswered anymore. In many successive discussions, the therapist continued to listen and respond to what was most important for Marsha. Although there were ups and downs and many other aspects of her treatment, a collaborative working relationship had begun, and Marsha ultimately went on to resolve her depression and successfully complete therapy.

The concept of "understanding the client" sounds simple enough. All the therapist has to do is listen carefully to what clients say, grasp the underlying accompanying feelings, and find a way to let clients know that the therapist understands and is touched by their experience. However, it is not easy for most beginning therapists to do this with clients. Most of us have been strongly socialized to "hear" in a limited, superficial way that denies the painful, conflicted aspects of people's communications. This was why Marsha's first counselor could not hear what she was truly saying and avoided the difficult emotions involved. Although the overt content of what the counselor said was apt, the process he enacted with her was problematic. By reassuring and trying to talk her out of her feelings, he metaphorically reenacted her developmental conflict of not being seen or heard.

Although most beginning therapists are aware that they also possess a "third ear"—that is, they already have a highly developed ability to hear the basic meaning in what people say—they often feel they must avoid acknowledging the true content of these underlying messages because of their emotional content. As a result, many beginning therapists have a pervasive habit of automatically switching to a more superficial level to avoid the emotional conflicts and closeness that accompany empathic listening.

Marsha's second counselor broke the social rules, however, and responded to the central affective meaning in her message "I feel empty." As a result, Marsha felt understood for the first time. In a small but significant way, this was a corrective emotional experience. The therapist joined her in her experience and approached her feelings. He did not move away from them by trying to talk her out of them, as had happened in the past. For many beginning therapists, an exciting but stressful component of clinical training is stepping out of the social norms they grew up with. This means that therapists can start to respond in this more direct, empathic way, use the ability they already possess to hear what is most important to the client, and take the risk of saying what they see.

To summarize, therapy offers clients an opportunity to be understood more fully than they have been in other relationships. When this understanding occurs in the initial session, clients begin to feel they have been seen and are no longer invisible, alone, strange, or unimportant. At that moment, the client begins to perceive the therapist as someone who is different from most other people and possibly as someone who can help. In other words, hope is engendered when the therapist understands and articulates the personal meaning that each successive vignette holds for the client. With this in mind, let us look more specifically at how the therapist can find the central meaning in what the client presents.

Identify Recurrent Themes

At the beginning of this chapter it was suggested that therapists start the session by encouraging the client's initiative, following the client's lead, identifying the meaning in what the client relays, and sharing this understanding with the client. Although this may sound simple to do, it is not. To accomplish it, *the therapist must give up a great deal of control over the direction of therapy and over the timimg of when issues are brought up for discussion. The therapist is placed in the far more demanding position of responding to the diverse and unpredictable material that the client produces, rather than simply directing what the client will cover.* This approach gives clients more control and responsibility in resolving their problems, but puts a greater demand on the therapist to understand the varied material that clients present. If the therapist can identify *recurrent themes* in the client's material, it will help the therapist make sense of the client's experience and better understand what is important to the client.

Suppose the client tells the therapist about her- or himself and the reasons for coming to therapy. As the therapist follows the different recollections and descriptions the client chooses to relate, the therapist needs to find an *integrating focus* for the wide diversity of material that the client is presenting. The therapist can do this by identifying a superordinate *theme, conflict,* or *affect* that recurs throughout the different material the client presents. For example, a client's various experiences are often linked together by a common *theme* (for example, "No one is trustworthy"; "I have no power"; "It's my fault"; "It wasn't fair"). Although the disparate material that clients present often seems unrelated and disconnected, synthesizing themes are usually present and can be found if the therapist listens for them.

Similarly, the different vignettes the client presents often contain a repetitive *conflict.* For example, the problems and concerns clients discuss often embody a central underlying conflict (for example, "I have to give up what I want in order to be close; if I follow my own interests and feelings, I have to be alone. Either way I lose."). Usually only two or three central conflicts recur throughout the varied problems that clients present.

Most important, there is often a repetitive *affect* that comes up again and again for the client (Mueller and Kell, 1966). As the therapist listens to the client, an overriding feeling such as sorrow, bitterness, or shame may pervade the client's mood or characterize the different experiences the client relates. Thus, if the therapist can identify the repetitive theme, central conflict, or primary affect that links together the client's experience, the client will feel that the therapist understands. We will explore these ideas further in later chapters, but for now, let us examine some issues that make it difficult for beginning therapists to understand their clients.

Performance Anxieties Impede the Therapist's Understanding

Therapists, like other people, often do not really hear what their clients are telling them. They are not accurately empathic and often do not capture the feeling and meaning in the client's experience. This section examines performance anxieties that make therapists less empathic and cause therapists to push clients to change prematurely.

Therapists will not be as effective with clients when they are burdened by their own excessive performance demands. Commonly, beginning therapists are trying too hard (to be helpful, to win approval from a supervisor, to prove their own adequacy to themselves, to be liked by the client). When therapists are trying too hard in one of these ways, it is almost impossible to decenter and be emotionally available to the client.

Too often, novice therapists are thinking about where the interview should be going next, wondering how best to phrase what they are going to say next, or worrying about what their supervisors would expect them to do at this point in the interview. This self-critical monitoring can immobilize student therapists, block their own creativity, and prevent them from being as sensitive and empathic to the client as they could be. Beginning therapists should slow down their own inner process of planning what to do and focus more on finding the meaning that this particular experience seems to hold for this particular client.

Beginning therapists' anxiety about their helping abilities can also be translated into a need to *do* something to make the client change. Novice therapists often believe they are supposed to make the client think, feel, or act differently within the initial therapy session. Paradoxically, when these unrealistic expectations come into play for the therapist, clients are more likely to drop out of therapy because they feel that the therapist is not with them or does not understand.

Therapists with excessive performance anxieties are less effective because they are responding more to their own internal need (to be helpful, competent, or liked) than they are to the client's need to be understood. Beginning therapists may be alerted to their own excessive performance demands if clients express that they are not being heard or are being told what to do, or hurried up. When this occurs, the most effective way for therapists to manage their performance anxieties is to discuss them with a supportive supervisor or colleague. We will elaborate on this point later.

Change Occurs in the Context of Care and Understanding

The therapist does need to help the client change, of course, but change is most likely to occur if the client first experiences the therapist as someone who understands and cares. In the initial sessions, the therapist's primary goal is to establish an emotional connection with the client and to begin a working alliance. This is more important than obtaining any specific information about the client or effecting any change. In this regard, one of the best ways to evaluate the success of an initial session is for therapists to ask themselves "Do I feel like I made contact with this person and have a genuine feeling for who he or she is?" Therapists are building an affective bridge to the client and creating the interpersonal context necessary for change when clients feel that the therapist is available, concerned, and sincerely trying to understand. If therapists provide this type of responsiveness throughout the initial session, they are already being helpful to the client.

Finally, we must address the most important component of what it means to understand the client. Therapists must *actively* extend themselves to the client and *directly* express their feeling and concern for the client. That is, therapists must articulate their understanding of the client's experience in a way that also communicates their compassion and care for the client.

This ability to articulate the client's experience in an accurate and caring way is illustrated beautifully in Selma Fraiberg et al.'s (1975) classic article, "Ghosts in the Nursery." The therapist in this case study is working with a very depressed young mother whom social services has judged to be at high risk for physically abusing her infant daughter. Early in treatment, the therapist is disconcerted as she observes the mother holding her crying baby in her arms for five minutes without trying to soothe it. The mother does not murmur comforting things in the baby's ear or rock it; she just looks away absently from the screaming baby. The therapist asks herself the question "Why can't this mother *hear* her baby's cries?"

As this young mother's own abusive history began to come out in treatment, the therapist realized that no one had ever heard or responded to the mother's own profound cries as a child. The therapist hypothesized that the mother "had closed the door on the weeping child within herself as surely as she had closed the door upon her own crying baby" (p. 392). This conceptual understanding led the therapist to a clinical hypothesis and basic treatment plan: when this mother's own cries are heard, she will hear her child's cries.

The therapist set about trying to hear and articulate compassionately the mother's own childhood experience. Her own mother had died when she was 5, and at age 11, her custodial aunt "went away." Responding to these profound losses and the mother's resultant feeling that "nobody wanted me," the therapist listened and put into words the feelings of the mother as a child:

> How hard this must have been. . . . This must have hurt deeply. . . . Of course you needed your mother. There was no one to turn to. . . . Yes. Sometimes grown-ups don't understand what all this means to a child. You must have needed to cry. . . . There was no one to hear you. (p. 396)

At different well-timed points in treatment, the therapist accurately captured the mother's experience in a way that gave her permission to feel and remember her feelings. As a result, the mother's grief and anguish for herself as a cast-off and abused child began to emerge. The mother sobbed; the therapist understood and comforted. In just a few more sessions, something remarkable happened. Usually when the baby cried, the mother ignored it. When the baby cried this time, the mother, for the first time, gathered the baby in her arms, held it close, and crooned in its ear. The therapist's hypothesis had been correct: when the mother's own cries were heard, she could hear her baby's cries. The risk for abuse ended as this beginning attachment flourished.

This case study illustrates how the therapist can use the therapeutic relationship to resolve the client's conflict. A corrective emotional experience occurred as the therapist responded to the mother's pain differently than it had been responded to in the past. This case study also illustrates how powerful it is when the therapist articulates an understanding of the client's experience in a way that also communicates the therapist's genuine feeling for the client.

Utilizing role models such as this one, beginning therapists need to go on to explore and develop their own personal ways of communicating that they are moved by the client's pain and are concerned about the client's life and well-being. Clients' inability to care about themselves is central to many of their conflicts, and most clients cannot care about themselves until they feel someone's caring for them (Gilligan, 1982). Therapists provide this care when they recognize what is important to the client, express their genuine concern about the client's distress, and communicate that the client is someone of worth and will be treated with dignity in this relationship. These are the therapist's goals in the beginning stage of therapy.

CLOSING

The interpersonal process approach tries to resolve problems in a way that leaves clients with a greater sense of their own capacities and abilities. This independence-fostering approach to psychotherapy can only be achieved through a collaborative therapeutic alliance. The client must be an active participant throughout each phase of treatment—not a "good patient" waiting for the "doctor" to cure him or to tell the client "what to do." This process dimension of how the therapist and client work together is more important than the theoretical orientation of the therapist or the content of what they discuss. This chapter has also underscored the profound therapeutic impact of listening and understanding. Perhaps because they are so simple, these basic, human responses are too easily overlooked. They are the foundation of every helping relationship, however, and the basis for establishing a collaborative therapeutic alliance.

SUGGESTIONS FOR FURTHER READING

1. Highly recommended is Chapter 3, "The Therapist's Stance," a marvelous exploration of the therapist's basic values and attitude toward the client, in H. Strupp, and J. Binder, "Psychotherapy in a New Key" (New York: Basic Books, 1984).

2. Illuminating ideas about the effects of multigenerational family relations on individual personality are found in these two articles on triangular coalitions: J. Haley, "Toward a Theory of Pathological Systems," in G. H. Zuk and I. Boszormenyi-Nagy, eds., *Family Therapy and Disturbed Families* (Palo Alto, Calif.: Science and Behavior Books, 1967), pp. 11–27; and especially, M. Bowen, "The Use of Family Theory in Clinical Practice," *Comprehensive Psychiatry* (1966): 345–376. Both of these articles will help therapists apply family systems concepts to the practice of individual psychotherapy.

3. For some, client-centered therapy connotes passivity on the part of the therapist and the lack of an effective treatment focus. However, Carl Rogers's original discussion of the therapeutic reflection (Chapter 4 of Carl Rogers, *Client-Centered Therapy* [Boston: Houghton Mifflin, 1951] remains an enormous contribution to psychotherapy that therapists should examine.

4. Chapter 1 of Ralph Greenson's book *The Technique and Practice of Psychoanalysis, Volume 1* (New York: International Universities Press, 1967), lucidly describes a collaborative therapeutic relationship. The reader does not have to be interested in psychoanalysis in order to glean valuable insights about this basic therapeutic dimension.

CHAPTER THREE

HONORING THE CLIENT'S RESISTANCE

J oan was nervous about seeing her first client, but the initial session actually went very well. The client talked at length about his concerns and, to her relief, she found it was easy to work with him. The client expressed some difficult feelings, and Joan felt that she understood what was important to him. She was sure they had begun a good working relationship when the client parted and said he looked forward to meeting again next week. One week later, however, Joan received a telephone message from the client saying that he was no longer interested in therapy. Confused and dismayed, Joan sat alone in her office wondering what had gone wrong.

CONCEPTUAL OVERVIEW

Just when the therapist feels that something important is getting started, some clients put their foot on the brakes. The client cancels his second appointment, shows up 25 minutes late, or asks to reschedule for Sunday at 7:00 A.M. This *resistance* is puzzling and frustrating for the novice therapist: "Why didn't he return; we had a great first session!" Although most clients will not be resistant in this particular way, other forms of resistance will occur regularly throughout the course of therapy. The purpose of this chapter is to help beginning therapists recognize, understand, and respond to client resistance.

All clients have both positive and negative feelings about entering therapy, although the positive feelings are usually more apparent initially. Clients are distressed and want relief from their suffering, and these painful feelings motivate them to seek therapy. We must look further into the complexity of the client's feelings, however. Clients also bring resistant feelings to therapy that must be acknowledged as well. Paradoxically, at the same time as clients are seeking help and trying to change, they are also fighting against

45

it. Why? Layers of fear become entwined with the original core of hurt, which makes it even more threatening for clients to approach their problems. The reasons for these fears differ for each client, but common themes include:

> If I let myself depend on the therapist, he or she might leave me, or take advantage of me, or try to control me as others have done when I needed them.
> I cannot ask for help or need anything from others because I must be perfect and in control all of the time.
> I am afraid of what I will see or what a perceptive therapist will learn about me if I stop and look inside of myself.
> Asking for help is admitting that there really is a problem, and if therapy does not help then I surely will be hopeless.
> If I cannot handle this by myself it means that I really am weak or dependent, just like they told me I am.

It is easy to respond to the *approach side* of clients' feelings, the hurt and pain that motivates them to enter therapy. If you gently scratch the surface it is usually right there in front of you, and the client wants you to respond to it. In contrast, the other side of the client's feelings—the reactive emotions to having a problem and needing help—may not be so accessible. These concerns over what it means to enter therapy or ask for help act as a countervailing force to the client's motivation to enter therapy. If unaddressed, these ambivalent feelings may draw clients out of therapy prematurely, as occurred in the opening vignette.

CHAPTER ORGANIZATION

The first section of this chapter discusses why it is difficult for both therapists and clients to approach resistance and work with this important aspect of clients' experience. The second section provides a working definition of resistance, clarifies when resistance is occurring, and suggests how therapists can conceptualize each client's resistance. The third section presents intervention guidelines for responding to some of the different types of resistance that clients may present. Common expressions of client resistance are illustrated at three different points in time: during the initial telephone contact, at the end of the first session, and during subsequent sessions. Sample therapist-client dialogues illustrate effective and ineffective responses at each point.

BOTH THERAPISTS AND CLIENTS WANT TO AVOID RESISTANCE

Imagine your client has missed, come very late for, or twice rescheduled her second appointment. Perhaps this has no significant meaning at all. Cars do break down, traffic jams occur, children get sick, and employees get called for work at the last minute. It is also possible, however, that this behavior reflects the client's ambivalence about some aspect of being in therapy. You may not know what this behavior means, but by trying to find out, you can increase the chances of the client's continued participation.

The Therapist's Reluctance to Address Resistance

To a greater or lesser degree, every client will be ambivalent, defensive, or resistant. This push-pull occurs at the beginning of therapy and will continue to wax and wane throughout treatment. Although therapists need to address signs of potential client resistance, this is difficult to do for many beginning (and experienced) therapists. Let us examine three reasons why therapists are often reluctant to approach their clients' resistance.

Many beginning therapists are not aware of the multiple meanings and conflicted issues that entering therapy arouses for new clients. In their initial therapy sessions, these therapists are surprised to find that their clients actually resist the help they are overtly seeking. For other therapists, the concept of resistance is more familiar, but it has a pejorative connotation. These therapists have observed that resistance can be used to keep the therapist in a superior position and to deny the validity of the client's own experience. This occurs, for example, when a therapist says to a working, single mother of three, "Hmm, I notice that you are four minutes late for our appointment today." Resistance does not have to be associated with this type of insensitive or hierarchical therapist-client relationship. Resistance can be used instead to strengthen the client's commitment to therapy and to enhance the therapeutic alliance.

There is another, more personal reason why therapists are often reluctant to approach their clients' resistance. Most novice therapists have strong needs for their clients to like them, find them helpful, and to keep coming to therapy. If the client does not show up or comes late, therapists often feel that they have failed. When this occurs, therapists become increasingly concerned about their ability to help others and overly invested in the next client's satisfaction with therapy.

In order to ward off unwanted criticism, therapists often do not inquire about signs of potential resistance. Most therapists, like their clients, are not eager to approach issues that arouse their own anxiety. Thus, the beginning therapist may be hesitant to invite clients to express negative reactions they may have toward the therapist or being in therapy. Although it is difficult to invite critical feedback and approach conflicts, it is necessary to do. The paradox is that if therapists allow their own anxiety to keep them from approaching clients' resistance, their clients will be more likely to end therapy prematurely.

The Client's Reluctance to Address Resistance

Unfortunately, the client usually shares the therapist's reluctance to address resistance. Clients are confused by their own contradictory behavior when they see themselves resisting. For example, clients often exclaim with dismay:

> Why do I go to all the trouble and expense of coming here to see you, when I can't think of anything to say as soon as I walk in the door?
> Why would I forget our next appointment after we had such a great session last week? It doesn't make sense!
> Why do I keep asking you for advice, and then say "Yes, but . . . " to whatever you suggest? What's wrong with me?

Clients also interpret their own resistance as being bad and project this critical attitude onto the therapist. When the therapist begins to inquire about resistance, most clients want to avoid the topic because they are afraid the therapist will blame them for not really trying, failing, or being unmotivated. The therapist must help clients reframe their critical attitude toward their own resistance and appreciate the fact that they originally learned this defensive behavior for very good reasons. Both the therapist and client must *honor* the client's resistance, as it originally served a self-preservative and adaptive function. We will examine below what it means to honor the client's resistance, and will view it as *the best possible response to an unsolvable conflict that the client had available at that point in her development.*

Past experiences with family members and other significant relationships have given clients very good reasons for not wanting to ask for help, not sharing a painful feeling, or not risking a disclosing relationship. If the therapist and client explore how significant others have responded in the past, the client's resistance will become understandable. The feelings that underlie the client's resistance always make sense historically, although they are no longer necessary or adaptive in most current relationships.

For example, suppose that a client is having trouble entering therapy. The therapist might ask:

> What might I do to hurt you or make things worse if you seek help from me?
>
> OR
>
> How have others responded to you in the past when you have asked for help or needed someone?

These types of questions will help the therapist and the client identify the aversive consequences that occurred for the client when help was asked for in the past. For example, clients may respond that they were ignored and felt powerless, were made fun of and felt ashamed, or were told that they were selfish and too demanding. They may have been told they didn't really need or want something, or felt there were strings or obligations attached to everything they received, and so on. In this way, therapists and clients can clarify both why and how clients originally learned to defend themselves.

Thus the first thing the therapist must do is help clients *understand* why they originally needed to defend themselves and how they are continuing to do that now in therapy. Second, the therapist must confirm or *validate* the necessary protection this resistance once provided. That is, the maladaptive resistance in the therapeutic relationship was once an adaptive response. The original defensive behavior minimized the hurt and allowed the client to cope with the painful interpersonal response that repeatedly occurred. Third, the therapist must also *differentiate* his or her own response in the current relationship from the aversive ways that significant others have responded in the past. For example, the therapist might respond:

> In the past you learned that if you allowed your____to help you or take care of you, she wanted you to remain a child and continue to need her. I would like to respond to your need, but I am different from your____. I do not need for you to remain dependent on me. I would like to help you achieve your own independence so that you will not need me any longer, and will be able to go on with your own adult life.

Therapists must follow this three-step sequence: identify the original transactional pattern, validate the client's unmet need and defensive adaptation to it, and differentiate the therapist's current response from the past dynamic. This three-step sequence will need to be repeated many times with different manifestations of resistance throughout the course of treatment.

We have seen, then, that clients are far more likely to become stalled in therapy, or to drop out, if their resistance is not addressed. One of the most important ways to keep clients in treatment, and to identify conflict areas in clients' lives, is to invite clients' negative reactions toward therapy and the therapist. The guiding principle is that if clients *talk* about their feelings of not wanting to be in therapy, or express what they do not like about the therapist, clients will be less likely to *act* on their ambivalence and drop out. Before going on to illustrate specific ways to implement this general principle, we must first learn how to identity and conceptualize clients' resistance.

IDENTIFYING AND CONCEPTUALIZING RESISTANCE

Early in their training, many therapists will have several clients drop out of therapy within the first few sessions. The main reason clients prematurely terminate is because they are *acting on*, rather than *talking about*, their conflicted feelings about entering therapy. In order to help clients remain in treatment, the therapist must be prepared to identify when resistance is occurring, directly approach this issue with clients, and help clients resolve these concerns. To do this, the therapist must first be able to identify when resistance is occurring.

The Client's Difficulty Participating in Treatment

How does the therapist know when a client is resisting treatment? Resistance is usually operating whenever clients have difficulty participating in treatment. For example, clients are probably resisting when any of the following occur repeatedly or in tandem:

The client misses the appointment or comes late.
The client needs to reschedule the appointment.
The client has very limited hours available for therapy.
The client cannot make a firm commitment to attend the next session.

It is important to stress that the same behavior often means very different things to different clients. Therapists never know for certain what any particular behavior means, but whenever clients have trouble attending sessions it is likely that some form of resistance is occurring. In such cases, the therapist should *generate working hypotheses* about the possible meaning this resistance holds for the client.

The Therapist's Formulation of Working Hypotheses

Therapists must formulate *tentative hypotheses* about clients' conflicts, central feelings, primary expectations, and interpersonal style right from the initial contact. One systematic way to do this is for therapists to formulate answers to three successive questions for each client.

What Do Clients Elicit from Others? The first question therapists can assess is "What does the client's interpersonal style tend to elicit from others?" Even in the initial telephone contact, clients' interpersonal style and what it tends to elicit from others is an important source of information. For example, if the client sounds helpless and confused on the telephone, might he or she adopt a victim stance and invite others' rescuing behavior? Or if the client presents in an angry and demanding way, might others often withdraw and leave him or her alone? If so, perhaps this client is testing whether the therapist can tolerate the angry challenges and still see the underlying need and hurt. As therapy progresses and the therapist learns more about each client, many of these initial hypotheses will prove inaccurate and will need to be discarded. Others will fit the client, however, and these formulations can be further developed and refined. It is important to formulate, evaluate, and revise hypotheses regarding each client's dynamics.

What Is the Threat? The second question therapists can ask themselves concerns the client's potential resistance: "What might this particular client find threatening about being in therapy?" Based on other information about the client's past relationships and interpersonal style, the therapist can begin speculating how this client could be averse to therapy. For example,

> Is it incongruent with this client's perfectionistic demands to need help?
>
> OR
>
> Is it difficult for this older Chicano male to seek help from a younger female therapist?

Therapists should formulate working hypotheses such as these about the feelings, issues, or concerns that are likely to be difficult for each client. Therapists must also keep in mind that resistance and defense are always reflections of fear. Although clients may or may not be aware of it, they are afraid that if they continue in treatment the therapist will hurt them in the same way their parents did when they were a child. Over time, the therapist will need to help clients clarify this fear and invite them to risk a new relationship and see if the therapist's response will be different from their past negative experiences.

How Will the Client Express Resistance? Finally, therapists should formulate a third set of hypotheses that anticipate how clients will play out or enact these concerns with the therapist. For example, suppose that a therapist has observed that her depressed client feels selfish and guilty whenever she does something for herself, or whenever someone does something for her. The therapist then hypothesizes that this client may withdraw from treatment as soon as she starts to feel better, or emotionally disengage from the therapist when she realizes that the therapist genuinely cares for her.

To illustrate further, let us look at working hypotheses for each of these three questions in the following example. Suppose that a male client whose problem is substance abuse telephones the therapist to schedule an initial appointment. During this initial telephone contact, the client tells the therapist that his alcohol and drug usage is more problematic than it has ever been and that his mother believes that he "really needs to be in therapy." Based on this information and other impressions the therapist has gathered, the therapist hypothesizes that an important part of the client's interpersonal style is to let others know he is hurting, elicit help from them, but then avoid taking responsibility for his own needs and behavior.

Continuing with the second question, the therapist hypothesizes that this client may become resistant to treatment when the therapist addresses the issue of how he meets his dependency needs, or when the client is given reality-based confrontations about how he eschews responsibility for his own decisions (for example, to enter therapy, continue drinking, and so forth). Third, the therapist hypothesizes that this client is impulsive and that he may act out his resistance by bolting out of therapy as soon as these anxiety-arousing issues are addressed.

Thus, the therapist must try to anticipate the concerns that might cause each client to drop out of treatment and the way each client is likely to express these concerns. This will enable the therapist to help clients antici-pate their own resistance before they act on it, and it will help the therapist to respond more effectively once clients have already begun to act on their resistance.

As the therapist spends more time with the client, the therapist will learn much more about this person, and many of these general, initial hypotheses will need to be discarded. Some of them will probably be accurate, however, and these can be elaborated to help understand this particular client. In this way, the therapist identifies the enduring issues that arise for the client. The therapist will then be better prepared to *center treatment around these re-peated themes,* which provides structure and focus for the ongoing course of treatment. As we will see in Chapter 7, this is part of the continuing process of formulating and refining one's conceptualization of client dynamics and treatment plans.

RESPONDING TO RESISTANCE

This section illustrates how therapists can respond to the types of client resis-tance that commonly occur at the beginning of therapy. Sample therapist-client dialogues illustrate effective and ineffective responses at three critical points. The first situation examines different ways of handling a telephone conversation in which the client has difficulty scheduling the initial appoint-ment. Next, we will examine several ways of inquiring about resistance and ambivalence at the end of the initial session. Third, we will examine sample dialogues with clients who have difficulty attending subsequent appointments. As before, student therapists should find their own words to express the principles embodied in these dialogues.

The Client's Resistance During the Initial Telephone Contact

The first situation in which resistance may be encountered is in trying to schedule the initial appointment. The therapist wishes to obtain a firm com-mitment from the client. The client, however, may be ambivalent about entering therapy and express this during the initial telephone contact. The therapist should be prepared to respond directly to this issue.

An Uncertain Commitment. In the first example below, the client is only somewhat ambiguous about attending the first session.

Therapist:
    It's been good talking with you, and I'll see you on Tuesday at 4:00.
Client:
    Okay, I guess I'll see you then.
Therapist:
    You "guess so." Does that mean you are not certain you will be there?
Client:
    Oh no, I will be there for sure.
Therapist:
    Good, I am looking forward to meeting with you. See you next Tuesday at 4:00.

An effective response to the client's ambiguity ("I guess so") is modeled above. The therapist hears the indecision in the client's commitment and addresses it directly. An ineffective response would be for the therapist to let it pass by unnoticed. Indeed, chances are that the client will still arrive at the appointed hour anyway. However, the chances of the client not arriving are far greater if the therapist does not directly address the signs of uncertain commitment.

Further, the therapist should mentally note this indecision as a possible sign of resistance to treatment. This is an instance in which the therapist can begin to generate working hypotheses about the possible meaning of relevant client behavior. Of course, it is very possible that this client's ambiguous statement means little or nothing. On the other hand, it may reflect that the client has difficulty making commitments, entering into new relationships, doing things to meet her own needs, and so on.

A More Ambivalent Client. Let us return to the topic of the client's resistance, but this time take it one step further with a more difficult client. Imagine that we have returned to the same telephone conversation:

Client:
    Okay, I guess I'll see you then.
Therapist:
    You "guess so." Does that mean you are not certain you will be there?

Client:

Don't worry, I'll be there unless something comes up.

Therapist:

I need a firm commitment from you to attend the first session before I will agree to meet with you. Maybe there is something about coming here that doesn't feel right to you. Can we talk about that for a minute?

OR

Can we agree to meet only one time on Tuesday at 4:00? At that time we can discuss what therapy is and any concerns you may have about it.

An ineffective response would be to accept the client's uncertain commitment ("Okay, I guess I'll see you Tuesday at 4:00") and deny that an important issue is being played out. In this dialogue the therapist has continued to push for a firm commitment from the client, even if that is only to attend the first session. The therapist has taken what may seem like an unnecessarily hard line: not making an appointment based on a response of "maybe." The therapist wants to accept the client's ambivalent feelings and to make them overt as a topic for discussion. However, the therapist wants to discourage the client from acting on the ambivalence as much as possible. So, although the therapist invites the client to talk about the ambivalence, the therapist wants the client to make a decision whether to enter therapy.

It is important to emphasize that the therapist does not stop with the requirement of a firm commitment to attend the first session. The therapist also makes an effort to address the client's difficulty in making a decision. In this example, the therapist offers to try to help the client ("Can we talk about that for a minute").

Why must the therapist take such a firm stance? Wouldn't it be more supportive to let clients leave the appointment a little bit tentative if that is what they need to do? Little or no therapeutic change will occur until clients take responsibility for the decision to enter therapy and work on their problems. Clients' commitments can be very short—for one session or for just a few sessions—to get a sense of whether therapy is for them. However, it is necessary for clients to take responsibility for this decision before therapy can progress. Without this commitment, the therapist has little to work with. In fact, it is better for the client to remain out of therapy than to enter without commitment and have an unsuccessful therapeutic experience. The therapist must be concerned about preventing failed hope in the client. If clients have one or more unsuccessful therapy experiences, it may discourage them from trying to seek help with their problems again.

Clients Who Try to Make the Therapist Responsible. Let us continue the conversation above and examine a particular response that many clients will give the therapist. At this point in the telephone conversation, some clients will try to make the therapist take responsibility for their decisions. The therapist does not want to resolve the client's ambivalence by assuming responsibility for his decision or by trying to provide the necessary motivation for therapy. Suppose the client says:

I'm not sure if I should start therapy or not, what do you think I should do?

Although well intended, it is not helpful to automatically tell the client to go ahead and begin. For example, it might be easy for the therapist to say:

Oh, I'm sure I could be helpful to you.

OR

Yes, you should definitely see me in therapy.

A more effective response is for the therapist to help clients take responsibility for their own decisions. The therapist does not want to cajole, coerce, or win the client into therapy. *The therapist must keep responsibility for the client's behavior squarely in the client's lap.* At the same time, however, the therapist does not want to leave clients stranded and alone. The therapist needs to reach out and work with clients on their ambivalence. If this is done skillfully, the therapist will help the client without taking the responsibility or providing an external solution for the client. Thus, a more effective response is for the therapist to say:

It seems as if one part of you wants to be in therapy, but another part of you doesn't. Tell me about both sides of your feelings.

In this example the therapist is inviting the client to express all concerns about entering therapy. Thus, the therapist is working with the client to reach a decision but does this in a way that leaves the client responsible for his or her own decision. Here again, we are working with the process dimension in psychotherapy. Although this process distinction is subtle, it will make all the difference in the outcome of therapy.

The client in the dialogue above is providing the therapist with potentially important information about himself. Just as before, the therapist should begin generating working hypotheses about what this behavior may mean. For example, uncertain clients may not have been supported when they have tried to take responsibility for their own actions. These clients may now try to avoid the aversive consequences they have experienced in the past by getting others to take responsibility for them. If so, this could make it difficult for clients to initiate new activities (such as applying for college) or follow through on their own wishes and interests (such as selecting the major or career choice they are most interested in). Being held back in this way may leave clients feeling resentful and frustrated as well.

Therapists can generate hypotheses such as these and be alert for evidence of these themes in other arenas of the client's life. If these prove to be enduring and pervasive issues, the therapist is better prepared to focus on them later in therapy. The therapist must not become wed to these early hypotheses, however, but be ready to discard them if further supporting data is not forthcoming. As therapists become more experienced, their initial hypotheses will become more fruitful.

Even these initial tentative formulations can help therapists respond more effectively, however. As noted in Chapter 1, the therapist does not want to recapitulate the client's conflict in the therapeutic relationship. This can easily occur in an encapsulated way in the initial negotiations between therapist and client. This is another reason why the therapist should not take over and tell the client seeking advice what to do—for example:

> Based on what you've told me, I'm confident that therapy can help you and believe that you should begin now.

Assuming such a directive stance often reenacts a prototypic and problematic interaction for clients. Clients often feel that they cannot act on what they want, or that they need to be dependent and let others assume responsibility for their decisions. Although clients often feel they need to ask the therapist to tell them what to do, it also makes clients feel that their own autonomy is being suffocated at the same time. Paradoxically, clients resist the control they have just elicited by avoiding or rebelling against the therapist. As this scenario continues, clients come to feel badly about themselves—confused as to why they are rejecting the help they have just asked for and guilty for rejecting the therapist who was trying to help. The therapeutic responses suggested earlier prevent this reenactment from occurring, and may provide clients with a new and different response to an old conflict.

The Client's Resistance at the End of the First Session

At the end of the first session, the therapist should ask clients how the session felt to them. The therapist should also ask about any dissatisfaction with therapy or difficulty with the therapist that the client may have had. The therapist should ask about these concerns even if they were not evident in the session.

Approach Interpersonal Conflict. Even if the first session went very well, five minutes before the end of it the therapist should ask:

> How was it to be here today?

Most clients will answer, "Fine." Thinking that the therapist may need some reassurance or to try to win approval, many clients will go on to tell the therapist how helpful the session has been. If so, the therapist might respond:

Good, I'm glad you've found our first session helpful. You've told me a lot about yourself today, and I feel we have gotten off to a good start too. But was there anything about coming today, or anything that I did, that did not feel good to you? If so, it is important that we talk about that.

Client:

Oh no, I was eager to begin and you have been very nice and understanding.

Therapist:

That's fine, but if in the future you ever have any uncomfortable feelings about me or therapy, I would like for you to talk with me about them. Would you be sure to do that?

In this vignette the therapist is trying to establish an important set of rules and expectations for what is going to occur in therapy. Unlike many relationships the client has experienced, the therapist is telling the client that the therapist can tolerate the client's angry or dissatisfied feelings. The therapist is also saying that the therapist is not afraid of conflict and wants to deal with problems between them straightforwardly. Although many clients will not be able to accept this bid initially, the therapist is laying the groundwork for an honest and direct relationship. Therapists want to establish these important expectations with their actions, not just their words, early in the course of treatment.

A More Assertive Client. Let us stay with the same situation, but imagine we have a more assertive client this time. What happens if the therapist raises the same type of query as before:

How has it been for you to talk with me today?

This time the client is critical of the therapist and says,

I thought you were trying to push me or hurry me up.

The therapist must learn to *approach* the conflict, rather than avoid it by moving on to another topic or ending it with a punitive response. The best way to approach the conflict is to encourage the client to express fully his or her critical reaction. For example, the therapist might respond:

I'm sorry that happened. Let's look at that together and try to understand what happened for each of us. Tell me more about your feeling of being pushed or hurried up.

Of course, it is often difficult for beginning therapists to do this. The therapist's anxiety may be aroused by such confrontations, especially if the therapist has strong needs for the client's approval. In order to help therapists approach such anxiety-arousing confrontations, therapists must become aware of their own characteristic responses to interpersonal conflict. For example, many therapists will want to avoid or ignore the client's confrontation or will readily agree with and apologize to the client in order to abate the criticism. Other therapists will automatically begin to defend themselves and offer long justifications and explanations to the client. A few therapists will counter with their own hostility. Every therapist must become aware of how she or he typically reacts to difficult confrontations.

One of the best ways to do this is to recall how the therapist's own family of origin dealt with interpersonal conflict. Regardless of age, the therapist's initial reaction to conflict usually follows closely from how his or her parents dealt with conflict in their marriage and how each parent dealt with conflict with the therapist as a child. Rather than reflexively following their initial propensity, therapists must learn to *approach* conflicts with clients.

After inviting clients to express fully their concerns, therapists must accept the validity of clients' perception. Perhaps the client is right and the therapist was rushing the client. The therapist must honestly examine his or her own behavior and see if the client's perception is accurate. If so, the therapist should not be afraid to admit the mistake to the client—for example:

Therapist:
  Yes, I think you're right. I was aware of the time going by and I wanted to touch on a few more issues before we had to stop. I probably was pushing you there, and I can see why that bothered you. I'm glad you made me aware of that; I'll try not to do it again.

It is liberating for beginning therapists to learn that they do not need to be afraid of making mistakes, although they may need to acknowledge them. In the example above, the therapist is responding to the client on the basis of reality and in an egalitarian way. The client's perception is validated by the therapist, which tells the client that the therapist is willing to have a genuine dialogue. It also tells the client that the therapist will respond to the client's concerns with respect and that the therapist-client relationship is going to be a two-way street. Too often, therapists and clients enact a relationship in which the client is the sick and needy one and the therapist is the healthy one who does not make mistakes or have problems. The response suggested above discourages this illusion. Overall, these messages can have a powerful effect on clients' expectations of therapy and accelerate the level of disclosure and exploration clients undertake in subsequent sessions.

In contrast, therapists can handle the confrontation in a way that hides their own humanity, keeps the relationship safely distant, and puts them in a superior position. For example, an ineffective response to this client's criticism would be to put it back on the client:

> So you saw me as hurrying you up; how was that for you?

This response is an abuse of the client-centered reflection or psychoanalytic *blank screen*. With this type of *deflection*, the message to the client is "It's always your problem, I will not look at my own contribution here, this will not be a genuine interpersonal encounter." This type of response limits the relationship to a superficial encounter and sets up a power battle between client and therapist. Little therapeutic gain will be realized as long as the relationship continues in this mode.

But what if the therapist does not agree with the client's complaint? The therapist should still accept the validity of the client's perception, but without agreeing to the comment. For example, the therapist can respond:

> I'm sorry you saw me as being impatient with you; that wouldn't feel very good to me either. I wasn't aware of being in a hurry or trying to push you, but I'll be alerted to that in the future. If you ever feel that happens again, stop me right then and we'll look at it together.

The therapist should never agree to something he or she doesn't believe is true. In the example above, the therapist is telling the client:

> I will take your concerns seriously even if I do not see it the same way. We can have differences between us and still work together.
> Your feelings about our relationship are important to me.

This type of response also tells the client that problems between them can be resolved, which lends hope that the therapist and client together will be able to resolve the client's problems.

Finally, it is very possible that the client is systematically misperceiving the therapist as being hurrying. For example, this client may readily experience the therapist and most other authority figures as demanding more than the client would like to produce and then being dissatisfied with whatever the client does produce. If so, this client may have grown up with a parent who repeatedly demanded that the client do everything on the parent's timetable and/or ignored the child's own wishes and accomplishments. Even if the

therapist has gained further evidence to support such a hypothesis, presenting this type of historical or transference interpretation should be done later
in therapy. Therapists stand to lose a lot if clients see them as sidestepping a
reality confrontation. However, the therapist can use this information to generate working hypotheses that can be utilized later.

Clients Who Test the Therapist's Adequacy. Because it is usually difficult for
beginning therapists to respond to client confrontations, we will examine another example of confrontation. In the following situation, the client challenges the therapist's competence. Although this taps into an anxiety-
arousing area for the novice therapist, the therapist still approaches the issue
and invites the client to express the concern more fully.

Therapist:
> You arrived late today. We should talk about that for a minute. I wonder if
> there is something about seeing me, or being in therapy, that doesn't feel
> right to you.

Client:
> Well, aren't you just a student here? Isn't that what you said the first time
> we spoke?

Therapist:
> Yes, I'm a second-year graduate student, working on my master's degree.

Client:
> Well, I don't really feel like a guinea pig or anything, but you really are
> just practicing on me, aren't you? Maybe you haven't had enough experi-
> ence to help me?

Therapist:
> Are you worried that if you go to all of the trouble of coming here and talk
> about difficult problems with me that I just won't know enough to be able
> to help you?

Client:
> Yeah, after all, you really are just a beginner, and I must be fifteen years
> older than you. What do you think—are you certain that you can help
> me?

Therapist:
> I certainly cannot offer you any guarantees, but I will do my best to try to
> help you. And as we continue to meet together a few times, you will be able
> to decide for yourself if I can help you or not. But for now, let's see if there
> are any questions I can answer for you about my training status, and then
> we should talk about how our age difference might get in the way.

In this vignette, the therapist was able to approach the client's concern,
even though this was difficult to do. The therapist did not act on initial im-

pulse, which was to try to assure the client of the therapist's competence and ability to help. Instead of responding to personal need, the therapist was able to respond to the client by inviting the client to express reservations directly and fully. By tolerating personal discomfort and discussing the client's concerns, the therapist *demonstrated* competence. This is always more effective than offering verbal reassurances, which would only sound hollow to the client and still leave the burden of proof on the therapist.

The Client's Difficulty Entering Therapy. In the previous two examples, the therapist inquired about resistance and the client expressed concerns that personally challenged the therapist. In the following example, the therapist addresses the client's resistance, and the client expresses concerns about entering therapy. This occurs more commonly than challenging the therapist and is usually far easier for the therapist to respond to. For example, a client may respond:

It's hard for me to ask for help.

OR

I'm a little embarrassed talking to a stranger. In our family, we kept our problems to ourselves.

First and foremost, it is crucially important to let clients know that you have heard their concerns, take them seriously, and want to do something about the problem. Again, the best way to communicate this respect and responsiveness is to invite clients to discuss their concerns more fully. For example, the therapist might say:

That does sound like an important concern for us. Let's talk more about it. What does it mean for you to need help?

OR

I'm glad you can tell me about your embarrassment. It is very different for you to talk to someone like me who you don't really know very well.

Taking this further, it is even more essential to listen and respond to the client's concerns when ethnic/cultural differences exist between the therapist and client (Pinderhughes, 1989). As before, the best way to work with these important differences is to acknowledge them openly and address them directly. For example, suppose a black client says, "I don't know if you can help me because you're white." The therapist can respond by accepting the client's concern and being willing to explore it further: "That's right, our cultural backgrounds are very different. Tell me some of the ways our color could keep us from working together well."

In all three of the examples above, the therapist is able to follow the suggested guidelines and *approach* the client's conflict. As the therapist and client discuss the conflict, some concerns will be taken away by educating the client more fully about the process of therapy. Other concerns will be resolved by correcting inaccurate assumptions about the therapist. However, some of the concerns that clients express cannot be assuaged so easily. The therapist can offer to be sensitive to these concerns and express a willingness to work with the client on them over the course of therapy. One of the best ways to do this is by enlisting clients' help in better understanding their background and experience. That is, *the therapist can invite clients to tell the therapist when they are not feeling understood.* The therapist can then ask clients to share their experience more fully and begin a mutual dialogue that will bring the therapist closer to clients' actual experience.

As before, when ethnic/cultural differences exist, this approach of enlisting the client's help is even more apt. It is counterproductive for the therapist to labor under the misconception that it is the therapist's responsibility to understand everything about a client from a different culture. Instead, the therapist can simply invite the client to educate the therapist whenever the client feels that the therapist is misinformed or does not understand. By welcoming this clarification instead of feeling threatened by it, the therapist wins clients' appreciation of the therapist's acceptance of their very real differences, openness to a true dialogue, and invitation for a real relationship. In sum, giving all clients an opportunity to express their concerns about treatment or the therapist and sincerely trying to accommodate them as much as possible will go a long way toward diminishing those concerns.

Approaching Resistance During Subsequent Sessions

The third and final section of this chapter examines therapeutic responses when a client cancels, does not show up, or comes late to subsequent appointments. The therapist must consider the possible meaning this behavior holds for the client. In most cases, clients are not fully aware of their conflicted feelings about therapy. When people have consistently had their feelings invalidated and perceptions disconfirmed, they will eventually lose awareness of many aspects of their experience. Thus, resistant clients are not lying or deceiving the therapist; they are simply unaware of the multiple contradictory feelings they have about seeking help and being in treatment. For example, clients may be unaware that:

Getting help is relieving, but may also arouse detested feelings of humiliation.
Feeling cared about is comforting, but can also evoke sadness about the many times this need went unfulfilled.
Being listened to and heard is reassuring, but sometimes may trigger guilt over not having a right to one's own feelings.

Unless addressed and clarified, these conflicted emotional reactions will cause some clients to leave therapy and prevent others from moving forward and resolving their problems. At the beginning of their clinical training, many therapists do not yet appreciate the ambivalent, push-pull nature of emotional conflicts. Let's examine this further by recalling Marsha from Chapter 2.

It was profoundly reassuring for Marsha when her second therapist approached her feelings directly and validated her experience. At the same time, however, this very positive experience also aroused other contradictory feelings that she "hated." Marsha now felt heard and understood but she also felt:

sad as years of unacknowledged loneliness welled up;
angry at not being heard so many times;
guilty and disloyal to her parents for feeling angry at them;
anxious as her ties to her internalized parents felt threatened.

Marsha did not want to experience any of these feelings. She did not understand them, felt threatened by them, and could not make them go away. Fortunately, her therapist was comfortable with the push-pull ambivalent nature of conflict. He continued to help her understand the different, contradictory aspects of her experience that emerged. Over time, Marsha was able to integrate these conflicted feelings and resolve them.

Clients are usually unaware of and threatened by their conflicted feelings about continuing in treatment. As a result, clients often feel blamed when the therapist inquires about potential signs of resistance. That is, clients often feel that the therapist's questions imply that they are doing something wrong or are not trying hard enough. Concerned that the therapist is angry or disappointed with them, clients may try to justify their good intentions (for example, "Oh no, you don't understand. I really do want to see you and get here on time. It's just that . . . "). Therapists do not want clients to feel blamed; rather, the client is invited to join the therapist in trying to understand the danger or threat that some aspect of treatment has aroused.

To achieve this, the therapist must be direct but gentle when approaching resistance. This may sound contradictory to some beginning therapists. Without gentleness, however, approaching resistance directly can be experienced as an aggressive "stripping away" of the client's defenses. Of course, this is never the intention. In actuality, few beginning therapists respond in this aggressive or intrusive way. Instead, many beginning therapists are too worried about hurting their clients and do not respond as forthrightly or strongly as they could. If beginning therapists are worried that their explorations may be too intrusive, aggressive, or exposing for the client, they can always stop and find another way to respond. Or better yet, they can check out their concern with the client by posing the question directly.

The therapeutic goal is to address signs of client resistance directly but in a collaborative, nonthreatening way. Thus, therapists can wonder aloud with clients about the possible meanings certain behavior may hold rather than insist on exploring a client's resistance. In other words, therapists must address resistance in a way that leaves clients' dignity intact. One of the best approaches is through a series of gradual steps that are progressively more direct. A three-step sequence for approaching resistance follows.

In the first step, the therapist offers a *permission-giving and educative response* to encourage clients to express their conflicted feelings about therapy. That is, the therapist tells the client that resistance and ambivalence are understandable and expectable feelings. If this permission giving does not work, the therapist can take a second step and encourage the client to explore the potential danger these feelings hold. This focuses on the *defense* (for example, "What could the threat be for you if . . . "). If the client continues to show signs of resistance but cannot talk about it, the therapist can draw on previous working hypotheses and try to interpret the *content* (for example, "I wonder if it is difficult for you to become involved in therapy because . . . "). This progressive sequence will work well in many cases. For example:

Therapist:
Mrs. Smith, I would like to talk about how it feels for you to see me in therapy. I noticed that you were 20 minutes late today and had to reschedule your appointment last week. I was wondering if there was something about coming here that didn't feel good to you. If so, it would be helpful for us to talk about that.

Client:
Oh no, I really do want to be here. And you've been very helpful already. It's just that my boss called.

Therapist:
Okay, but if in the future you ever find yourself having any difficulty about being in therapy, I want you to tell me about it. In therapy it is very important that we talk about any problems that come up between us. How would it be for you to tell me about something I did that you didn't like or something about being in therapy that didn't feel good to you?

Client:
Well, that might be kind of hard for me to do.

Therapist:
What about that would be hard for you?

At this point the therapist and client are off and running together. The therapist can help clients work through the issues that would prevent them from expressing dissatisfaction or disagreement (for example, clients' concern that the therapist or others will not like them unless they are always "nice"; clients' fear of the intensity and destructiveness of their anger, and so on). Not only will this help keep clients in therapy, it also provides an entreé into important conflict areas that need to be addressed in therapy.

In the example above, the therapist offered a permission-giving and educative response to try to free the client to talk about ambivalent feelings toward therapy. If the client continued to show signs of resistance (missing, canceling, rescheduling, coming late) without being able to talk about it, the therapist should continue to focus on the resistance. In the example below, the therapist does this by addressing the *defense*.

Therapist:
It's important that you feel free to tell me about critical or troubled feelings you may have, because they are bound to occur. Would you be able to tell me if something about me or being in therapy bothered you?

Client:
I think so.

Therapist:
I'm not so sure you would. I think it would be difficult for you to tell me if I did something that you didn't like or if there was something about being in therapy that was uncomfortable for you. Perhaps you believe "good clients" or "nice people" never have irritated, frustrated, or disappointed feelings, or at least that they don't ever express them.

Client:
Well, yes, that's probably true.

Therapist:
We need to look at that. You are having difficulty being in treatment, but you can't talk with me about that problem. What is the danger for you if you stop being "nice" and tell me what doesn't feel good about coming here? What do you think might happen?

In this example the therapist is trying to identify the threat that keeps the client from expressing conflicted feelings about therapy. The therapist is not trying to find out why the client is not showing up for therapy but why the client is having trouble talking about it. *It is more effective to address the defense itself than it is to probe for the conflict that is being defended against.* In most cases, this approach will prove effective. If focusing on the defense does not work, however, the therapist can try to interpret the *content* of the client's resistance as a last resort. For example, if the therapist thinks the client's ambivalence is about to pull her or him out of treatment, and the client cannot talk about the conflict, the therapist can draw on working hypotheses and interpret the resistance:

Therapist:
It's been hard for you to get here; you've missed the last two sessions. I don't think that you just forgot. I think there is something about being in

treatment that is difficult for you. Based on some other things we have talked about, I wonder if you are . . . ?

Why does the therapist only take this more direct interpretive stance as a last resort? The interpretation (accurate or not) is the therapist's issue and puts the ball in the therapist's court. Whenever possible, it is better to try to follow the client's lead or focus on the therapeutic process rather than trying to pull the client along in the therapist's direction. That is, it is usually more effective to explore why the client is resisting or make a process comment and address the current interaction than to make interpretations or tell the client what to do. Responses gained in this approach are more effective because they leave more responsibility with the client.

CLOSING

Listening to the client with concern and respect is the most powerful intervention the therapist can make in the beginning of therapy. Such listening is the basic tool the therapist uses to begin a working alliance with the client. Addressing ambivalence or resistance to therapy is the next step in maintaining the relationship that has just begun. Resistance will be more of an issue with some clients than others, but it will occur to some extent for every client. This chapter has emphasized that if the client expresses these ambivalent or resistant feelings and the therapist responds to them, they will be far less likely to pull the client out of therapy. Resistance will remain a concern throughout the course of therapy and repeatedly emerge as clients address difficult personal issues. Responding effectively to the many different types of resistance that will occur for clients is an important way to keep clients engaged and progressing in treatment. If therapists formulate working hypotheses, it will help them anticipate client resistance and respond more effectively when it occurs.

Resistance, ambivalence, and defense provide a window to certain inner aspects of the self. Each provides an opportunity to observe the fascinating workings of internal conflict. People do not possess a unified self—humans are so complex and multifaceted that it often feels as if "a part of me is working against another part of me." By resolving an internal conflict, a person becomes a little more integrated or whole. This process of integrating disparate parts of the self is the resolution of neurosis and the avenue to personal growth and change. When this process occurs around the topic of resistance, the therapist and client stride forward in therapy. This early success experience can show clients that they possess the internal resources, and have the helping person necessary, to go on to resolve the bigger issues that lie ahead.

SUGGESTIONS FOR FURTHER READING

1. Beginning therapists are encouraged to read further about the concept of resistance. For example, one classic reference in this area is Ralph Greenson's book, *The Technique and Practice of Psychoanalysis*, Volume 1 (New York: International Universities Press, 1967), chapter 2. This chapter provides a lucid introduction to the topic of resistance and offers informative case studies to illustrate effective therapeutic responses. Again, the reader does not have to be psychoanalytically oriented to be informed by this discussion.

2. There are many different ways to work with resistance and beginning therapists will find it useful to examine other approaches. For example, therapeutic responses to resistance have been especially highlighted in the family therapy literature. Therapists who are interested only in individual psychotherapy may still find it useful to examine basic texts in this area, such as C. M. Anderson and S. Steward, *Mastering Resistance: A Practical Guide to Family Therapy* (New York: Guilford Press, 1983).

3. An excellent discussion of cross-cultural issues in counseling can be found in H. Pinderhughes, *Understanding Race, Ethnicity, and Power* (New York: Free Press, 1989).

CHAPTER FOUR

AN INTERNAL FOCUS FOR CHANGE

CONCEPTUAL OVERVIEW

The first stage of therapy is complete when the therapist and client have established a collaborative relationship and begun to work together on the client's problems. This collaborative alliance is a necessary prerequisite to the beginning of the second stage of therapy—the client's journey inward. In order to change, clients must become less preoccupied with the problematic behavior of others and begin to explore their own internal and interpersonal responses. More specifically, this means that clients need to stop focusing exclusively on historical events, past relationships, and the problematic behavior of others in their lives. Instead, clients must begin to clarify their own thoughts, feelings, and reactions to the troubling events they are experiencing. Why? Although clients will usually fail in their attempts to change or control others in their lives, they can often resolve problems by understanding and changing themselves.

The therapist's task is to help clients make the transition from seeing the source and resolution of problems in others to adopting an internal focus for change. This is a twofold process. First, the therapist must help clients to look within. That is, the therapist must focus clients away from complaining about or trying to change others and toward identifying and understanding their own reactions. Second, the therapist must help clients become active agents in their own change process. The therapist does this by fostering the client's own self-direction and initiative within the therapeutic relationship. In adopting an internal focus for change, clients can begin to adopt new and more effective responses to old problems and claim a greater sense of effectance in their lives. It will be difficult for many clients to begin looking at their own issues, however, and they cannot take this journey inward without the support provided by a secure and caring relationship with the therapist.

CHAPTER ORGANIZATION

The first section of this chapter introduces the need for clients to shift from an external to an internal focus for change. It describes how clients often externalize their problems onto others, maintaining their feelings of helplessness, "stuckness," and/or depression. It shows how therapists can help clients focus inward and begin to change themselves rather than continue to try to change others. And it illustrates how clients often resist the transition to an internal focus and how therapists can respond to this resistance.

The second section discusses how clients can become active agents in resolving their own problems. It discusses how therapists can use the therapeutic relationship to foster the client's own initiative and sense of effectance. It examines specific intervention strategies that therapists can use to place the locus of change within the client. Sample therapist-client dialogues will illustrate effective and ineffective ways to achieve this.

The third section shows how therapists can actively enlist clients in understanding and changing their own problems. A case study will illustrate how therapists can help clients remain responsible, contributing agents throughout each phase of treatment.

LOOKING WITHIN TO ADOPT
AN INTERNAL FOCUS FOR CHANGE
Clients Externalize Their Problems

In the beginning stage of therapy, most clients see the source of their problems in others. Clients often want to spend more time describing the problematic behavior of others than their own experience of these problems. For example, many clients begin the first few therapy sessions by announcing that the problem is really with another person:

> My wife is always on my back.
> My husband won't pay any attention to me.
> My children are impossible; they won't do anything I say.
> My boss is a raging tyrant. If he doesn't back off, I'm going to have a heart attack.
> My mother won't stop criticizing me; I can't do anything right according to her.
> I'm twenty-seven years old, and my father treats me like a child.
> My boyfriend has a drinking problem.

When therapy begins with these externalizing complaints about the behavior of others, the therapist must respond to clients' immediate experience and acknowledge these complaints as valid concerns that are genuinely troubling. This is only the first step, however. After hearing and empathizing with clients, the therapist must begin to focus clients back on their own thoughts, feelings, and reactions to these problematic others. The following discussion examines why therapy is more productive when therapists focus clients inward and how this can be done.

In the examples above, the client is talking about the behavior of others that is troublesome for him or her. The client feels depressed, anxious, distrustful, enraged, or helpless because of the other person's behavior. In many cases, clients will try to get the therapist to join them in blaming, criticizing, or trying to change the other person. Therapy will not progress very far if the therapist joins clients in focusing on the other person's problematic behavior. Whereas clients' attempts to change the other person will usually fail, clients are much more likely to resolve the problem by changing their own way of responding (Wheelis, 1974). Thus, the therapist's task is to shift clients' focus away from the other person and back onto themselves.

One of the most effective ways therapists can help clients change themselves is by increasing clients' awareness of their own thoughts, feelings, and reactions in problematic situations. Each of the questioning responses below can be used to focus clients back on themselves:

How do you feel when your wife is nagging you?
What do you find yourself thinking when your husband is ignoring you?
What do you do when your children do not mind you?
What is it like for you when your boss is being so demanding?
Tell me the thoughts you were having as your mother was criticizing you.
How do you react to your father when he diminishes you?
What is most troublesome for you about your boyfriend's drinking?

Simple inquiries of this type serve two important functions. First, they tell clients that the therapist is listening to their concerns and is taking them seriously. The therapist has not changed the topic or brought up something that was discussed ten minutes ago but is responding directly to their concerns. Second, while inviting clients to say more about their concerns, the therapist is also shifting clients' focus away from others, encouraging them to look more closely at themselves. This bid to help clients become more aware of their own reactions is a critical step toward understanding and resolving their problems. As we will see throughout this chapter, the simple response of focusing clients on their own experience is a powerful intervention that will elicit strong feelings, memories, and associations.

In many cases, clients will welcome the therapist's offer to talk more about themselves. When clients begin to focus inward and learn more about *themselves*, they begin to change. Clients' active exploration of their own lives and problems will lead to new feelings of mastery and effectance that often result in growth and change. However, not all clients will respond so positively to the therapist's bid to look more closely at themselves. Clients may avoid or actively reject an internal focus, continuing to talk about the problem "out there" in others. The therapist can expect this and can continue to inquire about the personal meaning that this particular situation holds for the client. For example:

Therapist:
Where would you like to begin this morning?
Client:
My wife is impossible to live with. She complains constantly; nothing ever pleases her.
Therapist:
It sounds like you've had a difficult week with her. What's been the hardest thing for you?
Client:
Do you know how hard it is to live with an angry, demanding wife who keeps trying to tell you what to do all the time?
Therapist:
You're very angry at her. And I can see why—it would be hard to have someone after you like that. Tell me, how do you respond to her when she is trying to boss you around?
Client:
I don't know, I just hate it. I guess I yell back sometimes, or just try to get away from all of them. It's not just her, you know, her whole family is like that.
Therapist:
They really are very critical of you, and I can see how hard that would be to live with. But it seems like criticism, in particular, really gets under your skin. What's it like for you to be criticized so much?
Client:
I hate it. I just hate it. They make me feel like I can't do anything right— that I'm doing it wrong and failing all the time.
Therapist:
It sounds like her family's constant criticism taps into your own feelings of not measuring up or not being enough. And having those painful feelings of inadequacy aroused all the time would be infuriating.
Client:
Yeah, I hate them for making me feel that way. If I could make them stop, everything would be okay.
Therapist:
This is very important for you, and I want us to work together on it. I would like to understand better what you do when they criticize, so I can help you learn some more assertive, limit-setting responses. But your

own feeling of not measuring up is a big part of this problem that we need to work on too. If we can change that part of you, it would be much easier to handle all of this than it has been in the past.

Client:

Alright, I'm for that. What should I do?

Therapist:

Tell me more about your feeling of not measuring up.

Client:

Well, I guess I've always sort of felt like I'm not really good enough.

In this dialogue the therapist validated the client's experience while at the same time encouraging the client to look at his own reactions. Although the client kept trying to focus on the problematic behavior of his wife and her family, the therapist's repeated bids to have the client look at himself eventually served to mitigate his defensive, externalizing stance. As a result, the client moved closer to his own problematic feelings and contribution to the marital conflict. By gaining a better understanding of his own feelings of inadequacy, the client will not be so overreactive to others' criticisms and will learn to respond more effectively than yelling back or withdrawing.

Focusing clients on themselves is a simple but powerful intervention, and most clients have not experienced this before. Some clients will initially resist this internal focus, however, because it demands that they come face to face with those difficult feelings they have been unable to resolve alone. The paradox is that as long as clients avoid their own conflicts by externalizing their problems onto others, they will feel powerless, dependent, and out of control. We must look further at why it is more effective for clients to focus inward and try to change themselves rather than others.

Many clients who are struggling with neurotic conflicts are inappropriately invested in changing others as a means of managing their own problems or insecurities. In attempting to shape or direct others, the client is seeking an external solution to an internal problem. Beyond clearly and directly expressing our preferences and personal limits ("I would like . . ."; "I will not . . ."), the reality is that we are limited in influencing the way others think, feel, and act. For example, clients usually fail in their attempts to make their spouse stop drinking, smoking, or overeating. Similarly, some clients try for decades to win the approval or recognition from others that they never received from a parent. Others try unsuccessfully for years to have their grown offspring choose a different mate, friend, or job. As a result of these failed attempts to change others, many clients enter therapy with feelings of frustration, helplessness, and depression.

A therapist can offer clients the more productive alternative of decreasing their attempts to change others and gaining more understanding and control over their own reactions. This internal focus is a necessary prerequisite before clients can adopt new, more effective responses to old problems. Only when clients begin to focus on understanding and changing themselves will they begin to feel in charge of their lives and capable of change. These feelings are experienced by the client as *empowerment*. Thus, as we saw above, a consistent therapeutic response should be to gently focus clients back onto themselves to learn about their own thoughts, feelings, and reactions. The following types of questions will help clients explore their own responses:

What is the main feeling you are left with when . . . ?
Tell me the thoughts you were having when . . . ?
What was the most difficult thing for you when . . . ?
How would you like to be able to respond when . . . ?

Therapists Must Focus Clients Inward

Focusing clients on their own behavior often reveals how they are contributing to or participating in their own conflicts. Often clients will not have realized their own role in these conflicts. As we will see below, clients who can focus on themselves and see their own participation in a conflict are usually motivated to change their own part in it. This, in turn, may allow the other person to respond differently as well. To illustrate, we return to the previous example of the husband who complained about his critical wife and in-laws.

Although the client did begin to explore his own feelings of inadequacy and how he responded to his wife, he kept complaining about his "obnoxious" wife and "superior" in-laws. As before, the therapist was empathic, validated his experience, and supported his anger. But at the same time, the therapist did not join the client in focusing exclusively on the clients' wife or blaming her as the sole source of his problems. Instead, the therapist continued to lead the client away from his preoccupation with his wife's behavior and repeatedly focused him on his own reactions to her.

What would have happened if the therapist did not do this? If the therapist had responded to his eliciting pull to blame his wife, the client would have remained an angry but helpless victim. In contrast, if the therapist had emphasized just the clients' contribution to his marital conflict, without first validating his experience, it would have recapitulated his developmental conflict. Recall the discussion of client response specificity from Chapter 1. The client's feelings of inadequacy stemmed in part from rarely being supported by his parent and commonly being blamed for whatever went wrong. Thus, by validating the client's experience first, and not rigidly focusing him inward in an absolutist way, the therapist helped the client evolve a new and more satisfying response to an old conflict. And by coupling this validation with a consistent bid for an internal focus, the therapist allowed the client to become more aware of how his own reactions contributed to the conflict in his marriage.

For example, the client learned that he was quiet and unresponsive to his wife when he arrived home from work. The therapist helped him see that his silence escalated his wife's attempts to gain his attention, causing him to become even more unresponsive to her. Their problematic interaction escalated as the wife became more insistent and demanding of his attention, leading him to withdraw even further—by taking a nap, for example. Furthermore, by focusing on his own emotional reactions at that moment, the client realized that his wife's increasing requests for attention also made him feel overwhelmed by the prospect of trying to meet all of her needs. In this regard, he had held the unrealistic belief that if he did not always respond to her, he was failing as a husband and again being inadequate.

If the therapist does not join with the client in complaining about his wife but encourages the client to become more aware of his own internal and interpersonal responses to his wife, then the client is given an opportunity to change his part in the marital conflict. That is, this client stopped being a helpless and begrudging victim of his "obnoxious" wife only when he began to alter his part in their conflict. In this case, the husband began to express more directly to his wife when he would like to be close to her and when he would prefer to be alone. He also explained to his wife that he wanted thirty minutes alone to unwind when he returned home from work, after which they could then sit down and share their day together.

More important, as the husband gained a better understanding of his tendency to feel overwhelmed by the demands of others, he became less reactive to his wife's requests. He learned that he felt overwhelmed, in part, because he could neither say no to her nor express his wishes. If his wife wanted something from him, he thought that he was failing and felt bad if he didn't respond immediately. And because he couldn't set limits or ask for what he wanted without feeling selfish, he resented the "unfairness" in their relationship. The client also learned that he expressed this resentment to his wife indirectly—in critical and withholding ways. Over the next few months, his new awareness allowed him to respond to his wife's "demands" as if they were merely requests. He could choose to respond to them or not, without feeling controlled by them. As the client set these limits, he began to feel a new sense of control over himself in his relationship and was able to make some tentative steps toward greater closeness with his wife.

Thus, as soon as clients begin focusing on their own behavior, they will start to feel less "stuck," powerless, and depressed. Most clients will start to see more alternatives available to them and begin to feel more hopeful and in charge of their lives. Thus, the therapist's task is to discourage clients from passively complaining about others or from trying to manipulate and control others' behavior. Although clients usually fail in their attempts to change others, they can often succeed in resolving problems by gaining greater mastery over their own responses.

Both Therapists and Clients Avoid an Internal Focus

Therapists Join Clients in Externalizing. We have already seen that many clients externalize their problems onto others and that therapists can help clients change by focusing clients inward. However, at times therapists will find it difficult to work with clients in this way. Focusing the client inward means that the therapist is *drawing out* the client's fears and concerns rather than diminishing or assuaging them. Some therapists have difficulty approaching client conflicts so directly, perhaps because they confuse being direct with being critical, blaming, or unsupportive. Other therapists are reluctant to approach clients' internal conflicts so directly because they believe that "good people do not make others hurt or feel bad." These therapists try to make clients feel better by reassuring them about their insecurities and by emphasizing their strengths and successes. Moving away from client conflicts in these ways are well-intended but ineffective responses that keep clients from fully expressing and exploring their problems. Still other therapists avoid an internal focus in order to maintain client approval. This occurs because some clients will become angry as the therapist encourages them to explore the threatening internal conflicts that they have been defending against.

For these and other reasons, therapists often join with clients in looking away from the internal conflict. Therapists collude with the client to externalize problems when they repeatedly respond in the following ways:

Give advice and tell the client what to do or how to respond to others.
Interpret or explain what the other person's motives or behavior really mean.
Reassure clients that their problems will go away or are not something to be
     concerned about.
Disclose what the therapist has done to cope with a similar person or problem.

Although each of these responses may be effective at times, they cannot come to characterize the ongoing course of treatment. If they do, they will keep clients from exploring their own experience and, ultimately, from being able to resolve their own conflicts. Thus, therapists must help clients expand and elaborate their awareness of their internal experiences and interpersonal responses. This must be done repeatedly throughout each therapy session. As we will see below, however, this is difficult to do, because an intense focus on self and internal experiences may arouse clients' anxiety.

Clients Resist an Internal Focus. Why do clients often eschew an internal focus, and how can therapists work with this resistance? A shift away from the client's focus on others can make some clients feel that the therapist does not really understand them or is not sympathetic to their concerns. Other clients fear that if they give up their attempts to change others, they will either have to accept the blame for the problem or remain forever resigned to defeat. Still other clients may not yet be ready to approach the painful feelings or difficult choices that looking inside entails, or they may feel that it is unsafe to share their personal concerns with the therapist. Thus, the therapist should *work with clients to explore their reasons for not wanting to look within* (this is called *addressing the resistance*). The therapist should not insist, however, when clients are not ready to look at their own issues.

We must look more carefully at how the therapist can best respond when clients have difficulty looking within. One thing the therapist can do is to follow clients along for awhile, giving repeated bids to reveal a little more about themselves. If the client's externalizing stance does not begin to change, the therapist can make a process comment that simply describes the interaction. For example:

Therapist:

I've noticed that you talk very easily about your husband and your daughter, but you don't say very much about yourself. Are you aware that that happens?

OR

I think that we have been missing each other the last two sessions. I keep asking you what you were thinking about or trying to do in a particular situation, and you keep responding by telling me more about the other person. What do you see going on between us?

These process comments will help clients to become aware of their externalizing style with the therapist and to learn that they probably respond this way to other people as well. For example, if clients cannot share themselves in a personal way with others, many people will find them boring or aloof. The therapist and client may then have part of the client's presenting problem occurring in their relationship (for example, the client's complaints of loneliness, isolation, or lack of meaningful contact with others).

Although it is often frustrating and discouraging for clients to realize that they are reenacting their conflict in the therapy session, this reenactment provides the client the opportunity to resolve the problem by changing the distancing pattern *within* the therapeutic relationship. That is, the therapist can help clients become aware of how they interact with others and how others experience them, and then offer a new and more effective way of relating in the therapeutic relationship. For example, the therapist can describe the current interaction and offer to develop a more meaningful and sharing relationship with the client:

Therapist:

I feel that I am being held away from you when you keep talking about others rather than yourself. That doesn't feel very good to me. I would like to learn more about *you*! Can we work together to try and change that?

A significant response often occurs when the therapist uses questions or process comments to focus clients inward. Clients will often *reveal a variety of new and important concerns* that they had not talked about before. For example:

But there really isn't very much about me to know.
I'm not used to telling people what I'm feeling.
It seems like something always goes wrong when I try to get close to someone.
You wouldn't like me very much if you knew what I was really like.

In this way, the therapist's process comment has brought out important new concerns that can now be addressed in therapy. The therapeutic relationship and the content to be explored have deepened. *This process of helping clients to focus inward and to explore their resistance to looking within will provide some of the most important material to be addressed in therapy.* It is important to note that these new client concerns are far less likely to be brought up for treatment when the therapist does not focus clients inward. Thus, one of the most important reasons for adopting an internal focus is to *uncover* central conflicts that are operating in the client's life, and to do this in a way that makes them accessible for treatment. We will return to this uncovering aspect of the internal focus in the next section.

PLACING THE LOCUS OF CHANGE WITH THE CLIENT

The first component of the internal focus was to help clients *look* within and become more aware of their own reactions and responses. In addition to looking within, the client must also begin to *act* from within, by adopting an internal locus for change. This section examines how clients can gain a greater sense of *effectance* in their lives by becoming active agents in their own change process (White, 1959).

First, we will see how therapists can use the therapeutic relationship to foster the client's own initiative and self-direction. Second, we will examine specific types of therapeutic interventions that encourage the client's participation in and control over the change process. Throughout, the therapist's goal is to respond to the client's feelings, interests, and initiative and to thereby support the client's growing sense of effectance.

Using the Therapeutic Relationship to Foster Clients' Initiative

In the course of treatment, a therapist has the opportunity to convey to clients the broader message that they are able to take charge and effectively manage their own lives. Effective therapists of every theoretical orientation nurture clients' own sense of personal power and dignity. Rather than just using words to encourage clients' initiative and autonomy, however, therapists must provide clients with the experience of *acting* more effectively during the therapy session. When clients experience a greater sense of mastery and control in their relationship with the therapist, this generalizes to other relationships (Bandura, 1977). We will see below how therapists can help clients assume an active, initiating role in therapy.

The first way to help clients feel responsible for and capable of change is to encourage them to bring up the issues that they feel are most important to discuss. Therapists should repeatedly encourage clients to talk about whatever their primary concerns are, to explore their own motivations and wishes, and to generate their own behavioral alternatives and options.

Why is it so important to encourage and respond to the client's own initiative? In one way or another, most clients are unable to act on their own wishes, preferences, and interests. In past relationships, these clients have not had significant others respond to their own true feelings or support their own interests. As a result, it will be very exciting—but threatening—for these clients to feel the therapist's support for their own feelings, perceptions, and self-direction. Whenever therapists can successfully engage clients in pursuing their own interests and examining their own conflicts, therapy will become an intense and productive experience.

When the therapist is able to help clients explore and understand the material they produce, rather than merely directing them to the therapist's own agenda, change will often begin to occur. When clients provide the momentum and direction for therapy, they *experience* acting more effectively and being more in charge of their own lives. Once clients have begun to initiate and lead with their own concerns, the therapist can actively participate by contributing interpretations, behavioral alternatives, and interpersonal feedback to the client. However, the information and understanding that the therapist offers will be far more useful if the therapist is responding to the client's own agenda, interests, or concerns. This process dimension is one of the most important characteristics of the therapeutic relationship.

Hierarchical Relationships Keep Clients Dependent. We have already noted how clients often resist the therapist's attempts to make them active participants in treatment. Many clients will be troubled by expressing their own wishes, acting on their own initiative, and achieving successes. Because so many clients have not been supported in their own individuation and are threatened by self-direction, competence, or success, they continually elicit advice, direction, and explanations from the therapist. Therapy will not be productive if this helper-helpee mode is enacted. This will shift responsibility away from the client and onto the therapist, and create the hierarchical relationship discussed in Chapter 2. Clients will not be able to adopt a stronger stance in their own lives as long as this dependency is fostered.

Unfortunately, therapists often comply with the clients' subtle or overt request to tell them what to talk about in therapy and what to do in their lives. It is flattering to think that we know what is best and can tell others what to do; it appeals to the narcissism in every therapist. Although there will certainly be times when the therapist needs to take a directive stance, this cannot characterize the ongoing process of therapy. If it does, clients are passively healed by the powerful therapist and remain dependent on helpers to manage their lives. Because this occurs so regularly, we need to examine further this *dependency-fostering* approach to therapy.

Supporting Clients' Own Autonomy and Initiative. Effective therapy fosters and encourages clients' own autonomy. Therapists cannot just *talk* with clients about independence and autonomy. They must create a relationship in which clients *behave* independently. To do this, the therapist must first give clients permission to follow their own interests and to introduce the material that is most relevant to them. Then it becomes critically important for the therapist to identify the meaning and feeling in their concern and to encourage the client to expand and elaborate it further. In response to clients' increasingly specific exploration, the therapist can help clarify clients' experience and, together, they can begin to generate more effective ways to respond. When this interchange spirals on throughout several sessions, clients will become committed to treatment and find that meaningful change has begun to occur. Facilitating this growth process may be the primary challenge and satisfaction of being a therapist.

The model of therapeutic interaction described above is an *independence-fostering* approach to psychotherapy. Clients have the experience of sharing responsibility for the course of treatment by defining and addressing their own concerns and conflicts. The therapist encourages and supports clients in achieving this more assertive stance and secondarily contributes information and guidance to clients' own exploration.

A common misconception is that longer-term, dynamic, or relationship-based therapies are *dependency-fostering*, whereas short-term, problem-solving, or behavioral approaches are not. Actually, whether the therapy fosters dependence or independence is determined by the therapeutic process and not by the length of treatment or theoretical orientation of the clinician. In short- or long-term therapy, the client's dependency is inappropriately fostered when the therapist "cures" the client by repeatedly directing the course of therapy, giving advice, and prescribing solutions for the client. Let us examine an effective middle ground between the nonproductive extremes of directive and nondirective control.

Shared Control in the Therapist-Client Relationship. Therapy will be most successful when the therapist and client share control over the direction of therapy. It is overly controlling for the therapist to play the predominant role in structuring and directing the course of treatment, and it is ineffective to nondirectively abandon clients to their own confusion and frustration. In a more productive relationship, the therapist will encourage the client to take the lead but will contribute information, clarifications, and alternatives to the material the client has produced. It will be therapeutic for many clients to experience a relationship in which control is not competed over or held by one or the other party but is shared by both participants. For example, in Chapter 2 we stressed that in the beginning of treatment, the therapist should encourage the client to take the initiative and bring up whatever he would like to discuss. For example:

> I would like you to begin each session by bringing up what you want to talk about. I want to work on what is most important to you.

Some therapists will be frustrated by this approach because they feel an urgency to address problems and begin finding solutions. This practical, problem-solving orientation certainly has some very real advantages and is necessary in crisis situations. However, this approach has several important drawbacks. First, we have already seen how a directive approach prevents the therapist and client from uncovering conflicts that were not evident in the client's presenting problem. Second, the therapist is not to merely "fix" the client's presenting problem anyway. A much broader goal is desired, and the therapeutic approach suggested here facilitates it: *teaching clients that they possess the personal resources to resolve problems and effectively negotiate their own adult lives.* Working in this way, the client gains an increasing sense of autonomy and personal power, which does not occur when the client merely follows the therapist's lead.

Although personal power and autonomy are goals that most therapists would acclaim, the problem-solving therapist would assert: "What if you follow the client's lead and it takes you nowhere?" It is true that a nondirective approach requires an unrealistic amount of time and patience from the therapist and often results in a disorganized and unfocused therapy. As stated earlier, however, there is an effective middle ground of shared therapist-client control that therapists miss when they adopt a purely directive or nondirective stance. Next, we will examine some therapeutic interventions that enact or express this middle ground of shared control.

Therapeutic Interventions That Place the Client at the Fulcrum of Change

We have already noted how therapists can encourage the client's lead while still participating actively in shaping the course of therapy. The critical technique is for the therapist to intervene without taking the impetus away from the client. Three different examples illustrate effective and ineffective ways to intervene successfully. In the first example, the therapist is ineffective because she or he takes responsibility for the continuing movement of therapy away from the client.

Ineffective Interventions That Leave the Therapist at the Fulcrum of Change. Suppose that the client is filling the therapy session with seemingly irrelevant storytelling. The therapist cannot find a common theme to any of the client's stories or understand the emotional connection and personal meaning the stories hold for the client. It seems as if nothing significant is occurring. At that point, it is easy for the therapist to stop and direct the client toward a specific topic that the therapist thinks would be more fruitful. Although this needs to be done sometimes, the therapist must be careful to revitalize their interaction without shifting the impetus for therapy away from the client and onto the therapist. In the dialogue below, the onus for therapy comes to rest with the therapist, and the client loses an internal focus for change.

Therapist:
   I don't think this is taking us anywhere.
Client:
   Yeah, I'm not sure where I'm going with this either. What would you like me to talk about?
Therapist:
   You have had trouble asserting yourself in the past, and I think we need to look at that problem. Last week you said you wanted to ask your boss for three weeks of vacation instead of two. How are you going to handle that confrontation?
Client:
   I'm not sure, what do you think I should say?
Therapist:
   To begin with, you need to arrange a face-to-face meeting with him. It is important that only the two of you are present so you can have his full attention. Then use the "I" statements we have practiced to directly state what you want.
Client:
   Sounds good, but what would you say to him first?

This exchange will not be productive, even though the therapist has moved the client to a more salient topic and provided useful information about effective confrontations. The fulcrum of therapeutic movement has tipped from the client to the therapist, and a hierarchical teacher-student exchange has resulted. Most clients will not be able to incorporate and act on the therapist's useful information until the client picks up the momentum and begins to actively participate again. Furthermore, because the client remained in a passive, following role as the therapist continued to explain and inform, the client does not gain the increasing sense of mastery or effectance that comes from participating in successful therapeutic movement. Thus, a more productive intervention would be to direct the client to the new topic but wait for the client to become actively involved again before offering further information.

Effective Interventions That Place the Client at the Fulcrum of Change. Now we will see how the therapist can reorient the client toward more productive material and do so in a way that keeps the momentum for therapy with the client. One way is to use a process comment that makes their current interaction overt and a topic for discussion. For example:

Therapist:
> Are you using our time the way you want to right now? I don't have the feeling that what you're talking about is really very important to you.

Client:
> Yeah, I'm not sure where I'm going with this either. What would you like me to talk about?

Therapist:
> I think that we should try to identify what would be most important to you, and talk about that. What would that be right now?

Client:
> I'm not really sure.

Therapist:
> Let's just sit quietly for a moment, then, and see what comes to you.

This type of confrontation challenges the client to approach more substantial material but does so in a way that does not take the impetus away from the client. The therapist has directly intervened and confronted the client but has left the client an active participant in revitalizing the discussion. *Clients produce far more significant material when they are encouraged to lead in this way rather than to follow.*

Effective Confrontations Reveal New Conflicts. The final example shows how new client conflicts can be identified for treatment when the therapist intervenes without taking the locus for change away from the client. Imagine the following situation: A nineteen-year-old client in a college counseling center had been telling his therapist about his attempts in early adolescence to observe his mother undressing. The client had been detailing his voyeuristic efforts at great lengths, but the therapist did not feel that this was really much of a concern for the client. Unless the therapist could find the relevant meaning for the client, he wanted to move on to other more salient issues. In the dialogue below, the therapist refocuses the client in a way that keeps the locus for change with the client and opens up an important new conflict area for therapy.

Therapist:
Does this feel like an important topic to you that you want to discuss with me? As I listen to you I don't get the feeling that you are really very interested in what you are telling me. Is that the case, or am I not understanding the meaning this holds for you?

Client:
I thought therapists were interested in this Oedipal stuff. I figured you would want to hear about it.

Therapist:
I'm struck by the fact that you are telling me what you think I want to hear, rather than working on what is most important to you. That's something we should look at in therapy. I wonder if you find yourself doing this in other relationships as well—trying to sense other people's needs at the expense of expressing your own?

This is another way in which the therapist has confronted the client and redirected therapy without taking the impetus away from the client. In this vignette, the therapist has also used their current interaction to uncover a potential new problem area for the client. Because this arose from their joint interaction and not from the therapist's private agenda or personal directive, most clients will be responsive to exploring this new issue. Thus, the therapist has effectively focused the client internally, identified a new conflict area to be explored, and left the client a participant in directing the course of therapy.

As the client begins to work with the new problem areas that have developed out of the therapeutic relationship, important inroads will be made on the client's presenting problems as well. In most cases, significant progress cannot be made on the presenting problem until movement is made on other related conflicts that are not evident at the beginning of therapy. That is, clients have often been unable to resolve their presenting problem because they have not addressed other issues that interlock and impinge on the presenting problem. As noted above, adopting an internal focus will identify salient conflicts that clients did not realize were relevant to their presenting problem. We will return to this issue of expanding clients' conceptualizations of their problems in Chapter 7.

ENLIST CLIENTS IN UNDERSTANDING THEIR OWN CONFLICTS

In this final section, we will bring the internal focus into the therapeutic relationship. Once clients have begun to look within and express their inner world, the therapist can further clients' mastery over their own lives by engaging them in understanding their own conflicts. A common misconception about psychotherapy is that the therapist is completely responsible for figuring out what is wrong with the client. Many beginning therapists have unrealistic expectations that they must be very insightful and knowing, and then suffer under these performance demands. Here again, this places the impetus for change entirely in the therapist's lap and leaves the client a passive recipient, waiting to be enlightened. A more effective approach is to extend the collaborative alliance into the problem-solving phase of therapy as well.

Rather than setting the stage for therapists to announce interpretations and explanations, therapists will be more effective if they elicit client's active involvement in understanding their own conflicts. Although change certainly depends on the therapist's conceptual understanding of clients, clients must participate in a collaborative alliance as well. This frees the therapist to respond more effectively to what clients produce and gives clients the opportunity to become more effective in managing their own lives. Rather than trying to provide answers, therapists should develop the skill to help clients exercise their own strengths and resources. Real change has occurred when psychotherapy has not only resolved clients' presenting problems but has fostered clients' sense of effectance as well.

This third component of helping clients adopt an internal focus for change is illustrated by contrasting two different ways of responding to a client's dream. Although the interpretation of the dream remains the same, the therapeutic approaches differ and enact very different interpersonal processes with the client.

The Process Can Recapitulate the Client's Conflict

Anna is a twenty-two-year-old client who lives at home with her embittered and chronically embattled parents. For several years, Anna has been struggling with the developmental transition of emancipating from her family of origin. She cannot leave home and establish her own adult life. Anna has few friendships, dates little, and has no serious educational or career involvements. Anna's mother and alcoholic father fight constantly, and Anna feels it is her responsibility to stay home and help her mother cope with her problematic marriage. Anna entered therapy complaining of depression.

After several sessions, Anna volunteered a dream to her therapist that was of great importance to her. As the dream began, Anna was riding a beautiful horse across an open green savannah. She felt as one with this graceful and powerful animal as they glided effortlessly across the broad grasslands. Sunlit rivers, birds in flight, and herds of grazing elk flowed past as they sped toward a distant mountain. Anna felt strong and free as she urged the tireless animal onward.

The distant mountains held the promise of new life amidst green meadows and tall trees. Anna felt their promise quicken inside of her as she urged the horse onward. But as the mountains drew near, Anna and the horse began to slow. The horse's legs became her own and grew heavier with each step. Anna desperately tried to will them on, but their footing became unsure and they began to stumble. At that moment, menacing riders appeared on all sides, ready to overtake and capture her. Anna awoke with a scream.

"What do you think my dream means?" Anna asked

Her bright and concerned young therapist offered a lengthy and insightful explanation. The gist of the interpretation concerned Anna's guilt over leaving home. The therapist suggested that if Anna went on with her life and pursued her own interests, she would feel powerful and alive—just as she had in the dream. But before Anna could reach her goal and experience the satisfactions of having her own independent life, she would have to free herself from the binding ties of responsibility that she felt for her mother and her parent's marriage. Her loyalty to her mother threatened to entrap her in guilt and prevent her from having her own adult life.

Anna responded enthusiastically to the therapist's explanation: "Yes, I do feel as if I am being bad whenever I leave my mother. Is that why I dreamed that?"

Again, the therapist provided a provocative answer: "We've been talking about whether you are going to move in to an apartment next month. I think the dream reflects your conflict over taking this big step on your own."

Anna:

I want to move out, but I can't leave my mother with my father. She says she will divorce him if I move out, and it'll be my fault. What should I do?

Therapist:

I can't make that decision for you. You have to be responsible for your own decisions.

Anna:

But I don't know what's best to do, and you always do. You're so much smarter than me—I thought about that dream all day and I didn't know that's what it meant.

Throughout the rest of the session, Anna continued to plead for advice and expressed her discouragement about being able to resolve her own problems. The therapist kept refusing to tell her what to do and gave a lengthy explanation about autonomy, independence, and the need for Anna to find her own solutions. The hour ended with Anna feeling agitated and depressed and the therapist still explaining the need for Anna to make her own decisions.

Although the therapist was astute in linking Anna's dream to the current manifestation of her conflict over leaving home, this was an unproductive session. How did their therapeutic process go awry?

In this session, Anna metaphorically reexperienced the same conflict with her therapist that she is struggling with at home. In her family, Anna was trained to be dependent and believe that she didn't have the wherewithal to succeed on her own. Further, she was made to feel guilty whenever she did act independently. In the first fifteen minutes of their session, the therapist acted as the knowing parent who gave all of the necessary answers to the needing child. This interaction *behaviorally* communicated the message that Anna will be dependent on the therapist's superior understanding. On another level, however, this message was contradicted by the therapist's *verbal* message about independence. This mixed message about independence from the well-intentioned therapist immobilized the client. The therapist's direct interpretation may have worked fine for some clients, but recalling the notion of client response specificity, such an approach was problematic for Anna.

Anna reacted so intensely because she needed permission from the therapist to become more independent, yet simultaneously expected that the therapist needed her to remain dependent, just as her mother did. When the pattern of having to be dependent on the authority was reenacted with her therapist, Anna's fear that she was incapable of making her own decisions and having her own life was confirmed. Anna remained depressed until the therapist successfully reestablished a collaborative alliance. The therapist did this in the next session by soliciting Anna's ideas about a problem they were discussing. The therapist then expressed pleasure in watching her be so insightful and shared some related ideas. This time, Anna readily picked up the ideas and used them to further her own thinking.

The Process Must Enact a Corrective Emotional Experience

As a contrast to the response of the therapist in the preceding example, we will examine a different type of response to Anna's question "What do you think the dream means? Responses that engage the client in exploring the dream with the therapist will usually be more effective than the therapist providing explanations (no matter how accurate) to the client. Therapists can choose to respond in many different ways and can engage clients in exploring their own dreams as follows:

It sounds like a very important dream to me, too. Let's work on it together. Where should we begin?

What was the primary feeling you were left with from the dream? Can you connect that feeling to anything going on in your life now?

What was the most important image in the dream for you? Tell me what that image suggests to you.
I feel uncomfortable when you ask me to tell you what your dream means. It's as if you think I have all the knowledge and you don't have anything to contribute, and I know that isn't true!

Each of these responses encourages the client to participate actively with the therapist. Ultimately, the therapist may want to give the same interpretation of the dream. However, even though the therapist provides an explanation, the process will be entirely different and far more effective if it evolves out of their joint effort and is integrated into their continuing collaboration. This gives clients a relationship in which they are not one down or dependent on the therapist but are encouraged to exercise their own abilities and resources. When this occurs, clients' motivation to work in therapy increases, and their sense of effectance is fostered. Fostering independence is a corrective therapeutic experience, giving clients like Anna the permission they need to grow out of their dependence and act capably in their relationship with the therapist, something they have not experienced in the past.

CLOSING

Clients will not be able to resolve their problems unless they act out a different and more satisfying solution to their conflict in their relationship with the therapist. Adopting an internal focus for change provides clients with the type of experience that can produce change. By determining what material will be covered and by participating in finding solutions to their problems, clients gain an increasing sense of their personal power and uncover the interrelated constellation of feelings and beliefs that make up their problems. Bowlby (1988) comments that therapists facilitate this process when their stance toward the client is not "I know, I'll tell you" but "You know, you tell me."

As clients begin to reflect on their own experience and become less preoccupied with others, their affective world opens up and becomes available in a way that has not occurred before. This affective unfolding is a pivotal step in the process of change. However, the intensity of the affect aroused by pursuing an internal focus can be threatening for clients and intimidating to therapists. Thus, the next chapter examines how therapists can help clients master the deep-seated emotions aroused by looking within.

SUGGESTIONS FOR FURTHER READING

1. In his classic paper, "Motivation Reconsidered: The Concept of Competence" (*Psychology Review* 66 [1959]:297–333), Robert White introduces

the concept of *effectance motivation,* an innate drive that leads individuals to actively explore and master their environment.

2. In his book, *How People Change* (New York: Harper & Row, 1974), Alan Wheelis discusses the internal process of change. In particular, see the chapter "Freedom and Necessity," which uses the language of *responsibility* to clarify how clients must focus on themselves rather than others in order to change.

3. In a tour de force presentation, Albert Bandura argues that perceived self-efficacy is the underlying mechanism of change across all treatment approaches. In "Self Efficacy: Toward a Unifying Theory of Behavioral Change" (*Psychological Review* 84, no. 2 [1977]:191–215), he emphasizes that little enduring and generalized change results from verbal suggestion or persuasion. Instead, clients change when they have authentic experiences of *enactive mastery.* This occurs when clients have the actual experience of performing adaptive new coping responses with the therapist.

4. In his informative book, *Helplessness* (New York: W.H. Freeman, 1975), Martin Seligman discusses how learned helplessness operates in depression and anxiety. Seligman suggests that depression dissipates when clients can exert more control over their environment, and offers interesting suggestions for providing young children with experiences of control that teach them that they do have the power to influence their lives. Many of these ideas are readily applicable to helping clients gain greater mastery in their own lives.

CHAPTER FIVE

RESPONDING TO CONFLICTED EMOTIONS

CONCEPTUAL OVERVIEW

Conflicted feelings lie at the heart of enduring and pervasive problems. Change in therapy is a process of affective relearning, and this change occurs when the therapist responds effectively to the client's conflicted emotions. When the therapist focuses clients on themselves, the troubling feelings that are central to their problems will emerge. That is, looking within causes clients to feel more intensely, and express more directly, the emotions that accompany their problems.

This affective unfolding is a pivotal point in therapy because it brings the therapist and the client to the emotional basis of the client's problems. On the one hand, clients will welcome the promise and reassurance of having the therapist make contact with their problems on a deeper, more personal level. At the same time, however, clients also want to avoid feelings that are too painful, too intense, or that just seem hopelessly unresolvable. Thus, the therapist's response to the client's emerging feelings is critical and will greatly influence the eventual outcome of therapy.

Clients will not be able to change unless the therapist provides a more satisfying response to their conflicted emotions than they have received from others in the past. Unless the therapist effectively approaches the client's emerging affect, the therapeutic relationship will lose its vitality and therapy will be reduced to an intellectual rendering. Thus, the purpose of this chapter is to help therapists respond to the full range and intensity of feelings that are aroused when clients begin to look within. We will see that the therapist's ability to help clients change is in direct relation to how the therapist responds to their emotions.

CHAPTER ORGANIZATION

The first section of this chapter provides intervention guidelines for responding to clients' affect. Therapists need to approach clients' feelings and help expand the affective component of clients' problems. The second section continues the theme of approaching clients' affect and focuses on working with the predominant or characterological affect that clients experience.

The third section introduces the therapist to the interrelated sequence of emotions that comprise clients' conflicts. For many clients, three related feelings recur in an ordered sequence, and therapists must identify and respond to each feeling in the sequence. Too often, clients cannot resolve conflicted emotions because therapists do not address each of the distinct feelings that make up this affective constellation.

Once clients' conflicted emotions emerge, therapists must know how to respond effectively to them. The fourth section explains how therapists can provide a "holding environment" that enables clients to master and integrate painful emotions.

Finally, the fifth section discusses characteristics of therapists that influence their ability to work with clients' emotions. This is one of the most important issues in clinical training, since therapists' own personalities, needs, and current life situations will often keep them from responding to the strong emotions that clients present. All therapists need to seek consultation at times in order to manage their own emotional reactions to the material that clients present. If not, therapists will be less capable of responding to the full range and intensity of clients' emotions.

RESPONDING TO CLIENTS' CONFLICTED EMOTIONS

Many situational problems can readily be resolved by simply obtaining new information, trying out behavioral alternatives, or recasting problems in a new framework. In and of themselves, these brief interventions are sufficient to resolve many of the problems that clients present, and they comprise an important aspect of change for almost all problems. For many of the more enduring and pervasive problems that clients present, however, the conflicted emotions that accompany problems must be addressed as well.

In therapy, clients are often reluctant to work with the emotions that emerge for them. On the one hand, most clients hope that the therapist will be able to help with their emotional reactions, but at the same time, clients want to avoid the painful feelings that they have not been able to resolve alone. There are several reasons why clients may be reluctant to share these feelings with the therapist. To some clients, it may seem like reexperiencing the same hopeless pain for no reason, suffering needless shame or embarrassment for revealing their inadequacies or having to struggle with the fear of losing control of their unremitting rage or consuming need. As a result, clients will often resist the therapist's attempts to touch the emotional core of their conflicts, although they long for this contact as well.

It is understandable that clients have this resistance, but therapy will be reduced to an intellectual exercise—incapable of effecting enduring change that can be generalized to other situations—if the therapist complies and bypasses clients' emotions. Although conflicted emotions are the basis of most clients' problems, these emotions also provide the avenue to resolution and change. Therapists can respond more effectively to their clients' emotions by using the following intervention guidelines.

Approach the Client's Affect

In their moment-to-moment interaction with clients, therapists are repeatedly confronted with choices of how to respond to what the client has just said or done. For example, the therapist can respond by seeking more information, clarifying what the client has just said, relating this material to other issues the client has discussed in the past, and so forth. As a general guideline, however, the most productive response is to *respond to the feeling that the client is currently experiencing.* That is, the therapist's first priority is to acknowledge and approach the affective component of the client's response.

The following dialogue illustrates this guideline. Imagine that the therapist and client have just sat down together to begin their first session:

Therapist:
Tell me, Mike, what is the difficulty that brings you to therapy?
Client:
I'm having a lot of problems with my fifteen-year-old son. We disagree about everything and can't seem to talk to each other anymore. He doesn't do what I ask him to, and I don't like his values. I guess I'm pretty angry at him. His mother and I are divorced, and I'm thinking it may be time for him to go live with her. Do you think it's okay for a teenaged boy to live with his mother?
Therapist:
I don't think either of us understands what is going on between you two well enough to decide that yet. You said you were "pretty angry" at him. Tell me more about your anger.

In this example, the client has presented many different issues that the therapist could have chosen to pursue. Following the guideline above, however, the therapist approached the primary affect that the client presented. The therapist could have responded differently and inquired further about the issues that the father and son disagreed about, worked on values clarification with the father, obtained more background information about the father-son relationship or the divorce, provided research findings about the effects of mother-custody versus father-custody on boys, and so on. Although these and many other responses may work fine, responding to the client's feeling will usually produce the most information and intensify the therapist-client exchange.

In the dialogue above, the client spoke about his anger directly and the therapist responded to it immediately. In addition to responding to clients' overtly expressed feelings, therapists must also respond to the covert or unverbalized feelings that clients experience.

Strong feelings are usually aroused whenever clients discuss an issue that is conflicted for them. That is, overtly stated feelings or nonverbal affective signs such as tearing, grimacing, or blushing are signals that inform the therapist that the client is addressing a significant issue. Clients are often unaware of this, however, and therapists must help clients explore these emerging feelings more fully. In the example below, the therapist responds to the client's nonverbal cues and draws out the affect that this situation holds for the client. Imagine that the client has been discussing her marital problems with her therapist:

Client:
I don't know if I should stay married or not. I haven't been happy with him for a long time, but I can see how hard he's trying to make our relationship work. And our four-year-old son would be devastated if we ever broke up. I don't know what's right to do, and it's so important for everyone that I make the right decision.

Therapist:
As you speak about this your face tightens. What are you feeling right now?

When the therapist responds to the client's feeling in this way, whether it is overtly or subtly expressed, it often serves to clarify the client's central concern. For example, this client may express concerns such as:

I'm so sad about hurting the people I love.
I'm afraid everyone will think I'm selfish for leaving and they'll blame me for the divorce. They'll all hate me.
I don't want to be alone. I don't want to be married to him anymore, but I'm afraid I can't leave and make it on my own.
I'm furious that I'm the one who has to make this decision. I'm responsible for every decision we make, and I always pay for it. It's not fair.

Throughout every session, clients will have an emotional response to the issues and concerns that matter most to them. Sometimes the client's affect will be presented forthrightly; often it will be subtle and elusive. If the therapist can approach and draw out the client's affect, as in the example above, it will usually bring further disclosure from the client and clarify the content of the client's conflict.

Expand and Elaborate the Client's Affect

We must look further at how the therapist can best respond to the client's feelings. At times, it can be helpful to anticipate or label a client's emerging feeling (for example, "You must have been furious" or "You're frightened"). As a general guideline, however, a more effective response is to give clients an *open-ended bid* to explore the feeling further. For example, an open-ended response is when the therapist encourages clients to explore or express *what they feel is central* in their affective experience. A simple response such as "What are you feeling right now?" or "Tell me more about that feeling" is remarkably effective in eliciting the client's affect. This open-ended bid to elaborate the feeling *in any way the client wishes* is also more effective than trying to label the client's feeling in an either-or fashion. For example, if the therapist were to say, "Were you feeling _____ or _____ in that situation," the choice may restrict the client rather than invite a free range of responses. The open-ended bid is more effective in drawing out just exactly what the client is feeling, especially as the client often experiences something that the therapist has not anticipated.

This type of open-ended response is also more effective than asking clients why they are experiencing a particular feeling. That is, more information is disclosed if the therapist replies, "Help me understand your anger better" or "Tell me about your anger" than if the therapist asks the client to explain his feeling by asking "Why were you angry about that." By inviting the client to express more fully whatever feeling he is having, therapists are giving the message that they are interested in the client's own subjective experience and they are comfortable sharing whatever the client is experiencing. Most clients have not had permission to share their emotions so freely or honestly in the past, which is why this is one of the most important responses therapists can give their clients.

Clarify the Client's Subjective Feeling. Giving clients an open-ended bid to explore their feelings will also help clients clarify what this particular feeling means to them. Too often, therapists erroneously assume that a particular affective word such as *angry* or *sad* means the same thing to their clients as it does to them. Therapists should not assume that they understand what a particular affective word means to a client without clarifying what it means to this particular client. Therapists must actively encourage clients to elaborate the personal meaning that this feeling holds for them. This is especially true if clients repeatedly use the same affective word to describe themselves, or if there is cross-cultural disparity between therapist and client. Finally, having every client elaborate affect in this way will also safeguard therapists against becoming overidentified with the client and seeing the client's experience as being the same as their own.

Clients are often uncomfortable and therefore unfamiliar with many of their emotional reactions. As a result, clients also need to clarify the broad *undifferentiated feeling states* they often experience. For example, the following questions suggest several ways that therapists can help clients learn more about the emotional reactions that comprise their problems:

Can you bring that feeling to life for me and help me understand what it is like for you when you are feeling that?

Do you have an image that captures that feeling, or is there a fantasy that goes along with it for you?

Is there a particular place in your body where you experience that feeling?

Is this a familiar or old feeling? When is the first time you can remember having it? Where were you? Who were you with? How did the other person respond to you?

How old do you feel that you are when you experience that feeling? Can you attach an age to it, such as being 7 years old or 13 years old?

Does this feeling have its own sound or movement? Can you make a sound that would let me hear what it's like or a gesture that would help me see it?

Some of these exploratory questions will work well with a particular client and not at all with another. Therapists will need to find what works best for each client. In general, however, these responses are all ways of approaching the client's emotions and clarifying the subjective meaning they hold for the client. These types of responses also tell clients that the therapist is concerned about their feelings—who they are and what is important to them. Further, they tell clients that the therapist is different from many other people they have known and is comfortable with their emotions.

Exploring feelings in these ways also creates an opportunity for therapists to confirm the client's personal experience. Clients have often had their feelings and perceptions invalidated by others and these types of responses give the therapist a chance to validate their emotions. In sum, it is profoundly important for clients to receive each of these messages. Together, they comprise a caring, concerned response that reassures clients about the therapist's ability to understand and help with what is most important in their lives.

Experiencing versus Talking about Feelings. Another reason for approaching clients' feelings in these ways is to *intensify* the affect. The exploratory responses suggested above are also attempts to amplify the client's emotional reactions. Although many clients are adept at talking about their feelings (especially psychologically sophisticated clients), it is a very different matter to feel or experience one's emotions. Little change occurs until clients are able to stop talking about their emotions in an intellectualized or objective manner, and actually experience their conflicted emotions with the therapist. Let us examine the critical difference between talking about and experiencing feelings further.

As stated above, the previous ways of approaching feelings are also intended to intensify the client's immediate affective experience. These therapeutic responses will help clients experience or get in touch with the emotional content of what they are discussing. Another way to help clients experience their feelings more fully is to *mirror* the client's emerging affect. For example, if a client's feeling is on the verge of coming through, clients may blink back tears, open their eyes wide in terror, clench their jaw in anger, tighten their lips to keep them from trembling, slowly turn their head from side to side in protest, rock or hold themselves for comfort, drop their heads and cover their eyes in shame, hold their breath in fear, and so on. The therapist can mirror or match the client's posture and expression as a way to clarify, amplify, and invite the full intensity of the client's emotional reaction.

It is important to draw out the client's affect because the greatest opportunity to help clients change occurs at the moment clients are experiencing the full emotional impact of their problems. It is the therapist's ability to be available and compassionate to clients *while they are experiencing their conflicted emotions* that allows clients to move through their conflicted feelings. Clients cannot do this when they are alone with their feelings or when they are insulated from the full intensity of them, as the following case example illustrates.

Throughout the session Jean had been telling her therapist about her hopelessness and despair. She described her life as a merry-go-round of endless ups and downs that always returned to the same hopeless conflicts. This past week she had dropped out of school, as she had done "so many times before," and gave in to pressure from her abusive boyfriend to let him move back into her home again. Jean described her hopelessness about ever being able to do or have anything for herself. Sooner or later, she acknowledged, the only way out of her misery would probably be suicide.

The therapist could feel Jean's despair and was deeply moved by her pain. The therapist tried to work with Jean's feelings by acknowledging her pain and validating her experience ("Of course you feel hopeless and defeated—you haven't been able to do what you wanted to do for yourself again. Like so many times before, you felt that you had to meet someone else's needs rather than say no and do what you wanted for yourself.")

Just as Jean had done in all of their previous sessions, however, she was not able to "feel" her feelings with the therapist. That is, Jean would not share her actual feelings with the therapist or let the therapist be emotionally connected to her *while she was experiencing the sadness.* Because this critical connection to the therapist was missing, Jean still felt helplessly alone with her feelings and hopelessly alone in her life. In part, because she could not allow herself to be comforted by or revealed to a caring other, Jean had not been able to resolve the helplessness and hopelessness that she felt in this crisis and that she had experienced throughout her life.

The upsetting setback of the previous week had intensified Jean's distress. The therapist recognized that this crisis provided an opportunity to make contact with Jean's feelings for the first time:

Therapist:

It just seems hopeless.

Jean:

[long pause, nods]

Therapist:

You don't want to try anymore. You don't want to hurt anymore. You just want it to stop hurting, and suicide seems like the only way out.

Jean:

[nods]

Therapist:

You are so sad. You have been sad inside all of your life.

Jean:

[nods, looks at therapist]

Therapist:

I can see how very painful this is for you right now.

Jean:

[looks away, puts hands over eyes]

Therapist:

I want to be with you in your sadness. I can't take your sadness away, but you don't have to be alone with it anymore. I want to be close to you while you are feeling this.

Jean:

[looks at therapist sorrowfully, and slowly begins to cry]

Therapist:

Yes, I see your sadness there and how much this has hurt you. I feel very close to you right now.

Jean:

[begins sobbing and reaches to the therapist]

For the first time, Jean was able to let the therapist be available to her while she experienced her despondency. The therapist acknowledged the risk that Jean had taken and they discussed how it felt to share her sadness with the therapist. Later in the session, Jean volunteered that she felt "lighter" and her depression lifted for the next few days. We will return to Jean later in this chapter and see how this issue continued to unfold for her over the next few sessions.

IDENTIFY AND PUNCTUATE THE PREDOMINANT AFFECT

Clients often feel confused, trapped, or defeated by their emotions because they seem irrational or inappropriate to the current situation. Clients often think that their feelings seem to occur for no reason or are stronger or different than the situation calls for. This inability to understand their own emotional reactions is the source of tremendous insecurity and distress. One of the most important ways to help clients achieve a greater sense of adequacy and mastery in their lives is to help them make sense of their emotional reactions. Therapists can do this by working with the client's *predominant affect*.

Clients usually enter therapy in response to one of two situations. First, a current life crisis echoes or recaptures an earlier emotional conflict that origi- nally occurred years ago. That is, the current stressor taps in to a preexisting vulnerability or *old wound*. Second, clients may enter therapy in response to feeling overwhelmed by *too many stressors* that have occurred in a short pe- riod of time. These stressors have overwhelmed the client's usual coping strategies and defense mechanisms. We will see below that the client's experi- ence often revolves around a central affect and that therapists need to identify and punctuate this predominant feeling.

An Old Wound

The first reason many clients enter therapy is because of an old wound. This occurs, for example, when clients experience a painful loss such as through divorce or death. It is especially difficult for clients to cope with this current loss when it arouses unresolved feelings from other significant losses in their past. For example, clients may have a predominant feeling about the current loss such as emptiness, betrayal, abandonment terror, or intolerable sadness. The current feeling becomes both understandable and manageable when it can be linked to similar feelings that have been aroused by other losses in their lives. Thus, the therapist needs to identify the central affect that the current crisis has aroused and link it to the original "wound." This is one way to help clients make sense of their seemingly irrational feelings and thereby gain greater mastery of them.

Multiple Stressors

Second, clients often enter therapy when they have suffered too many stress- ful events in a short period of time. Most individuals have adaptive coping mechanisms to help them manage a single crisis event unless the current stressor taps into a preexisting vulnerability. If a second or third stressful event closely follows the first, however, it becomes much harder for individuals to cope. The client's usual coping strategies fail, and the cumulative stressors precipitate symptoms and maladaptive, defensive maneuvers.

When multiple stressors have occurred, clients often enter therapy describing themselves as overwhelmed, defeated, or broken. The stressful events that have precipitated the client's crisis and request for help often reflect a central theme, and therapists are more effective if they can identify and articulate this unifying theme. For example, clients often repeat a *compacted phrase* that encapsulates their emotional responses to the stressful events that have occurred:

> I want everyone to go away and leave me alone.
> It's too much for me; I just can't stand it.
> I don't care anymore; there's no point in trying.

As noted in Chapter 2, therapists must look for recurrent affective themes and try to unlock the emotional reactions that have become encapsulated in these compacted sentences. Underlying each repetitive, compacted sentence are one or two central feelings that capture the impact these stressors have had on the client. Like spokes around the hub of a wheel, the various problems and stresses that occurred are often connected by one or two central feelings. For example, in response to losing too many people or things, the client may have an overriding feeling of being despondent, empty and alone, powerless and hopeless, or afraid of any further losses, changes, or new commitments. When therapists articulate the underlying feeling that links the impact of several different crisis events, clients feel understood and invest further in the therapeutic relationship.

A Characterological Affect

In the beginning of this chapter, therapists were encouraged to respond to the client's current affect. In addition to tracking the client's moment-to-moment affect, therapists can also listen for a recurrent feeling that pervades the client's life, a *characterological affect*.

Once therapy is underway and the therapist has learned more about the client, the therapist can often identify a predominant feeling that captures the client's current conflict and also characterizes his or her life. That is, if the therapist is empathic and sees things from the client's point of view, the therapist can usually find a central feeling that reflects the fabric of the client's life. Clients often have two or three core feelings that are familiar and continuous throughout their lives. When the therapist can identify these central feelings that capture the client's characterological conflict, the client often responds: "Yes, that's how it has always been for me," "That's what it's like to be me," or "That's who I really am." Clients experience these central feelings as their fate because they have "always been there and it seems like they always will be." One of the most significant interventions therapists can make is to accurately reflect these generic feelings to the client.

For example, after listening to the client for several sessions the therapist may respond: It seems as if you have always felt:

. . . *burdened* by all the demands you feel you have to meet.

. . . *afraid* that people are going to "find you out" and point up your true inadequacies.

. . . *resentful* that no matter how much you do, it's never enough.

. . . *wary* that others are trying to put you down or take advantage of you.

The therapist must be prepared to respond to all of the varying emotions that clients experience in the course of therapy. However, therapists will be most effective when they can identify the repetitive feelings that have recurred throughout the client's life that are considered by the client to be central to his or her sense of self.

THE COMPLEXITY OF CLIENTS' FEELINGS

It is difficult and sometimes discouraging to work with clients' conflicted emotions. Some clients are adamant in wanting to avoid their emotions, and others talk endlessly about the same feelings without any change resulting. One reason for these problems is that therapists have only responded to the client's single, presenting affect. To be effective, therapists must work with the three-tiered constellation of feelings that make up the client's emotional conflict.

If the therapist acknowledges the client's current affect and invites the client to explore it further, a sequence of interrelated feelings, a constellation of emotional reactions that are central to the client's conflict will often occur together as a predictable, patterned sequence. Although different variations occur for each client, a triad of interrelated feelings that repeat thoughout the client's daily life can often be identified. The process of change involves mastering each of the feelings in this affective constellation. This section examines the two affective constellations that most commonly occur. We will see that therapists help clients change by responding to the entire sequence of feelings that occur, rather than just responding to the first feeling in the sequence—the client's primary, presenting affect.

Anger-Sadness-Shame

The first affective constellation we will examine consists of anger, sadness, and shame. The predominant feeling-state for many clients is anger. These

clients often experience and readily express angry feelings including irritation, impatience, criticism, and cynicism. However, the client's anger is often
a *reactive* feeling to an original or primary feeling of sadness, hurt, or vulnerability. That is, the anger is a secondary feeling that occurs in response to an
original experience of sadness, hurt, or pain.

The therapist must acknowledge the client's anger, locate its source and
target, and help the client find an appropriate way to express it. Therapists
often stop at this point, however. If so, clients will remain obsessively "stuck"
in their angry, blaming, or critical feeling-state and no change will result.
Why does this occur?

Clients remain fixed in their angry stance because the anger response is a
*reactive feeling to an original hurt that has not been expressed and to which no
response has been given*. The therapist must help the client bring out the
original emotional response of sadness or hurt that led to the reactive feeling
of anger. Said again, the anger response is a secondary feeling that occurs in
response to the primary feeling *that is more threatening or painful for the
client to experience*.

One way to reach the original affect is to wait for clients to spontaneously
ventilate their anger and immediately afterward invite them to examine what
they are feeling now. Following expression of the reactive feeling, there is
often an *open window* to the original feeling of hurt or sadness. For example,
the therapist might respond, "What are you feeling right now, after you have
just expressed how angry you are?" The original feeling of sadness, hurt,
vulnerability, or helplessness will often surface at this moment. The therapist
can then acknowledge this feeling as well, which will often dislodge the client
from the familiar reactive feeling of anger.

There is another way to approach the primary feeling underlying the predominant reactive feeling. If the client's original feeling is not accessible in the
moment after expressing his anger, the therapist can inquire directly about the
original experience that led to the client's anger—for example, "Something
must have hurt you very much for you to remain so angry about that. Tell me
how you felt when that happened." If the client again begins to express anger,
indignation, or a sense of injustice about what occurred, focus the client back
on the original experience: "Yes, I know how unfair that seemed to you, but
how did it feel to you when . . . ?" This type of query also helps to elicit the
original hurt that underlies the reactive response. As the client's original feeling
of sadness or hurt is expressed and the therapist responds, the client *comes in
contact with the internal aspect of the conflict*. It is this internal aspect of the
conflict that has kept the client from being able to change.

Next, we will restate this reactive-primary sequence and take it one step
further by bringing in the third feeling in the sequence. When this type of
client experiences anger, sadness often follows. Although the anger is easily
experienced, the client has learned that it is unsafe to experience and/or

share the original sadness-hurt-vulnerability. To avoid the original painful feeling, the client defensively returns to the reactive feeling of anger in an obsessive or repetitive manner that could cause others to describe him as being "an angry person."

The therapist's task is to help these clients experience the sadness-hurt-vulnerability underneath their repetitive anger. But as soon as the original hurt is activated, the client will defend against this feeling and reflexively return to the safer expression of anger. Thus, the therapist must explore the client's resistance to the original painful affect. Although clients resist the original feeling for different reasons, it is often because *the original affect of pain or sadness arouses a third, aversive feeling of shame, anxiety, or guilt.*

For example, if the therapist inquires about the client's resistance to the original hurt or pain, clients will often say something like: "If I let the pain be there, it's admitting that she really did hurt me," "They won," or "I really am weak." As soon as clients who express these types of concerns experience the hurt that underlies their anger, they usually have painful feelings of shame or humiliation. To repeat, if the therapist draws out the original pain that under-lies the anger, a third feeling of shame or humiliation that is associated with being hurt is aroused as well. The client will defend against both the original sadness and the shame associated with it by reflexively returning to the "stronger" anger.

Instead of shame, other clients will experience anxiety or guilt in re-sponse to feeling the original hurt. For example, some clients will say that if they let themselves feel sad/hurt/vulnerable, then "no one will be there," "others will go away," or "I will be empty and alone." These clients feel painful separation anxieties on experiencing their hurt or pain and avoid this anxiety by reflexively returning to their anger. Still other clients will say that if they let their sadness be real, it is admitting that they really do have a need—which makes them feel selfish, bad, or unworthy. For these clients, a third accompanying feeling of guilt emerges as part of their regularly occurring affective constellation.

For many clients, a triad of feelings exists such as frequent anger, which defends against unexpressed sadness, which, in turn, is associated with shame, guilt, or anxiety. *Significant and enduring change results when clients can expe-rience, express, and contain each feeling in the triad.* More specifically, clients resolve their internal conflicts when they can (1) let themselves experience the full intensity of each feeling; (2) express the feeling and share it with the thera-pist so that they are no longer alone with it or hiding it; and (3) contain, hold, or tolerate the difficult feeling rather than having to move away from it.

When clients can integrate their conflicted emotions in this way, they have internally mastered their conflict. They no longer need the same mal-adaptive response patterns they have employed in the past. Clients are then prepared to adopt new, more adaptive responses that they could not incorporate previously. Although other steps are important, this is a pivotal experience in the process of change.

Sadness-Anger-Guilt

The other commonly occurring affective constellation consists of sadness, anger, and guilt. This time a case study will be used for illustration.

Whereas some clients lead with their anger and defend against their hurt, another type characteristically leads with their sadness and avoids their anger. This type of client presents with an undifferentiated feeling-state of sadness-helplessness-vulnerability-depression. These clients do not experience or express anger, avoid interpersonal conflict, and tend to respond to other's needs at the expense of their own. To illustrate this contrasting affective constellation, we return to Jean—the client in the previous case study.

Earlier we examined a sample dialogue in which the therapist invited Jean to share her sense of hopelessness: "I can see how painful this is for you right now." For the first time, the client was able to let someone respond to her pain and be emotionally connected to her *while she was experiencing it*.

Later in that session, the therapist explored why it had always been so difficult for Jean to share her pain with others. Jean responded that her painful feelings, memories, and needs were all sickeningly real if someone else saw them. Jean had experienced these sad-empty-hopeless feelings all of her life, but they had always been ignored or invalidated in her family of origin. Jean had internalized her family's taboo against unhappy and angry feelings. As a result, she had denied to herself the reality of the deprivation and disparagement that she had suffered throughout her childhood. And, as so often occurs, as an adult Jean went on to reenact her childhood conflict through the abusive men with whom she chose to become involved.

When Jean returned to therapy the following week, she had made a significant change. For the past several months, she had been involved with another irresponsible, exploitative man. This week, when the boyfriend again borrowed her car and arrived two hours late to pick her up from work, she expressed her anger for the first time. Jean also told him that she deserved to be treated with more respect and that she had the right to have her own needs considered as well. Jean had remained in this relationship for several months because she was "afraid to be alone." At this point, though, she decided that this relationship was destructive to her and ended it.

Once the therapist was able to touch Jean's sadness and hurt, her anger was activated and subsequently expressed in an appropriate manner. Jean had remained locked in her sad and helpless victim role, in part, because the direct expression of anger and the assertive expression of her own needs were both unacceptable. As often occurs, *Jean began to claim her own personal power once her feelings were expressed, and she received validating responses to them.* We must look more carefully, however, at the sequence of feelings that unfolded for Jean.

Although Jean began the next therapy session by sharing her good news about ending the destructive relationship, she had difficulty staying with this feeling of strength. Jean gradually retreated from her indignation at how badly this man had treated her, began to feel concerned about how she "may have hurt him," and wondered if she had been selfish to end the relationship. The therapist anticipated that Jean would feel guilty on experiencing her anger or responding to her own needs, however, and helped her explore her guilt.

Just as before in the anger-sadness-shame sequence, Jean defensively avoided her anger because it aroused a third aversive feeling. In Jean's affective constellation, a third affect of guilt served to reflexively return her to her characteristic affect of sadness/helplessness. As the therapist helped Jean integrate all three of these interrelated feelings, she was able to relinquish her victim stance for longer periods.

With the therapist providing a supportive "holding environment," Jean could let the deprivation that she originally experienced in her family become real to her. As this occurred, Jean stopped defending against these painful memories in her past by reenacting them in her current relationships. Jean could also accept her anger at the hurtful ways she had been treated and stopped feeling guilty when she asserted her own needs. Coming to terms with each component of this affective constellation eventually left Jean feeling stronger and more in control of her life than she had ever felt. As before, significant life changes followed from Jean's internal resolution of her conflicted emotions. In this way, therapists help clients resolve their conflicts by responding to each feeling in their affective constellation.

HOLDING THE CLIENT'S PAIN

So far, this discussion has addressed ways to approach and draw out the full range of clients' feelings. If the therapist follows the guidelines suggested, painful feelings will emerge. The therapist's primary concern then becomes how to respond most effectively to these feelings. The purpose of this section is to answer this question. We will see how the therapist can provide a "holding environment" that gives clients a new and more satisfying response to their feelings than they have received before. When this corrective emotional experience is provided in response to the client's core painful feelings, it is the most powerful intervention therapists can make.

Clients Resist Painful Feelings

Just as we saw in Chapter 3 that clients have resistances to treatment, they also defend against painful feelings. As before, the therapist does not simply want to push through these defenses in order to reach the client's sadness or other significant feelings. That would be winning the battle but losing the war. Recall that all resistance and defense is ultimately about fear. Thus, it is a safer, more effective interpersonal process to enlist the client's participation in trying to understand why it is dangerous to experience or share certain feelings. To illustrate, rather than pressing the client to disclose a difficult feeling, the therapist may work with the resistance by using responses such as the following to explore the threat:

> Let's not talk about how you feel about this but about what will happen for you if we did.
> If you cried or let me see your vulnerability, what might go on between us that wouldn't feel good to you?
> What is the danger for you if you let me see your sadness? Help me understand why that is so unsafe for you.
> How did your parents respond to you when you were feeling _____? What did they do?

Thus, the therapist does not push for the content (the specific feeling) but clarifies the defense against it. As in Chapter 3, the therapist is honoring the client's resistance by trying to understand why this defense was once necessary. Therapists' basic orienting assumption is that clients' fear does indeed make sense historically, although it is no longer necessary or adaptive in many current relationships. If the therapist and client can clarify how the client's defense was necessary and adaptive at another point in time, and the therapist can differentiate him- or herself from how others originally responded, it will soon be safe enough for the client's conflicted affect to emerge. Before going on to look at how the therapist can respond to these emerging feelings, we will further explore the interpersonal nature of defenses against affect.

Clients regularly tell the therapist that they just do not want to experience painful feelings—that it "isn't any fun to feel them" and it "doesn't do any good anyway." An interpersonal threat is usually far more important than just their own discomfort, however. The discerning therapist can usually find very good reasons why clients learned in their families of origin that certain feelings were unsafe. For example, one interpersonal theme commonly found in clients' defenses against their feelings is protecting their parents.

Many clients have learned to avoid or deny painful feelings in order to *protect* their parents. This loyalty is carried out at their own expense, however, and at too great a price. As adults, these clients are still complying with delimiting familial rules and enabling their parents by denying the impact of hurtful parental actions. These clients are not allowing their own painful feelings to be real. This protects the (internalized) parents from seeing what they are doing that is hurting the child. If the client participates in this denial, avoids the internal conflict, and idealizes the parents, homeostatic family rules are maintained, and the client remains emotionally connected to split off, all-good parents. If painful feelings are permitted expression in therapy, however, chronic depression or other symptoms may lift but familial rules are broken and emotional ties are threatened. Interpersonal themes such as this often underlie clients' defenses against their painful feelings. Clarifying them is one important step in freeing clients up to experience and share their conflicted emotions.

Therapists Must Provide a Holding Environment

Once painful feelings emerge, what can the therapist do to help clients resolve them? When clients' core feelings are expressed, they anticipate that they will receive the same problematic response from the therapist that they have received in the past. *Clients fear this even though the therapist has never responded to them in this problematic way.* A corrective emotional experience occurs when the therapist responds in a new and safer way that resolves, rather than metaphorically reenacts, the client's original conflict. The therapist can achieve this result by providing a "holding environment" that "contains" the client's feelings.

While growing up, the client had certain developmental experiences that were painful or frightening. Enduring conflicts arose, in part, because parents could not provide a safe, understanding context to help the child contain emotional reactions. The child is contained by being psychologically held in a close, interpersonal "envelope" of empathic caring. *Before the child can develop the capacity to manage feelings on her or his own, someone must first provide this holding context.* Too often, however, this essential developmental experience is not provided. For example, suppose the child was sad or hurt. In some families, the child's sadness:

Aroused the parent's own sadness, and the parent withdrew—leaving the child emotionally alone.

Made the parent feel guilty, and the parent tried to cheer the child up and deny the child's experience—leaving the child confused and alienated from her own experience.

Made the parent feel inadequate, and the parent responded punitively toward the child's sadness—leaving the child ashamed of her or his vulnerability.

In these and other scenarios, the child's sadness cannot be heard and supported, which is necessary to allow these feelings to run their natural course and come to their own resolution. As emphasized above, young children cannot contain or hold a strong, painful feeling by themselves without support from an emotionally available parent. As a result, the child will have to devise ways to deny or avoid this painful feeling. Years later, when this young child is an adult client and risks sharing the sadness with the therapist, the therapist must provide the holding environment that was missed developmentally. We have already seen two examples of this in Chapter 2. Marsha's second therapist, who finally heard and responded to her experience of emptiness, and the therapist of the depressed young mother, who affectionately articulated the mother's own unanswered cries, both provided this holding environment. We now turn to specifics and first look at what therapists should not do; then we closely examine what therapists can do to help clients contain and resolve their painful feelings.

Too often, therapists avoid or move away from clients' painful emotions, *leaving them again unrelated to others while they are experiencing their emotions.* The most common reason why therapists do this is because they assume too much responsibility both for causing and for alleviating clients' pain. In this regard, beginning therapists often say, "I got the client into this, so now it's up to me to put them back together again." Both parts of this belief are false. By responding in the ways suggested in Chapters 4 and 5, *therapists reveal feelings that are already present; they do not cause the client's pain.* Further, it is demeaning for therapists to think they can "fix clients," "get them out of their feelings," or "put them back together again." In actuality, the therapist never has the power to manipulate another's feelings in this way, and any attempt to do so often recapitulates the parent's controlling, dependency-fostering stance with the client.

Therapists often inappropriately assume responsibility for the client's feelings, feel inadequate to respond, or are threatened by the feelings aroused in them by the client. In such situations therapists are likely to respond to the client's affect in these ineffective ways:

- Become anxious and change the topic
- Fall silent and emotionally withdraw
- Become directive and tell the client what to do
- Interpret what the feelings mean and intellectually distance themselves
- Self-disclose or move into their own feelings
- Reassure and explain that everything will be all right
- Diminish the client by trying to rescue him or her
- Become overidentified with the client and insist that the client make some decision or take some action to manage the feeling

When these ineffective responses occur, there is no holding environment. As when the client was a child and could not contain her or his feelings without parental support, the client still cannot hold or tolerate painful feelings alone. Therapists' avoidance, as reflected in these responses, will usually recapitulate the client's developmental deficit. For example, this is what occurred when Marsha's first therapist tried to talk her out of her feelings. And, as sometimes happens when clients express strong feelings, Marsha's first therapist went even further to avoid Marsha's feelings by, in effect, sending Marsha away. That is, when Marsha got near her sad, empty feelings again, the therapist suggested that she join a group and talked to her about seeing a psychiatrist for antidepressant medications. Although referrals such as these are certainly appropriate and necessary at times, in this case they were used to distance the therapist from the client's feelings by sending the client away. This occurs far more commonly than one would expect.

If these distancing responses are ineffective, what should the therapist do instead? The therapist needs to welcome the client's painful feelings and approach them directly. For example, in contrast to the first response, the therapist could say, "I'm concerned about you and want to know more about your empty feelings. Tell me about your sadness."

Further, therapists also want to find genuine ways to express their understanding, acceptance and concern. In particular, therapists want to be emotionally connected to clients while they are experiencing their feelings. There are many ways that therapists can do this; much of this communication is nonverbal or uses only a few words. The following discussion presents some of the elements found in effective responses that create a supportive, holding environment. Of course, these guidelines are only general suggestions, and therapists will have to tailor their own responses to fit each particular client.

Initially, the therapist's primary goal is to stay emotionally present and connected to clients while they experience painful feelings. As discussed in Chapter 2, the therapist may also want to articulate what clients are feeling and acknowledge the reality of clients' emotional experience. This can be done as simply as acknowledging "You're very sad right now." With some clients, it may also be helpful to further validate their experience by saying: "Of course you are feeling sad right now. It hurt you very much when he did that." It will also be helpful for therapists to find a way to express their own sincere concern or compassion for clients (for example, "I can see how sad you feel. It makes me feel very close to you to see this more vulnerable part of you.").

In addition, therapists also want to demonstrate behaviorally that they can tolerate the full intensity and range of clients' feelings. In other words, therapists want to communicate overtly or by manner that they are in no way hurt, burdened, or undone by clients' painful feelings. For example, therapists can do this by saying: "I'm honored that you choose to share this with me. I feel with you right now and we're going to stay together in this until we have worked our way through it." As we will see below, *it is essential that clients see that the therapist is not overwhelmed or threatened by their feelings, does not need to move away from them in any way, and is still fully committed to the relationship.*

As the client recovers from a wave of emotion, the therapist may also want to observe succinctly what parents and others have done in the past when the client felt a similar way. The therapist can then clarify that this relationship is different than others in the client's past and that the therapist is comfortable with or accepting of this part of the client. In this regard, it is important to debrief clients by asking them how it has been to share their feelings with the therapist. Because transference-laden misperceptions usually occur in these sensitive moments, it is helpful to ask clients what they think the therapist was thinking or going through while they were feeling so sad or hurt. Long-standing transference distortions can be identified and resolved in these special moments (for example, the therapist might say, "No, I wasn't thinking that you "looked silly" and "sounded like a baby" at all. I was deeply moved by how sad you were, and I am still feeling very much for you right now."). Finally, when traumatic/abusive memories are being recovered, it may be useful to share the comforting reality that the painful event is over and the client has survived it and to emphasize that the client and therapist are living through the emotional reactions to what has already happened, not the crisis itself.

These simple, uncomplicated responses mean much to clients when given sincerely. Unfortunately, however, beginning therapists are often afraid that they have to do much more than this to respond adequately to the client's pain. At times, these concerns reflect the therapist's own unrealistic expectations to provide "perfect" responses. That is, beginning therapists often labor under the immobilizing burden of believing that they have to respond in some precisely correct way to something as sensitive as the client's pain. In reality, the client does not need the therapist to provide eloquent, crafted responses in a calmly self-assured manner. This perfectionism is unnecessary and may, in fact, serve to keep the therapist from trying to respond to the client's pain at all. As Winnicott (1965) says, the child needs only "good enough" mothering. The therapist provides a "good enough" substitute and a satisfactory holding environment when the therapist finds genuine ways to enact these guidelines. Clients will be thankful for sincere efforts and find them comforting, even if they are expressed in a sometimes fumbling, halting way.

Change from the Inside Out

Clients improve markedly when therapists provide an effective holding environment that allows them to contain feelings that have been too painful to integrate. How does this come about? A corrective emotional experience occurs when the therapist can stay emotionally connected to the client's pain without denying, minimizing, or otherwise moving away from it.

Almost all clients hold a primary irrational belief about their most central, painful feelings. In its most primitive expression, the fear about their feelings is either "I will be destroyed" or "You will be destroyed." That is, clients learned in their families of origin that their painful feelings are "too much" or "overwhelming" or that they "won't be able to stop crying," "will go crazy," or "won't be able to breathe." Or clients may think that the therapist/parent will be "overwhelmed," "hurt" or "burdened," or will "go away" or somehow be impaled by the intensity or unacceptability of their feelings.

The therapist disconfirms these "grim, unconscious pathogenic beliefs" and provides a corrective emotional experience when the therapist can (1) accept; (2) stay emotionally connected to; and (3) not be injured, burdened, or overwhelmed by the client's painful feelings. If the therapist does this, clients learn that neither they nor others are being hurt by these powerful feelings.

Further, when there is a supportive context for their feelings, the feelings can run their course and come to a natural close. This often occurs in just a matter of moments, and clients by themselves recover and readily reestablish their own internal equilibrium. Through this corrective emotional experience, clients learn that their feelings (and they themselves) are not dangerous, disgusting, or bad. As they have the experience that they can remain in a caring relationship even though these feelings are a part of them, their feelings no longer compel them to be isolated or ashamed. As a result, the client no longer needs to maintain elaborate defensive structures, because the feelings that had to be warded off can now be experienced, understood, and integrated. When the therapist can hold clients' pain and allow them to tolerate experiencing and sharing it, their developmental deficit is resolved and they will become able to contain their feelings on their own. This is change from the inside out. Emotional healing occurs when this interpersonal process is enacted, and the healing will propel far-reaching and enduring behavioral change. Long-standing symptoms often drop away at this point. Ironically, *when clients risk exposing their pain, vulnerability, or shame and the therapist responds with kindness and understanding, clients become more powerful.* One of the most satisfying things about being a therapist is facilitating this empowering process. Below, a brief case study highlights some of the principles discussed in this section.

Sherry, a first-year practicum student, was struggling to assimilate all of the new ways of thinking about therapy that she had been learning. It was an exciting but difficult year, as her entire world view was shifting. Part of the difficulty was that different instructors and supervisors were suggesting very different ways to respond to clients. Having grown up with combatative divorced parents, her own conflicts about trying to please "both sides" were being aroused and making the already complex reality of clinical training even more difficult to manage. At times Sherry was immobilized as she tried to sift through these competing ideas, find what made sense to her, and come up with something that she thought would be useful to say to her clients. Two-thirds of the way through her first practicum, she felt more self-conscious about responding to people than she was when she started the program!

Despite her insecurity, Sherry actually was learning a lot and had been responding quite effectively to her client Cathy. Near the end of their weekly session, Cathy began to disclose a very painful memory. With tears in her eyes,

Cathy recounted the frightening experience of a date rape that she had suffered fifteen years ago when she first went to college. As Sherry listened to Cathy's painful story she felt sad and angry. But as she began to think of all the things she should and should not say, and what her supervisor would want her to say, she got "all balled up" and could not find the words to say anything at all. The silence grew awkward as Cathy finished speaking and waited for Sherry to respond. Sherry felt terrible; her worst fear was being realized as she sat there immobilized. Shaken by Cathy's painful story and thinking of all the different ways that she "should" respond, she just could not say anything at all.

After an awkward pause, Cathy tried to take care of Sherry and started talking again, but this did not last long. After a few minutes, Cathy angrily charged: "Don't you have any feelings! He hurt me a lot when he did that!" Understandably, Sherry had made a "mistake," but she recovered quickly and validated Cathy's experience.

Therapist:

Yes. He did hurt you very much. It was frightening and painful for you. I'm very sorry that happened. And I understand why you are angry at me for not responding to you. I was touched by what you said, but I just couldn't find the right words for a minute.

Client:

You couldn't?

Therapist:

No, I wanted to because I felt for you, but I just couldn't find the words. I'm really sorry that happened. I feel embarrassed about it and know it must feel bad to you.

Client:

It's okay. I don't know what to say either sometimes. I don't know why but this makes me think of my daughter when she was little. If I would take the time to stop and pick her up and really listen to her when she needed me, we would get through it pretty quick. My husband called it "collecting her." But if I was in a hurry and tried to ignore or speed her up, she would escalate and it would go on for a long time.

Therapist:

You're a very good mom. I think you're remembering that right now because that's what you needed from me—to be attended to, cared about, "collected." You needed me to give you what you gave your daughter.

Client:

Yeah, I think that's just exactly what I needed. *[Crying]* You know, I never dreamed of telling my mother what happened to me. She never seemed to listen to me when . . .

Sherry recovered from her "mistake" very well and began providing the holding environment that the client herself had articulated so well. As often occurs, such support often leads clients to further related feelings or to resolution of the experience. By having her painful feelings effectively responded to the second time, Cathy was given a corrective emotional experience that allowed her to progress in treatment.

In sum, when the pain associated with the client's central conflict emerges, therapists have the best opportunity to help the client resolve problems and change. The most important corrective emotional experiences occur around the therapist's new, more satisfying response to the client's pain. However, the beginning therapist has probably already intuited that this powerful sword can also cut the other way. That is, the client's conflict is also most likely to be reenacted in these intense, affect-laden moments. Why? The client is vulnerable, expecting the same hurtful response from the therapist that he or she received in the past, and can easily distort or misperceive the therapist's response. In addition, the therapist's own countertransference issues are most likely to be aroused in these intimate moments. Thus, the next section addresses countertransference issues and turns to factors in the therapist's own life that make it difficult to respond to clients' emotions.

PERSONAL FACTORS THAT PREVENT THERAPISTS FROM RESPONDING TO CLIENTS' EMOTIONS

Finally, we must turn our attention away from the client and examine personal characteristics of the therapist that prevent therapists from responding to their clients' emotions. This is an especially important dimension of therapy, yet it often receives too little attention. Just as it is easier for clients to externalize and focus on others rather than themselves, it is also easier for therapists to focus on the client than it is to look within at their own issues and dynamics. If therapists are not prepared to work with their own emotional reactions to the feelings that clients present, however, they will tend to avoid or intellectually explain their clients' feelings. Thus, the purpose of this section is to help therapists anticipate and manage their own reactions to the evocative material that clients present.

In the previous sections we have seen how therapists can elicit the client's affect and anticipate a sequence of interrelated feelings. In addition, an essential component of helping clients resolve their conflicted feelings is for them to receive a caring and accepting response from the therapist. No enduring change occurs without respect and compassion for the emotional conflicts with which clients are struggling. This is fundamental to helping clients change but, in actual practice, it is often difficult for therapists to respond to all of their clients' feelings. Why? Every therapist brings his or her own personal conflicts, developmental history, and current life stressors to the consulting room. This section will show how these factors in the therapist's own life can keep the therapist from working effectively with the client's emotions.

The Therapist's Need to Be Liked

The first issue we will examine is the therapist's need to be liked. Most students who are drawn to clinical practice are genuinely kind people who are sincerely concerned about others and ready to give of themselves. They are often nurturing, caring people who can readily respond to other's hurt and pain. At the same time, however, many therapists also have strong needs to be liked by others and may have difficulty accepting the anger, bitterness, and distrust that some clients will feel toward them. Or some therapists have strong needs to nurture others who are dependent on them. These therapists enter clinical practice, in part, in order to fulfill these needs, and they may have difficulty supporting the client's healthy individuation at times. The following discussion encourages all therapists to assess their own motivations for becoming clinicians and to examine what needs of their own are being fulfilled by doing therapy. The issue is not whether therapists will have their own needs and countertransference propensities, but how they will deal with them. All therapists have certain countertransference reactions, and this self-examination is one way to manage them effectively.

Beginning therapists are often taken aback when their well-intended attempts to approach the client's affect meet with anger, rejection, or ridicule. Beginning therapists often absorb the client's rebuff, comply with the defensive side of the client's feelings, and stop approaching the client's conflicted emotions. This is most likely to occur when the therapist's own needs to nurture or to be liked have been frustrated. To be effective, however, the therapist must continue to work with the client's resistance and approach the conflicted feelings.

To do this, the therapist can adopt the same strategies for working with the client's resistance that were presented in Chapter 3. That is, the therapist should not push clients to express a feeling they are reluctant to share but instead should explore what is the threat or danger for them if they do so (for example, "What are you afraid will happen if you let yourself feel ____"). The therapist must forgo winning the client's approval and not be a "nice" person who does not approach difficult feelings or awkward interpersonal situations. Instead, if the therapist goes ahead and addresses the client's resistance, the client will often become able to share the feelings that have been held away.

In sum, the feelings that therapists are most likely to have difficulty working with are clients' angry and critical feelings toward them. However, these emotional reactions will occur at times if the therapist approaches each of the feelings in the client's affective constellation. Therapy is most likely to falter at the point at which the therapist cannot respond to a particular feeling that the client is struggling with. Because it is so important for therapists to be able to respond to all of the client's feelings, we will continue to address this in the examples that follow.

The Therapist Assumes Responsibility for the Client's Feelings

Another factor that keeps therapists from responding to their clients' feelings concerns the issue of responsibility. Too often, therapists erroneously believe that if they respond to a client's feeling it means that they are responsible for *causing* the feeling or for *taking the client's pain away*. Three related problems occur when therapists assume such inappropriate responsibility for clients' feelings.

The first problem with assuming such responsibility is that therapists tend to avoid their clients' feelings because they do not want to hurt them or make them feel bad. These therapists mistakenly believe that responding to a painful feeling in the client is the same as causing that feeling to exist in the client. Therapists must keep in mind that they did not cause the client to have this feeling originally—it was present before the client met the therapist. The therapist has simply responded to the feeling that the client was experiencing. The unrealistic belief that the therapist is to blame for causing the client's feeling leads the therapist to feel *guilty*. This guilt over "making the client hurt" will immobilize therapists and prevent them from responding effectively.

A second problem occurs when therapists confuse their legitimate responsibility to respond to the client's feelings with an inappropriate belief that they are responsible for causing the client's original feeling. If the therapist inappropriately accepts responsibility for causing the client's feeling, it follows that the therapist must also be afraid of the client's angry retaliation for having to reexperience the painful affect. Clients will hurt when painful feelings are aroused, and anger often accompanies painful feelings. Thus, if the therapist accepts responsibility for causing the client's original feeling, both the therapist's guilt and fear of the client's retaliation may keep the therapist from approaching the client's conflicted emotions. The therapist can respond to clients' anger without accepting responsibility or blame for causing this pain, however.

A third problem results when therapists labor under the impossible burden of having to fix the hurt they have caused the client to feel. That is, when therapists take responsibility for causing the client's feeling, they also assume responsibility for making the client feel better. This is always a myth, however, as therapists can never take away clients' hurt or fix their pain.

If therapists should not shoulder this inappropriate responsibility, what should they do for their clients? The therapist's appropriate response to the client's feelings is threefold. First, the therapist must help clients identify, experience, and express more fully whatever feelings they are having. Second, the therapist must also be empathic or emotionally available to clients so that they can share their feelings with a concerned other rather than have to experience them alone as they often have in the past. Third, the therapist needs to confirm the validity of the client's feelings. The therapist does this by helping clients understand their feelings and make sense of why they are experiencing the particular feeling now. If the therapist accepts this challenge, but does not assume responsibility for causing or changing the client's feeling, the therapist will be able to respond effectively to whatever feelings the client presents.

Assuming responsibility for clients' feelings is one reason therapists may adopt the ineffective approaches of telling clients what to do, reassuring them, or explaining and interpreting clients' emotions before they can experience them. Even if the therapist is not prone to assuming too much responsibility for the client's feelings, however, most therapists will struggle with this issue when the client's affect becomes very intense.

For example, a therapist was treating a young boy who was dying of leukemia. The therapist would sit with the boy in the hospital and talk with him about his impending death: "What is the scariest thing about dying; what are you most afraid of?" The therapist approached the child's feelings in this direct way, and the boy responded by screaming, "I don't want to die, I don't want to die! I'm afraid to die, I want to live!" Sitting there feeling helpless, seeing the terror in this young child's eyes, the therapist felt like a sadistic, perverse monster to be making this child feel such anguish.

But the child went on to say, "I don't want to be alone, I'll be all alone if I die!" Inviting the child's feeling revealed his concern that he would be "all alone." As the therapist heard the separation anxieties and abandonment fears that were gripping this young boy, the therapist understood his primary concern and was able to talk with him in a helpful way. More important, the therapist was able to help his mother understand his central fear and reassure him that her love for him would last forever. Talking with the mother and son together about his fear of being left alone also allowed them to be closer during his illness. This closeness greatly alleviated the child's abandonment terror and subsequent fear of dying.

Working with such intense emotions as these will often lead therapists to feel that they are responsible for causing the client's pain. When this occurs, therapists tend to avoid these profound feelings. To keep this from occurring, therapists must consult with a supervisor or colleague to help them manage their own exaggerated feelings of responsibility that are aroused by the client. If not, these countertransference reactions will prevent therapists from responding effectively to the client. In the example above, the therapist could not have stayed with the intensity of the boy's fear or the mother's loss without a colleague to help manage the therapist's own emotional reactions.

Family Rules

Another reason why therapists may not be able to respond to certain feelings that clients present is because of *family rules* about emotional expression that were learned in the therapist's family of origin. Every family has unspoken rules that govern how emotions are dealt with. That is, emotional expression in families is governed by a rule-bound *homeostatic system* that prescribes what feelings can be expressed and which are unacceptable. The rule-bound system also prescribes when, how, and to whom certain feelings can be expressed. Further, the intensity or degree of emotional expression that is allowed is also gauged by the family homeostatic mechanism. For example, if too much conflict, independence, or closeness is expressed in the family, a corrective homeostatic mechanism automatically occurs to bring the level of emotional expression back within acceptable limits. The following example illustrates how homeostatic mechanisms operate to keep family emotional expression within prescribed limits.

Suppose that in the Smith family a moderate degree of hostility and conflict can exist between the older sister and the younger brother. A lesser degree of frustration and irritation can mutually be expressed between the father and both children. However, anger is rarely expressed between any family member and mother, and never between the father and the mother. What is the homeostatic mechanism that serves to keep this system operating within these boundaries? Whenever a child begins to express angry feelings toward mother, or have direct conflict with her, mother stops the child's emotional expression by looking sad and hurt. If the child's anger continues, father then intervenes and says something like, "Don't talk to your mother that way," or mother figuratively brings father in as a regulatory influence by saying, "I'm going to tell your father about this when he comes home."

In contrast, when anger, conflict, or differences of opinion begin to escalate between mother and father, the children serve as homeostatic regulators and respond in predictable, patterned ways to terminate the parental conflict. For example, the oldest child, eight-year-old Mary, serves as a go-between in the parental relationship. She tries to make peace between her parents by carrying messages back and forth between them. This mechanism usually succeeds in terminating parental conflict except in periods of exceptional family stress. If the parental conflict continues, the younger son may then provide a diversion to the parental conflict by acting out in some predictable way, such as by breaking something or having an accident. By becoming a problem that mother and father must now jointly address, their rule-breaking level of conflict is terminated, and the family's emotional equilibrium returns to within acceptable levels.

This example can be linked to the case study of Jean that we have been following throughout this chapter. Imagine that we have just turned the clock ahead 20 years. The oldest child in the Smith family, Mary, who was serving as the mediator to assuage parental conflict, is now a graduate student in clinical training. Mary is an intern at a community mental health agency and has been seeing Jean in therapy for the past four months. The family rules that Mary has learned in her family of origin will influence her ability to respond to Jean's emotions, just as the family rules that all therapists have learned in their families will influence how they respond to their clients.

Earlier, we observed the critical incident in which Jean was able to let Mary respond to her pain and share her sadness for the first time. Things had gotten somewhat better for Jean since then, but her problems still continued. Jean was able to end the abusive relationship with her boyfriend and felt better for awhile, but she soon became depressed again and fell back into a victim role. Jean was still unable to say no to the demands of others or to follow through and act on her own wishes and interests. Frustrated by her continued depression, Jean angrily criticized Mary for the first time: "I keep coming here every week, but I'm not getting better. You make me have these awful feelings and it doesn't help like you said it would. I don't think you know what you're doing or care how I feel!"

Mary was stunned by Jean's angry outburst even though it was short-lived and Jean quickly apologized. Mary was especially surprised by this criticism because she thought they had been much closer in recent weeks. Throughout the rest of the session, Mary backed away from Jean's anger by offering Jean reassurances. Mary tried to convince Jean that she really did care for her, and that she would get better if she would continue to come to therapy and work with the difficult feelings they had been sharing. Mary felt terrible that Jean had gotten angry at her and anxiously sought help from her supervisor as soon as the session was over.

Mary's supervisor was responsive to her distress over Jean's anger and was able to help Mary understand what went on for her during the session. In reviewing a videotape recording of the session, the supervisor helped Mary recognize how she had tried to assuage Jean's anger with reassurances rather than allowing Jean to feel angry with her or disappointed about her lack of progress. The supervisor explored with Mary why she tried to assuage Jean's anger, rather than encouraging Jean to express her concerns fully and responding to her frustration.

With her supervisor's help, Mary realized that she had been unable to tolerate Jean's anger. She had indeed tried to assuage it, just as she had always done before with her mother. Mary's old role was to "take care of" the conflict rather than allow others to express their dissatisfaction and listen to their concerns. In addition to clarifying Mary's old response pattern, the supervisor also helped Mary to generate working hypotheses about what this critical response may have meant for Jean. The supervisor noted that Jean's expression of anger followed sharing her hurt, and hypothesized that the anger may be part of her affective constellation, which needed to be addressed. That is, Jean needed the experience of being able to express her anger at someone who would take her concerns seriously and would not abandon her. In part, Jean may have been testing to see if she could be critical of Mary and still remain in relationship with her.

Without this helpful consultation, Mary and Jean probably would have become stuck in their relationship and therapy would not have progressed further. Jean could not move forward with her conflicts as long as Mary could not respond to the anger component of her affective constellation. In their next session, however, Mary was able to recover and asked Jean to discuss her frustration and anger. Although Mary still felt an anxious compulsion to reassure Jean and move on, Mary was able to contain her own discomfort and discuss Jean's concerns with her.

Clients will not be able to resolve long-standing conflicts unless the therapist can respond to each component of their conflicted affective constellation. As we noted before, therapy usually stops progressing at the point at which the therapist cannot respond to a particular feeling that the client is experiencing. Family rules about emotional expression are one important factor that influences how therapists respond to their clients' emotions. With this in mind, all therapists should examine the rules that governed how emotions were dealt with in their own families, and how they are bringing their own familial roles and rules for emotional expression to their clinical work. For many therapists, their own therapy will be the best way to change ineffective family rules that they are still enacting with their clients.

Situational Conflicts in the Therapist's Life

Another factor that may keep therapists from responding effectively to their clients' emotions is situational stresses in therapists' own lives. For example, when therapists are struggling with personal problems in their own lives that are similar to those their clients are experiencing, therapists may have difficulty approaching their clients' affect. Or, more likely, therapists will not be able to allow clients to experience fully the feelings they are struggling with. That is, if therapists are having difficulty coming to terms with the feelings aroused by a problem in their own lives, they may not be able to give the client permission to experience or express similar feelings. Here again, these countertransference reactions will occur for every therapist. The issue is not whether they occur but how they are dealt with.

Therapists' own reactions to their clients are the biggest obstacles to responding effectively to their clients' emotions. Therapy is a very human interchange. Although the personal availability of the therapist is the greatest asset in helping clients change, it will also be an obstacle at times. More specifically, the therapist's own countertransference issues are operating when the therapist fails to accurately identify the feelings that the client is presenting, avoids rather than approaches the client's feelings, or becomes personally invested in changing how the client responds or feels about an issue.

Countertransference reactions occur for every therapist. When they do, therapists must consult with a colleague or supervisor to better understand and manage their own reactions. When therapists find that they are repeatedly having difficulty with the same type of affect or supervision does not free them up to respond to the client's feelings, therapists should seek therapy for themselves. Because change is predicated on the relationship that the therapist provides the client, therapists must make an ongoing, lifelong commitment to working with their own dynamics. Without this willingness to work on their own personal reactions to clients, the help therapists can provide will be limited. Furthermore, those therapists who are unwilling to work on persistent countertransference reactions are those most at risk to be a danger to their clients. It is a privilege to be able to help people change, and therapists honor that privilege by acknowledging their own limitations and personal involvement in the therapeutic process.

CLOSING

As seen in Chapter 4, clients' conflicted emotions will not emerge in therapy unless the therapist focuses clients inward. An externalizing focus will lead therapists into a problem-solving and advice-giving mode that precludes the client's affective exploration. As the client talks about the problem out there with others, the therapist's complementary role is to give advice, reassure, or disclose what the therapist has done to solve similar problems. Although these responses can be helpful at times, little change will occur if they characterize the ongoing course of therapy.

But if the therapist does not tell the client what to do, what does the therapist really have to offer the client? The most important way to facilitate change is to help clients master their conflicted emotions by reexperiencing and integrating feelings that have been too painful to tolerate in the past. All clients have experienced tragedies in their lives that will be entwined with the symptoms and problems they present. The therapist helps clients resolve their presenting problems by sharing the full intensity of whatever feelings they are experiencing. The most important aspect of therapy is responding to clients in these deeply personal ways. Yet therapists must also be aware that their biggest obstacle to providing clients with a relationship that can produce change will be their own discomfort with certain client feelings. Thus, therapists must make a lifelong commitment to working with their own dynamics and examining how their own personhood influences their clinical practice.

Part III will next show how therapists can use the client's conflicted emotions to help conceptualize the client's dynamics. Then, in Part IV, this conceptual formulation will be applied to helping clients resolve their conflicts and change.

SUGGESTIONS FOR FURTHER READING

1. One way for therapists to increase their effectiveness with clients is to explore their motivations for becoming therapists and to examine how their own dynamics are expressed in their clinical work. It is just as important to focus on the personhood of the therapist as it is to focus on client dynamics and intervention strategies. Two sources that can help therapists explore these issues are: Chapter 21 of J. Bugental's *The Search for Authenticity* (New York: Holt, Rinehart & Winston, 1965) and A. Guggenbuhl-Craig's *Power in the Helping Professions*, (New York: Springer Publications, 1971). See especially the concept of the "wounded healer."

2. At times, techniques can be useful to elicit and clarify the client's affect. A book that describes Gestalt techniques for intensifying client affect is W. Passons, *Gestalt Approaches in Counseling* (New York: Holt, Rinehart & Winston, 1975).

CHAPTER SIX

FAMILIAL AND DEVELOPMENTAL FACTORS

CONCEPTUAL OVERVIEW

The previous chapters have focused on the interaction that occurs between the therapist and the client. The next three chapters step back from this intensive tracking of the therapeutic process and help therapists conceptualize their clients' dynamics. In order to be effective, therapists must be able to formulate a clear conceptualization of the client's personality and problems. The fact that beginning therapists have had little training or experience, however, makes it difficult for them to conceptualize their clients' dynamics or to apply this conceptualization to treatment. Although no single book, supervisor, or theory is sufficient to teach therapists how to recognize the pattern that exists in their clients' dynamics, helpful guidelines are available.

How can therapists understand what their clients' problems mean and use this conceptual understanding to guide their treatment plans? One way to understand problematic development is to examine what occurs for offspring in families that function well. Once the basic familial processes that produce healthy offspring are identified, it is easier to understand how normal development can go awry and lead to the enduring personality conflicts that clients present. Thus, this chapter will help therapists recognize the familial antecedents of clients' problems. Family systems concepts that clarify the genesis of many characterological problems will be introduced in order to aid therapists in conceptualizing their clients' dynamics. The discussion in this chapter lays the foundation for the comprehensive conceptualization model presented in the next chapter.

CHAPTER ORGANIZATION

This chapter examines three fundamental dimensions of family life. The first part discusses the structure of family relations and the nature of the parental coalition. The second part examines the separateness-relatedness dialectic that was briefly introduced in Chapter 1. The third part explores childrearing practices. Problems in each of these areas lead to developmental conflicts that are central to the symptoms that clients present. Understanding how these familial factors shape personality development will enable therapists to respond more effectively to their clients.

STRUCTURAL FAMILY RELATIONS

Structural family relations are the basis for family organization and define how the family operates as a social system (Minuchin, 1974). This term refers to the relatively enduring patterns of alliances, coalitions, loyalties, and alignments that exist in the family. Structural family relations shape family communication patterns and the roles that family members adopt. Among the different structural family relationships that exist, the parental coalition is the pivotal axis of family life and shapes much of how the family functions (Teyber, 1981). In particular, the nature of the parental coalition primarily determines how well children adjust.

The Parental Coalition

In healthy families, the marital relationship is the primary two-person relationship in the family. That is, both spouses have a primary loyalty commitment to each other, and the marital coalition cannot be divided by grandparents, children, friends, employers, or others. Parents will still have differences and conflicts between themselves—and they will be committed to others as well—but the marital relationship is a stable alliance that cannot be disrupted by others. In contrast, families in which the primary emotional bond or involvement is not between mother and father often produce offspring with enduring personality conflicts. In these problematic families the primary alliance is between a grandparent and parent, a parent and a child, or within some other dyad.

How does a primary parental coalition develop? Both parents must have been able to psychologically separate from their families of origin, have achieved an autonomous identity in early adulthood, and have been able to make a primary loyalty commitment to a peer relationship. Said differently, as young adults, these offspring have been able to transfer their primary loyalty commitment from their parents in the previous generation to a spouse in the same generation. The question here becomes "Who comes first?" Does one choose the parent or the spouse?

If young adult offspring have not been able to shift their primary loyalty commitment from their family of origin to their spouse, a primary marital coalition will not develop. The primary loyalty of one or both spouses will remain with their parent. When this occurs, the primary dyadic relationship in the family is a cross-generational alliance between a parent and the adult offspring, rather than a primary marital coalition between the husband and the wife. This cross-generational alliance (for example, maternal grandmother-mother) usually repeats in the next generation with the birth of children and results in a primary parent-child coalition as well (for example, mother-child). Before going on to see why these cross-generational alliances are so problematic for offspring, we must better understand the important psychological processes that are being enacted in forming a primary parental coalition. We will do this by examining the wedding ceremony as a cultural rite of passage.

The wedding ceremony is a familiar ritual for illustrating these concepts about shifting loyalty bonds from the family of origin to the spouse and forming a primary marital coalition. A central purpose of the wedding ceremony is to publicly mark a transition in loyalty bonds from the parents and family of origin to the new spouse. How does this occur? Once family, friends, and clergy are all assembled for the ceremony, the father walks the bride down the center aisle to the front of the church. In front of all, the father symbolically gives the bride away by placing her hand in the hand of the waiting groom. The father then leaves the couple by stepping back from the front of the church and sitting down beside his own wife. The bride and groom, who have now been separated from the parental generation, turn away and step forward to be married. In this ceremony, the bride and groom are shifting their primary loyalty commitments and publicly defining themselves to family and friends as an enduring marital couple.

This shifting of primary loyalties from the previous generation to the new spouse is a major developmental task. Although this transition is usually difficult for most families, it becomes especially conflict laden in families that have not had a primary marital coalition. The question of who comes first, parent or spouse, may be painfully enacted in conflicts that surround planning for the wedding day. Offspring embroiled in cross-generational alliances often find that their wedding day, and the preparations for it, are a wrenching battle between conducting the ceremony the way the couple being married want it done and doing it the parent's way. The underlying conflict is over shifting loyalties from the previous generation to the spouse, but it is played out in arguments over who will be invited to the wedding, where it will be held, how it will be conducted, who is financially responsible, and so on. In contrast, young adults who enjoy their wedding day have been able to switch their primary loyalty from parents to each other. These couples are not being pulled apart by competing loyalty ties that induce guilt. We will now extend this discussion to other family forms.

How does this model of a primary parental coalition apply to single-parent families? Are they inherently problematic because there is not a primary marital coalition? No, but this structural model is still useful in helping us understand why some single-parent families function effectively whereas others have problems.

In single-parent families that function well, there are clearly defined intergenerational boundaries that separate adult business from child business. By necessity, children in single-parent families usually need to take on more household duties, and there is often more emotional sharing between parent and child than in two-parent families. Even so, roles and responsibilities are clearly differentiated between adults and children in healthy single-parent families. This means that the single parent still performs executive ego functions for the family, such as providing a well-organized household with predictable daily routines for children, making decisions and plans for the family, and setting limits and enforcing rules. Further, although parents certainly have legitimate needs for companionship and support, these are met primarily in same-generational peer relationships rather than through the children.

In contrast, single-parent families will have more problems when adult and child roles are not clearly distinguished, when intergenerational boundaries are blurred, and when too many adult needs are met through the children. With this general background in mind, we now turn to how the parental coalition influences child development and examine why primary marital coalitions are more effective than cross-generational alliances.

How the Parental Coalition Influences Child Adjustment

Why is the nature of the parental coalition so crucial for family functioning and child adjustment? This section examines four reasons why children are better adjusted if the primary coalition in the family is between mother and father rather than between any other dyad.

First, when mother and father have a stable alliance, children cannot come between their parents and play one parent off against the other. For example, if a primary coalition exists between mother and 8-year-old daughter, father will have trouble setting and enforcing limits with his daughter. If father tries to put his daughter to bed at 8:00 or have her pick up her room, she can often defy these attempts at discipline by appealing to her mother. The daughter learns that she does not have to do what dad says because mom is likely to take her side against dad. When children can play one parent off against the other in this way, children learn that rules do not apply to them. That is, these children learn that they do not have to conform to adult rules in general, and they will often disobey teachers and try to manipulate other authority figures in their lives. These problems with limits and authority will carry over into adulthood and are especially likely to lead to problems in the work sphere where adults must be able to conform to rules and cooperate with others. A tragic illustration of this principle is found in Woodward's (1984) biography of the late comedian John Belushi.

As an early adolescent, Belushi's authoritarian father would work for long hours in the restaurant business while John stayed home and did chores for his mother. By making up humorous but hostile imitations of his father and performing these "routines" for his mother, he could get her to laugh at his father and manipulate her out of enforcing household duties. With his mother and siblings in stitches, Belushi would escape his chores and head out the door to meet with his friends. Among other problematic messages here, John learned that by successfully playing one parent off against the other, limits and rules did not apply to him. Despite his talents, his life was a study in compulsively pushing limits and being out of control with food, money, sex, and especially drugs. After chronic drug use, he predictably and tragically died from an overdose of cocaine and heroin.

Therapists will not see large numbers of clients with this background unless they work in alcohol and substance abuse programs. Clients who learn that they can manipulate controls by dividing the marital coalition will often develop impulsive, acting-out symptoms. When therapists do see them in treatment these clients will push limits, eschew responsibility, and be demanding of the therapist. For example, they will often arrive late for appointments, expect to be able to stay beyond the scheduled time, be delinquent in or try to avoid payment of fees, be insistent on calling the therapist at home, and so forth. These challenging clients receive a corrective emotional experience when therapists can set firm limits and not be manipulated out of their usual treatment parameters. At the same time, however, therapists must do this in a nonpunitive way that maintains their emotional commitment to the client and compassion for the very real fear and loneliness that has been engendered by these developmental experiences.

Second, children in families with a primary marital coalition are more likely to gain a realistic sense of their own power and control than are children raised in cross-generational alliances. When children form the primary emotional bond with a parent, they become too important to the parent and exert too much influence over the parent's well-being. As a result, these children gain an exaggerated sense of their own importance and a grandiose sense of their own ability to influence others. Children cannot gain a realistic sense of their own limits and capabilities when they are encouraged in the illusion that they can prop up a parent's sagging self-esteem, maintain their parent's emotional equilibrium, or make important decisions for the parent.

It is highly reinforcing for children to feel so powerful vis-à-vis their parent, and they will be extremely reluctant to give up their special role. These clients will presume this special status with the therapist and are often effective in reestablishing this relational configuration. In this regard, the client may offer the therapist a subtle but all-too-easily accepted invitation to establish a mutual admiration society. That is, these sophisticated clients are often adept at flattering the therapist and establishing an elite sense of mutual, shared superiority. In this cozy, shared aggrandizement, the client is very responsive to nuances in the therapist's mood, is skilled at making the therapist feel special, and, in turn, expects to be treated as special by the therapist. Once this unspoken deal is struck, however, the therapist feels constrained, as if he or she is betraying the relationship by confronting or disagreeing with the client or by focusing the client inward on internal conflicts. Such a reenactment, of course, will keep the therapist and client from contacting the client's real conflicts and unmet needs.

On the other side of their grandiosity, however, these clients also have a parallel sense of their own inadequacy. This inadequacy, which is a constant source of anxiety, arises because they as children were never capable of actually meeting their parents' needs. These clients often suffer from extreme performance anxieties and feel deeply inadequate to meet the exaggerated demands they now place on themselves. As before, the therapist's task is to remain compassionate toward both sides of their dilemma. On the one hand, these clients suffer from profound feelings of inadequacy and anxiety over all of the things they must control. On the other, relinquishing these demands they are struggling to meet takes away these clients' special role and identity. Further, to get healthier in this area threatens to destroy their (internalized) parent, who has convincingly communicated for decades that she or he cannot survive without them. Thus, getting better in treatment arouses both guilt for leaving their parents to manage their own lives and anxiety over disrupting these clients' primary modality for being in relationships with their parents.

Finally, the therapist must not be overreactive to the client's compliments, criticisms, or distress. The therapist needs to be affected by clients, but these clients will get worse if the therapist's own personal equilibrium can be too readily influenced. In the past, these clients were able to exert too much control over their parent's well-being, and the therapist does not want to reenact this situation in the therapy relationship.

A third problem for many children caught in cross-generational alliances is emancipation conflicts. If the mother and father have a primary marital coalition, children are free to grow up and become successful young adults who can leave home. Why? Parents do not need the child to remain dependent on them in order to fulfill their own lives. In contrast, if the primary coalition is between parent and child, these offspring may feel guilty about forsaking their parent to the unfulfilling relationship with the other spouse. As a result, they associate anxiety and guilt with achievements and outside commitments. In this regard, guilt over emancipation frequently underlies academic failure in college, as well as many other symptoms and problems that students present in college counseling centers (Teyber, 1983). Thus, cross-generational alliances impose binding loyalty ties that make young adults feel guilty about leaving home, successfully pursuing their own career interests, and establishing satisfying love relationships in adulthood.

Many clients, such as Anna in Chapter 4, struggle with intense separation guilt. These clients may feel guilty about being happy, succeeding in life, or even getting better in therapy. It is important with all clients, but these in particular, that therapists enjoy clients' happiness and express pleasure in their success. Some beginning therapists are set back and unsure of how to respond when such a client begins the session by saying, "I feel really good today; I don't have any problems to talk about right now." The therapist expands the ways in which these clients can be connected to others by enthusiastically responding: "That's great! What's the best thing going on for you today?" These clients cannot improve in therapy if the therapist does not actively support and encourage the successful side of their lives as well. Without such support, therapy will bog down and become stuck as these clients repetitively share deprivation, emptiness, sadness, or pain without any progress or resolution.

Conflicts over independence and success will be activated for many clients around the time of terminating therapy. In particular, these clients, who characteristically are struggling with separation guilt, will feel especially guilty about no longer needing the therapist and heading off successfully on their own. Therapists must find multiple ways to give these clients permission not to need them, to leave when they are ready to go, and to enjoy their own successful lives. Guilt over separation, success, and becoming stronger will be a common but important issue for many clients, although few will recognize it as such.

A fourth type of problem develops for children when the primary coalition is between a parent and a child rather than between the mother and father. Cross-generational alliances frequently result in the *parentification* of children. That is, a role reversal occurs in which children take on the role of meeting their parent's emotional needs rather than the parent responding to the child's needs. When certain emotional needs of these parents are not met by their spouse, they inappropriately turn to one or more of their children to meet their own adult needs for affection and intimacy; for approval and reassurance; or for stability, direction, and control. These parents will often describe their parentified children as their best friend, lifeline, or confidant (Teyber, 1992).

It is problematic for children when they become responsible for, or take care of, the emotional needs of their parent. The problem with this role reversal is that offspring must give to their parents rather than receive. The natural flow of nurturing from parent to child is reversed and children's age-appropriate dependency needs go unmet. These parentified children grow up to feel overly responsible for others, afraid of depending on others, and guilty about having their own needs met. As adults, parentified offspring often describe themselves as feeling empty or "having a hole inside of me" as a result of having given rather than having received throughout their childhoods. Parentified children initially enjoy having such a special and powerful role vis-à-vis their parent. As adults, however, they ultimately come to resent having been used by their parent and having been deprived of their own childhoods.

Parentification is common in the background of clients and therapists alike. Perhaps as many as one-half of all clients seeking outpatient psychotherapy have been parentified to some extent. Because their basic relational orientation is to take care of others, parentified children select careers as nurses, ministers, and therapists. Although kind and capable, they are guilty about saying 'no', setting limits, and meeting their own needs. Because they do not draw boundaries well, they tend to become overidentified with others' problems and are prone to experience burnout. Since they grew up having to take care of their parent, it is now threatening to relinquish this control in their current lives. For example, it will be hard for them to let others share in meeting demands, although they resent "having to do everything myself" at the same time. These control issues may also be evidenced in symptoms such as airplane phobias, for example, where these individuals must temporarily relinquish control to the pilot. These clients also have problems in their personal lives, because it is too threatening to relinquish the control necessary to be intimate with someone.

Clients who have been parentified will be highly attuned and responsive to the therapist. It can feel great to work with these clients in the short run, because they astutely discern what the therapist needs them to do so that he or she feels competent or secure. If the therapist does not collude in reenacting this relational pattern, however, clients can begin to explore the consequences of having missed their childhood. It will be both relieving and anxiety arousing when the therapist begins this exploration by making such process comments as: "Here again, you are taking care of me. I appreciate your thoughtfulness, but I don't really need that from you. In fact, it leaves me wondering what happens to your needs—if there is any place where you can ever be responded to." The following case study illustrates this important concept.

Carol was a highly regarded psychiatric nurse. An utterly dependable and take-charge person, she could seemingly handle every situation that arose. In a hospital emergency setting where very disturbed patients were brought in crisis, her rapid assessments, accurate judgment, and compassion for highly disorganized patients had earned her the respect of the entire staff. Although considered a "superstar" at work, Carol sought therapy for her recurrent depressions and loneliness.

Carol was bright and engaging and was skilled at getting the therapist to lead, talk about herself, and become involved in interesting discussions about abstract clinical issues. The therapist was usually effective in resisting Carol's strong pulls to externalize, however, and repeatedly focused Carol inward. Carol was outspoken about it being new for her to attend to herself and her inner experience in this way, saying that it made her feel "uncomfortable" and that she did not really like the therapist's approach. The therapist was genuinely sympathetic and open to talking about what this was like for Carol, but stuck to the approach and continued to focus Carol in on her own experience. Both soon agreed, however, that important material was emerging.

Only seven weeks into treatment Carol disclosed for the first time to anyone that her stepfather had sexually assaulted her when she was fifteen years old. Carol successfully fought him off, although she was scratched, had her blouse torn open, and suffered a bloody nose when she literally pushed him off of her. Carol recounted her ordeal in detail but without emotion, and the therapist responded effectively in caring and validating ways. The therapist, herself a mother of two daughters, soon asked what was the burning question for her: "You have kept this awful secret for almost twenty years. I'm glad that you can share it with me now, but I'm sorry that you had to be alone with this much pain for so long. What kept you from telling your mother?"

Carol's poignant response illustrated the plight of the seriously parentified child: "I didn't want to put more on her. She couldn't have done much anyway, and I didn't want her to worry." In this, as in many other aspects of her relationship with her mother, Carol's own profound needs for protection and comfort were set aside in order to meet her parent's need.

In sum, these are just four of the many ways in which children are better adjusted in families with a primary marital coalition than with cross-generational alliances. Therapists will see the consequences of these structural family relationships operating with many of their clients. As we will see, the nature of the parental coalition also influences two other basic dimensions of family life, the separateness-relatedness dialectic and child-rearing practices.

THE SEPARATENESS-RELATEDNESS DIALECTIC

The second basic dimension of family life that informs therapists about the nature and source of client conflicts is the *separateness-relatedness dialectic*. This family systems term refers, in part, to the family's ability to respond to both the child's need for closeness and for autonomy. Recall the dialectic of separateness-relatedness that was introduced in Chapter 1. As children develop, each family faces the task of having to provide both intimacy and individuation—to be close and separate at the same time. Infants and very young children must be provided with a symbiotic union with a nurturing parent. Children progressively become more independent and, by adolescence, must be supported in their further individuation and emancipation from the family. In healthy families, there is an *experiential ranging* between the poles of symbiotic union and individuation (Farley, 1979). That is, parents in these families have the breadth and flexibility to range back and forth along this continuum of separateness-relatedness and meet children's needs both for closeness and for autonomy.

In contrast, less effective families are more restricted in their experiential ranging. That is, they do not have the flexibility and personal resources to function well at both ends of the continuum. These less effective parents cannot move back and forth along this continuum to meet the changing needs that children present at different developmental stages. As noted in Chapter 1, enmeshed families cannot support the child's developmental movement toward individuation, whereas disengaged families cannot meet offspring's needs for closeness.

How does the separateness-relatedness continuum relate to the parental coalition? The following example shows how families without a primary marital coalition are more restricted in their experiential ranges.

Following Solomon (1973), suppose that a young married couple has not separated psychologically from their families of origin. Such newlyweds are likely to have a high degree of conflict in their marriage that they are both unable to resolve. In many cases, the couple will attempt to deal with their relationship problems by having children. Without being aware of it, the parents will experience the children as extensions of themselves and project their own conflicts onto the children. That is, rather than address their own internal conflicts and marital problems, they attempt to control their conflicts by externalizing them onto their children. Through this "family projection process," children are scripted into roles, and delimiting family rules and myths are established, to help parents defend against their conflicts.

To illustrate, if the mother's need for closeness cannot be met by the father, she may turn to the child to have her emotional needs met. This solution will work well in the short run, but it establishes the basis for long-term family problems. Typically, the mother could not emancipate psychologically from her own parents, and she is made anxious by individuation. As long as the child remains dependent on her, her need for closeness is met and her anxiety over individuation is managed. On the other hand, the father is made anxious by closeness. The primary mother-child coalition allows him to gain greater distance from the anxiety-arousing demands of closeness from both the spouse and the child. In this way, the child becomes both a wedge that holds the marriage together and, at the same time, ensures distance between the couple.

This type of solution eventually poses a dilemma for the child's continuing development, however. The child's innate push for growth will disrupt the neutralizing wedge in the marital relationship, and this will arouse each parent's conflict. Thus, these parents need to encourage nongrowth, dependency, or incompetence in the child in order to maintain the marital status quo. At the same time, however, parents will also express anger and frustration to the child about the child's refusal to grow up and act responsibly. This family's limited experiential range is most likely to come to a head during adolescence when offspring face the developmental hurdle of emancipating from the family of origin. The mixed messages the child has received about growing up and remaining dependent will often erupt in psychological symptoms and acting-out behavior at this time. Furthermore, these underlying conflicts have been internalized by the child and often continue to be expressed in symptoms and problems throughout adulthood as well.

This example is just one illustration of how the parental coalition and the family's experiential range shape the conflicts that clients present in therapy. Although large cultural differences occur, the separateness-relatedness dialectic does orient the therapist to formative developmental experiences. Further, just as the separateness-relatedness dialectic helps therapists conceptualize client dynamics, it can also help therapists intervene more effectively with the process dimension. Later, in Chapter 8, we will return to the separateness-relatedness dialectic and use it to help understand the interpersonal process that therapists and clients are enacting. For now, however, we will remain with familial characteristics and turn to childrearing practices, a third dimension of family life that influences child adjustment.

CHILDREARING PRACTICES
Three Styles of Parenting

The third dimension of family life that is relevant to understanding how personality conflicts develop is childrearing practices. Most families employ one of three parenting styles: *authoritarian, permissive,* or *authoritative.* This section examines these three styles of childrearing and shows how each is related to the problems that clients present in therapy. Part of this discussion draws on research by Baumrind (1967, 1971) on the effects of childrearing practices.

Authoritarian parents are firm disciplinarians. Children are given unambiguous prescriptions for acceptable and unacceptable behavior. Parental rules are clearly explained, and the consequences for violating them are consistently enforced. Authoritarian parents also hold high expectations for their children to behave in a responsible and mature manner. Children are expected to perform up to their abilities and to be competent and contributing family members.

Authoritarian parents do not give children reasons or explanations for the rules they set, however. Compromises or alternatives are not discussed with children. Children of authoritarian parents cannot ask why a rule is set—they must simply obey. Furthermore, although authoritarian parents discipline their children and expect much of them, they do not provide their children with much warmth or affection.

In contrast, permissive parents are lax disciplinarians. Children often do not know what behavior is expected of them, and they do not know what consequences will occur if they violate parental norms. Most important, permissive parents do not consistently enforce the rules that they do set. As a result, children of permissive parents learn that they do not have to obey because parents will not follow through and enforce the rules they set anyway.

Thus, authoritarian parents exert a high degree of control over their children. However, these limits and rules are not coupled with warmth and affection, with parental explanations for why the rules have been set, or with opportunities for the children to discuss compromises and alternatives with their parents. In contrast, permissive parents are often expressive, loving, and communicative with their children, but their children are not disciplined nor are they expected to behave in a mature, responsible manner. Before looking at the problems that result from these two ineffective childrearing styles, let us contrast them with the more effective, but less well-known, authoritative style.

The authoritative childrearing style produces the most healthy, well-adjusted children. Authoritative parents possess a wide range of parenting skills that allows them to combine firm discipline with nurturant child care. Although authoritative parents set and enforce firm limits, they also communicate with their children. Authoritative parents give reasons and explanations for the rules they set, and they will negotiate compromises and discuss alternatives with their children. While authoritative parents expect mature, responsible behavior from their children, they also provide a great deal of physical affection and spoken approval. In short, authoritative parents combine the most effective features of the other two parenting styles. They are nurturing parents who communicate with their children, but are also firm disciplinarians who place high demands for maturity on children. Research has found that authoritative parents produce children who are independent, self-controlled, successful with peers, and generally have a positive, happy mood.

We have seen that the authoritarian parent sets limits but does so harshly, whereas the permissive parent cannot take charge and place appropriate controls on children. Most parents are unable to both set rules and do so in a caring way, believing that they have to be either strict or loving. In contrast, authoritative parents have a wider experiential range and are effective in both domains. Despite the best of intentions, balancing these two domains is very hard for most parents. Authoritative parenting requires that parents have diverse personality strengths to be both nurturing and emotionally available to children and still being able to set rules and tolerate children's disapproval for firmly enforcing these rules. Authoritative parents also make an effort to talk with children and explain what the rules are and why certain behavior is encouraged or discouraged, to entertain alternatives and compromises, and to follow through and enforce the rules that have been set. Further, parents must also be highly discriminating in order to assess the upper level of children's abilities. Because children are constantly changing, it is difficult to determine what demands for mature and responsible behavior will challenge children yet allow them to succeed. It is understandable, but unfortunate, that only 10 to 12 percent of parents can provide such effective authoritative parenting.

Beginning therapists will find that most of their clients have been reared by authoritarian parents. Offspring from permissive parents have substantial problems, but they are less likely to seek help. What about children of authoritative parents? These healthier offspring will not usually be seen in longer-term treatment for enduring personality conflicts, although they may seek help in crisis situations (such as a child's major illness) or for negotiating developmental hurdles (such as premarital counseling). The following section examines more fully how childrearing practices are reflected in the conflicts that clients present in therapy. Following this discussion, we will examine further the most significant parenting style for therapists—authoritarian childrearing.

Consequences of Childrearing Practices

In socialization, young children gradually give up their own immediate demands for gratification in order to maintain parental approval. It is the threat of parental punishment and withdrawal of parental love that leads young children to inhibit their own impulses and conform to parental standards. If all goes well, children's conflict between the desire to gratify their own impulses and the fear of parental punishment will be successfully resolved. A successful resolution is one in which children learn to obey, but without sacrificing their own initiative and positive self-regard. That is, healthy children can become self-controlled and self-reliant without inhibiting their own initiative or losing their sense of being prized by their parents (Wenar, 1990).

For children of authoritarian parents, however, the trade-off between giving up their own wishes to maintain parental approval is too severe. Because authoritarian parents provide too little nurturance and affection, too much of the child's own initiative and positive self-regard is forsaken in order to secure parental approval. These children are obedient, but they are also anxious and insecure, complying with parents out of fear.

This interpersonal conflict between the authoritarian parent and young child has been internalized by the time the child is school aged. What was originally an interpersonal conflict becomes an internal or intrapsychic conflict. These well-behaved, insecure children become harsh, critical, and demanding toward themselves, just as their parents have been toward them. Many of these offspring will seek therapy as adults, and they are likely to present with symptoms involving guilt, depression, unassertiveness, anxiety, and low self-esteem.

Offspring of permissive parents will also have adjustment problems, but their symptoms are different. These offspring are more likely to develop acting-out or externalizing problems, and they are less likely to seek therapy as adults. Why? Children of permissive parents learn that they can avoid the consequences of their own behavior by manipulating others. Rules and limits do not apply to them, and wishes can be gratified without delay. Research has found these children to be dependent, immature, demanding, and unhappy. They have little self-control, low frustration tolerances, and do poorly with their peers. As adults, these offspring tend to be impulsive and to avoid taking responsibility for their own behavior. As a result, they are more likely to develop acting-out disorders such as alcohol and substance abuse. They also tend to be more self-centered and demanding in their interpersonal relations and less capable of making commitments and following through on obligations.

Authoritarian Parenting, Love Withdrawal, and Insecure Attachment

Because beginning therapists will be working with so many clients from authoritarian backgrounds, we must examine this childrearing style more closely. Another aspect of authoritarian parenting that therapists need to understand is love withdrawal discipline techniques. These occur when parents do not communicate that they disapprove of the child's behavior but are so angry and rejecting that they communicate essential disapproval of the child's basic self or personhood. This communication is often nonverbal, being done by inflection, gesture, and facial expression as much as by words.

As a method of punishing or shaping the child's behavior, or of communicating their anger (or even disgust), these parents withdraw their warmth, feeling, and emotional connection to the child (for example, "Get out of here; I don't even want to have to look at you."). To some extent, many parents will respond in these ways at times, but this is not what we are addressing here. With authoritarian parents, withdrawal of approval, warmth, and emotional contact is frequent and intense, and the child's emotional ties to the parents are disrupted. When this occurs, the child will have to develop symptoms and defenses to cope with the separation anxieties this disruption engenders.

A Continuum of Authoritarian Responses. Authoritarian childrearing and love withdrawal techniques occur on a continuum of severity. In families that are only somewhat authoritarian, disruption of ties from love withdrawal may occur only when parents are stressed, tired, or frustrated. If love withdrawal does not occur routinely, if there are other points of connection between parent and child, and if the break in relatedness is not too severe, ties can soon be restored. The anxiety may still be intense, but through compliance, the child can restore contact.

In families that are more severely authoritarian, however, the disruption will occur more often. As we will explore later, children in these families will be repeatedly exposed to experiences of interpersonal loss, emotional isolation, helplessness, and blame. In highly authoritarian families, and especially in abusive families, children may be exposed to the parent's intense anger, contempt, and emotional withdrawal on a daily basis. These parents not only withdraw approval of the child's basic self but also ridicule or debase the child. Affection and warmth are also withdrawn to an extreme degree. This leaves the child psychologically alone, feeling cold and empty inside and believing that he or she is bad.

At an even further end on this continuum, some seriously disturbed parents are so completely removed psychologically that they become dissociated. For a few moments, usually while they are enraged, these more highly disturbed parents lose absolutely all feeling for or awareness of the reality of the child's actual experience. Beginning therapists may not be familiar with these dissociative ego states, but important principles necessary for working with clients from less dysfunctional families can be learned from exploring the basic dynamics in these more disturbed families.

It is terrifying for children when angry, threatening parents become dissociated in this way and are no longer emotionally present or psychologically reachable. Offspring may describe their parents in these moments as being "possessed," "not there," or "somebody else." Much child abuse occurs when parents are in these altered ego states. These parents are usually reenacting with their children abusive events from their own childhoods that they may or may not be able to remember. However, as long as they are compulsively reenacting their past abuse, the painful feelings that accompanied the abuse they originally experienced will be unavailable to them.

Thus, these parents' reenactment is a primitive psychological defense against the painful feelings associated with their own past abuse. By externally reenacting the trauma over and over again with their children, abusive parents do not have to remember or experience internally their own painful feelings. The abusive adult often performs this defensive reenactment by evoking the same terrified feelings in the child that the parent was once made to feel. Through this primitive defense of "turning passive into active," abusive parents' own terror and shame is expressed, but vicariously through the child, so that they do not have to experience the trauma and defeat of abuse as their own. In sum, for children in families at the more severe end of this authoritarian continuum, these experiences pose a constant threat and organize these children's daily experience and, ultimately, their psychological adaption to life.

Effects of Severe Love Withdrawal. Love withdrawal as a discipline measure is primarily associated with authoritarian parenting, but it occurs in other families as well. For example, different variations of this dynamic can be seen in parents who act like martyrs. These parents indirectly communicate their hurt and disappointment in the child with a sigh or long-suffering look, turning away and withdrawing emotionally from the child. Or, some parents demand perfection from or excessive control over the child and withdraw their love when the child does not fulfill their excessive expectations. In these moments of parental love withdrawal, however they occur, the child in effect loses the parent, as the parent's feeling for the child is suspended. The child's emotional connectedness to the parent is temporarily broken, and the child is psychologically abandoned. Before going on to look more closely at the emotional sequelae of this all-too-common experience, we must emphasize again that all children's ties to their parents will be threatened at times. Significant problems only occur when disrupted ties *characterize* the relationship.

A constellation of significant emotional reactions occurs when parents angrily cut off their emotional connection to young children. To begin with, the child is psychologically isolated and experiences separation anxieties that may be intensely painful. Profound helplessness is also engendered by this withdrawal of warmth, approval, and relatedness. The child is made to feel bad and alone, and desperately wants to restore the relationship but is powerless to do so until the parent reengages. Further, *the child is also immobilized by being made to feel responsible for the parent's anger, rejection, and withdrawal.* In this immobilizing double bind, the child believes that by being "bad" he or she has caused the parent to go away, which is the thing most feared because it threatens already insecure ties to the parent.

The child is angry about this, of course, but the child's anger elicits further threats from the authoritarian parent. Through power assertion, the authoritarian parent does not allow the child to disagree, let alone find appropriate means of expressing anger (for example, "I'm your father. You will never be angry at me. Do you understand that? Look at me and say, 'Yes, sir.' "). Thus, the child cannot protest interpersonally, or even experience anger internally, because such reactions will further threaten already tenuous ties to the parent. As a result, the child internalizes or turns the anger inside and expresses it indirectly, often through self-deprecation and low self-esteem. This tendency is exacerbated as the child comes to identify with the parent and hold the same critical attitude toward her- or himself that the parent originally communicated. Just as the parent loses touch with the child's feelings in these angry moments, the child in turn loses touch with important aspects of the self and of internal experience. Repression, denial, and splitting defenses develop. When they enter treatment as adults, such clients often describe their parents in idealized, conflict-free terms.

Low self-esteem, internalized anger, helplessness, and loss of love constitute a prescription for depression, as well as engendering anxiety symptoms and the control conflicts found in eating disorders. Identity conflicts also develop for these offspring because their feelings have been so pervasively invalidated. Because authoritarian parents are so rigidly demanding of conformity and obedience, children soon lose all touch with their own internal experience. They have no idea what they like and dislike or even what does or does not feel good to them. Their own experience is overridden at such a young age that they have no basis for later developing their own belief systems, differentiating their own values, or formulating occupational interests in late adolescence and young adulthood.

In sum, therapists will frequently find themselves working with the types of emotional conflicts and family dynamics described above. With such clients, the therapist's task is to validate their subjective experience; encourage their initiative and follow their lead in therapy; and help them to begin attending to their own feelings, interests, and preferences for the first time. To better understand these dynamics, we will look further at the developmental experiences that result when parents are highly authoritarian and when emotional ties are disrupted by severe love withdrawal techniques.

Constancy of Parental Relatedness. There is already too little affection or nurturance in authoritarian families. Adding fuel to the fire, these already thin threads of connection are repeatedly disrupted when parents in a state of anger emotionally disconnect from children. When young children are unable to secure and dependably maintain parental affection, they will not grow up to feel loveworthy. These children have missed the essential developmental experience of "constancy" in their attachment bonds. This developmental deficit has two aspects.

First, these children missed the experience of someone actively reaching out and choosing them. They do not feel loved, cherished, or even wanted in most cases. The critical feature of such love is that it must occur independent of the child's efforts. The child needs to feel that the parent prizes him or her *without being responsible for eliciting the parent's love.* Because this feeling is not provided in authoritarian families, and the little parental warmth that is provided can be withdrawn on a whim, these children must find ways to cope with the intense anxiety generated by their insecure ties. They try to establish more secure bonds by attempting to control or manipulate parental feeling for them, employing, in part, interpersonal strategies to win or earn parental response (for example, by being compliant and pleasing, compulsively striving for achievement, or perfectionistically trying to be "good"). As we will examine in Chapter 7, this attempt to win approval and love often becomes a characterological coping style.

Second, just as children should not feel responsible for making the parent love them, neither should they feel they have the power to destroy the parent-child tie. That is, the child cannot be powerful enough to disrupt the parent's loving commitment to the child. For example, children in authoritarian families learn that their anger, tears, or even their questions can provoke their parent to anger and disrupt the parent-child tie. This occurs, for example, when the authoritarian parent threatens:

> Get that angry look off your face. You will do what I say, and like it, or else!
> Stop those tears right now or I'll give you something to really cry about!
> Never ask me "why." Just do what I say, when I say it.

Children in authoritarian families learn that if they do something the parent does not like, it can (seemingly) destroy the relationship (for example, Parent: "Now you've really done it. This time I've had it with you for good."). Derivatives of the preceding love withdrawal threats recur when adult clients report that their parents now threaten:

> If you marry him, we won't come to the wedding or visit you anymore.
> If you get a divorce, we are going to disown you and take you out of the will.
> If you do that, no one in this family will ever speak to you again.

Authoritarian parents who use severe love withdrawal techniques to control their children do not just set limits on unacceptable behavior, they also threaten to cut off fundamental relational ties. To cope with the intense fear this arouses in attachment-seeking children, compliance becomes a generalized trait, pervasive personality constriction and inhibition occur, and obsessive/compulsive defenses often develop.

A Diversity of Attachment Configurations. In their initial caseloads, most beginning therapists will work with some clients from authoritarian backgrounds. For beginning therapists who have had better developmental experiences, it may be hard to appreciate the emotional severity of highly authoritarian parenting when their own parents were so different. These therapists often wonder how the ostensibly normal looking and, in many other ways, decent parents of these clients can be so rejecting in moments and have caused such profound insecurities and self-hatred in their clients. For other beginning therapists, these client dynamics are threatening because they evoke the therapist's own authoritarian background. To help therapists cope with this difficult material, illustrations of a range of secure/insecure attachment configurations are given below.

In response to the question, "How did your mother respond when she was angry with you?" Molly described secure relational ties without fear of love withdrawal. Molly recalled an incident when her mother was angry for something Molly had done when she was about 7 years old. Her mother made very strong eye contact with her, reached out and touched her on the shoulder, and said in a calm but firm voice, "I love you, but I do not like you very much when you act this way." Molly felt "confused" and protested, "But you *have* to like me—you're my Mom!" Her mother went on to explain that it was Molly's behavior that she did not like, and Molly recalled that she began to understand that concept.

Her mother was angry, and she got her point across that she did not like what Molly was doing, but Molly also felt secure in her mother's love. Looking back, Molly thought that her sense of secure attachment in this conflict was maintained primarily by the nonverbal messages that accompanied her mother's restrictions and explanations. Because of these secure relational ties, Molly was able to internalize stable, loving self-object relationships and develop object constancy, as discussed in Chapter 1. As an adult, Molly is now an especially well-functioning person.

Often, children will be secure in their emotional ties with one parent but struggle with a lack of constancy with the other parent. For example, Ellen recalled that she always felt secure with her mother—even when her mother was mad at her. Her father was highly inconsistent, however, being at times affectionate and available and at other times overtly rejecting. Ellen recalled happy memories of her father patiently painting lady bugs on her rollerskates as well as painful memories of her father angrily yelling, "Get out of here—I can't stand having you around!"

Ellen's "secure base" with her mother allowed her to cope well with this intensely ambivalent relationship with her father. With the constancy of emotional contact provided by her mother, she could learn to anticipate her father's moods and stay away from him when necessary. Her feelings about herself were not based on the unstable yo-yoing of her father's moods. Now, as an adult, Ellen is especially perceptive and interpersonally aware. In this regard, personality strengths often develop from such conflict-driven demands for adaption. Ellen's brother, however, was not so fortunate. Ellen's mother seemed to "like girls better than boys," and her brother did not receive the secure emotional base with his mother that Ellen enjoyed. As a result, he was left to bob about unconnected, at the mercy of his father's stormy emotional seas. Ellen describes her brother as always feeling "very bad about himself" and being depressed a lot. Now in his late 20s, he has been unable to make commitments to relationships or career and cannot find a life for himself. Ellen says she "worries" about him a lot.

Finally, we will look at insecure attachments. Therapists should ask clients about the constancy of parental affection:

How did your parents respond to you when they were angry?
What did they say and do when they were upset with you?
Were you more likely to feel that you had just done something wrong and

disappointed them when they were angry with you, or were you made to feel that you were bad or in some way unlovable?

In response to queries like these, many clients will describe love with-drawal disciplinary techniques that threatened their ties to their parents. Of-ten, the only way for them to become emotionally reconnected again was to accept the role of being "bad" or defective in some way. Listed below are some sample comments that clients reported receiving from their authoritar-ian parents. Along with these comments, bracketed in parentheses, are the clients' statements about the impact these parental messages had on them. Although these clients could remember many such comments, the deep pain accompanying them was often unavailable:

Stop it or I'll send you to live with your [alcoholic] father! (This client said this threat made her feel like her mother did not really want her or care about her; however, the threat was not often voiced because the client as a child was "good all the time" and "stayed away" from her mother to avoid this threat.

How could you do this to me! Can't you think of anybody but yourself! What's wrong with you!" (This client said she always felt guilty and was trying to "earn love" by figuring out what her parent wanted and trying to provide it.)

I've had it with you! Just you wait until your dad gets home! (This client said her mother would then withdraw and not speak to her for the rest of the day. She said it made her feel "horribly alone.")

Look what you did—get away from me. I don't want anything to do with you. (This client said he felt that he was a "terrible person.")

You did it wrong again; you always do it wrong. You are such a difficult child; you ruin so many things for me! (This client said she "hated" herself.)

Another client said simply, "If I ate wrong, my Dad wouldn't say any-thing, he would just slap me in the face. I don't remember having any feelings about it though."

In these moments, highly authoritarian parents are threatening their chil-dren, breaking emotional contact with them, and, in tone or actual words, often communicating contempt or disgust for them. As adults, these clients report feeling "isolated," "alone," and "terrible" about themselves. As we have begun to see, *these offspring have also developed elaborate interpersonal strategies to cope with this trauma,* such as "being good," "taking care of my mother," or "being quiet and going away inside." The therapist needs to identify and address these interpersonal defenses in order to keep them from being acted out in the therapeutic relationship. If so, the pain these defenses have protected the client from experiencing will emerge. A confirming and comforting response from the therapist will allow these clients to reexperience and begin integrating these warded-off feelings for the first time. Only then can these clients stop protecting their parents, denying their own feelings, and maintaining family myths of happiness and togetherness at the expense of their own defenses and symptoms.

Clinical Implications for Working with Disrupted Ties. Parenting is probably the most challenging task in life. The great family therapist, Salvadore Minuchin, says parenting has always been more or less impossible. Most of the authoritarian parents described earlier, who adversely affect their children, are not psychopathic, sadistic, or "bad" people. In parenting, as in other aspects of personality, most people are uneven in their development. Most of these parents do other things well for their children, live by moral standards, and believe they are doing what is right and best for their children. Although children are certainly hurt by such childrearing practices, they usually love and still seek their parents' approval. The therapist's role is not to make these parents "bad," encourage clients to reject them, or replace the parents with idealized therapeutic substitutes. Instead, the therapist's role is to help clients come to realistic terms with their actual experience, change their own responses to problematic others in current relationships, and affirm their legitimate, unmet needs for more secure, positive attachments that are not fraught with excessive love withdrawal. Important guidelines for negotiating therapeutic relationships follow from these parenting practices.

Therapists provide a corrective emotional experience when they remain emotionally available to their clients in a *consistent* manner. An essential process feature of the therapist-client relationship is to provide clients with a continuously available point of contact. Such constancy over the course of treatment has more effect on client change than do more dramatic but isolated incidents of compelling insight, important self-disclosure, or other significant therapeutic interventions. As in parenting, however, this is much harder to do than it sounds, as we will see.

For the clients we have been discussing, parents characteristically withdrew or failed to provide an emotional connection to the child at certain specific times. This developmental deficit can be recapitulated in the therapeutic relationship in many ways. For example, some therapists have trouble being emotionally available to clients' pain and vulnerability. It may not be possible for them to stay with a certain affect, such as the client's shame or intense fear. For other therapists, the client's individuation, emancipation, or achievement may be threatening. These therapists may withdraw from or compete with the client rather than take pleasure in the client's successes. Both of these reactions by therapists occur regularly, and when they do, clients are again left unconnected in their experience. Clients' pathogenic belief that being sad or successful causes others to emotionally leave them is confirmed, and the anxiety generated by this therapeutic reenactment becomes further linked to these past experiences. As a result, rather than experiencing and working through their painful feelings or striving to succeed, clients will be reinforced in defending against these anxiety-arousing experiences.

In addition, factors in the client also make it difficult for therapists to remain consistently available. For example, many clients will tell the therapist that they like, trust, and find the therapist helpful and understanding. At the same time, however, such a client may also believe that if the therapist and others "really knew me," they would not respect, care about, or stay with the client. These clients believe they have deceived the therapist or "manipulated" the therapist's positive feeling for them. This is why it is necessary for the therapist to take an internalizing stance and attempt to draw out the full range of clients' feelings. Unfortunately, clients often experience their unacceptable, bad, or split-off emotions as their real selves. These conflicted emotions are resolved only when such vulnerable, dependent, shameful, or otherwise "unacceptable" parts of them are made overt *and they find that they still remain emotionally connected to the therapist.* That is, they still feel cared about, accepted by, and in relationship with the therapist even though the therapist now knows that this "unacceptable" part is a part of them. A powerful learning experience occurs when the emotional withdrawal and rejection that has occurred in the past is not reenacted. To repeat: clients believe these despised emotions reflect their true selves. It is the therapist's emotional connectedness to clients while they are experiencing these despised emotions that allows clients to integrate and resolve these feelings.

Finally, as we will explore later, some clients are also adept at eliciting the same problematic responses from the therapist that they received in the past. For all of these reasons, it is challenging but necessary for therapists to try to remain consistently attuned to all aspects of the client's experience. The following case study illustrates this.

A basic tenet of the interpersonal process approach is that the client's conflict will usually be reenacted with the therapist along the process dimension. In the following example, the client began to reenact his conflict with the therapist, but she was able to provide a corrective emotional experience by remaining emotionally connected to him during their relational crisis.

John, a 14-year-old client, was being treated in a strict, physically punishing manner by his authoritarian stepfather. His mother passively accepted her husband's harsh corporal punishment and hostile derision of the boy, often walking away and leaving the room when the stepfather was angry at John. In treatment, John defied the female therapist and repeatedly tried to push her away. Near the end of an especially frustrating session in which he had repeatedly pushed every limit, John was unwilling to speak. Trying to find some way to remain in contact with him, the therapist agreed that they would not have to talk together if he did not want to and that he could just throw the ball as he wished. Trying to join him in his chosen activity, she asked if she could silently play catch with him. He agreed but, of course, began throwing the ball too hard. Throughout the session, this situation continued, with John testing and the therapist setting limits (for example, "You have to throw the ball below my knees.") but still working hard to try and find some way to connect with him.

Near the end of the hour, the therapist invoked their standing rule and asked him to help her pick up the room. John refused; the therapist insisted. Exasperated, she held him firmly by the arms, whereupon he recoiled. At this moment, the same conflicted emotions that John struggled with at home were operating in the session and about to be reenacted with the therapist. The therapist had been sorely pushed, but even though she was frustrated with John, she was able to find another way to relate. She did not withdraw in resignation as his mother did nor physically dominate him as his stepfather did. Instead, she met his eyes and slowly said, "You're a good boy . . . I still like you . . . I want us to work this out together." Even though she was upset, the therapist could still communicate that she felt for John and was remaining emotionally connected to him. A turning point in treatment occurred here when John was not able to elicit and reenact with the therapist the painful drama of domination and isolation that had been played out so many times at home. John grudgingly helped the therapist pick up the room, and therapy progressed.

In closing, clients will present in therapy with an extraordinarily rich diversity of developmental experiences and family dynamics. Many clients' dynamics, of course, will be unrelated to this discussion. However, authoritarian childrearing practices and love withdrawal techniques will be among the most common experiences clients report in therapy. Read Alice Miller's compelling book on authoritarian childrearing, "For Your Own Good" (Farrar, Straus, & Giroux, 1984), to learn more about these issues.

RELATING THE THREE DIMENSIONS OF FAMILY LIFE

This section draws some relationships between the three basic dimensions of family life: the nature of the parental coalition, the separateness-relatedness dialectic, and childrearing practices. Authoritative parents have the emotional flexibility and range of parenting skills necessary to meet both children's needs for closeness and for individuation. Authoritarian and permissive parents have a more limited experiential range than authoritative parents. Specifically, the experiential range of authoritarian and permissive parents is limited to opposing halves of the separateness-relatedness continuum. For example, the range of authoritarian parents does not extend to include intimacy and closeness. These parents do not meet children's age-appropriate dependency needs for warmth and affection, although their emphasis on mature, responsible behavior does allow children to individuate.

In contrast, permissive parents meet children's emotional needs better, but they do not foster their children's individuation by expecting competent and independent behavior from them. Children of permissive parents are further stifled in their individuation because permissive parents are especially likely to embroil children in cross-generational, parent-child alliances. Of the three parenting styles, permissive parents are least likely to establish a primary marital coalition, most likely to embroil children in cross-generational alliances, and most likely to parentify children.

The family dynamics presented in this chapter offer a parallel to the relationship between the therapist and the client. Therapists, like authoritative parents, must develop their own abilities to respond at both ends of the separateness-relatedness continuum. On the one hand, effective therapists are those who have a flexible experiential range that allows them to nurture and care for clients. On the other hand, therapists must also be able to set limits with clients, challenge and confront them when necessary, and tolerate clients' anger and disapproval at times. For example, therapists need to be able to respond to the deprivation and emotional needs of clients who have been reared by highly authoritarian parents. At the same time, therapists must also be able to set clear rules and limits with the provocative, demanding, or testing behavior of clients who have been reared by permissive or inconsistent parents.

Thus, the personal challenge for therapists is to examine their own experiential range that has been shaped in their families of origin. Therapists must identify their own limitations and work to develop a flexible interpersonal range that allows them to respond to the diversity of problems that clients present. In order to achieve this, therapists must do their own "family-of-origin work."

An integral part of training in family therapy is learning about one's own family of origin. More so than in other modalities, family therapists emphasize that clinicians must be willing to work with their own family dynamics. In particular, Murray Bowen (1966) has written extensively about how clinical trainees can systematically study and sometimes change repetitive patterns of interaction in their own families of origin. This new understanding of their own family background, in turn, is often one of the most important influences on therapists' clinical skills. One useful way of becoming a better therapist is to read about family-of-origin work (see Bowen, 1966) and, especially, to prepare a family genogram—a three-generational map of family roles and structural family relationships (see Hartman, 1978). Learning about one's family of origin in this way is one of the best ways for beginning therapists to learn about their own countertransference propensities, their clients' dynamics, and the profound influence of familial experience on adult life.

CLOSING

This chapter has provided an introduction to three basic dimensions of family functioning: structural family relations and the parental coalition, the separateness-relatedness dialectic, and childrearing practices. These three aspects of family life will help therapists understand the genesis of clients' personality and emotional problems. The next chapter leaves this general discussion of how normal development goes awry in families and provides a detailed model for conceptualizing client dynamics.

SUGGESTIONS FOR FURTHER READING

1. Basic information on child development and child psychopathology will help therapists understand their adult clients' personalities and problems. One outstanding text is C. Wenar, *Psychopathology from Infancy through Adolescence: A Developmental Approach*, 2nd ed. (New York: Random House, 1990). (See especially Chapters 5 through 8.)

2. Structural family relations provide an illuminating road map for understanding family functioning. Seminal work in this area has been provided by Salvadore Minuchin in his book *Families and Family Therapy* (Cambridge, Mass: Harvard University Press, 1974). (See especially Chapters 3 and 5.) For a general review of structural family relations and how the parental coalition serves as the principal axis of family functioning, see E. Teyber, "Structural Family Relations: A Review," *Family Therapy* 1 (1981): 39–48. An empirical study of these structural concepts is also found in E. Teyber, "Effects of the Parental Coalition on Adolescent Emancipation From the Family," *Journal of Marital and Family Therapy* 9, (1983): 89–99. Finally, Bob Woodward's biography of the late comedian John Belushi also illustrates the effects of cross-generational alliances on child development. See Chapter 2 of B. Woodward, *Wired* (New York: Simon & Schuster, 1984).

3. *Parentification* is an important concept for therapists to understand since so many clients have been scripted into this familial role. Further information about this far-reaching concept can be found in Chapter 9 of E. Teyber, *Children and Divorce: A Practical Guide for Parents* (New York: Lexington Books/MacMillan, 1992).

4. The terms *separateness-relatedness dialectic* and *experiential range* are useful family systems concepts that are readily applicable to individual psychotherapy. One informative article that can also lead to further reading in this area is J. Farley, "Family Separation—Individuation Tolerance: A Developmental Conceptualization of the Nuclear Family," *Journal of Marital and Family Therapy* (January 1979): 61–67.

CHAPTER SEVEN

A MODEL FOR CONCEPTUALIZING CLIENT DYNAMICS

CONCEPTUAL OVERVIEW

This chapter provides a model for helping therapists conceptualize how client conflicts are expressed, maintained, and resolved. This model for conceptualizing client dynamics is based on the client's generic conflict and interpersonal strategy for coping with this conflict. The term *generic conflict* refers to a central or underlying conflict that pervades the client's life and links together the different problems that the client presents. Therapists will be far more effective when they can identify the client's central conflict, understand how the client defends against this conflict, and recognize how this conflict is expressed in current relationships. If the therapist can formulate the client's generic conflict and interpersonal adaptation to it, this conceptualization will lend structure and organization to the disparate material that clients present. In turn, this conceptualization will effectively guide the therapist's intervention and treatment strategy.

If formulating a conceptual understanding of the client's dynamics is essential to change, why has discussion of it been delayed to this point? Shouldn't the therapist have been formulating a conceptual picture of the client's personality and problems earlier? As noted in Chapter 2, client conceptualization is an ongoing process that begins with the initial client contact. General hypotheses about client dynamics are formulated early in treatment, and these tentative working hypotheses are further refined or discarded as the therapist learns more about each particular client. It is not until the client's conflicted emotions emerge, however, that the central conflict underlying the client's problems becomes clear. That is, the therapist often cannot identify the client's generic conflict until the client's conflicted emotions emerge. Just as initially focusing clients inward elicits affect, clients' emotions now serve as guideposts to signal generic conflicts.

CHAPTER ORGANIZATION

The first section of this chapter provides a model for conceptualizing the client's generic conflict—how it originally developed, the client's interpersonal adaptation for coping with it, and how it is being expressed in current symptoms and problems. This model of conflict expression includes (1) the client's unmet developmental needs, (2) the original environmental block that created the conflict, (3) the client's intrapsychic defenses against the blocked need, (4) the client's interpersonal strategy to rise above or overcome the blocked need, and (5) an interpersonal resolution of the generic conflict. Together, these five components of the conflict model provide an initial framework for conceptualizing client dynamics.

This model for conceptualizing clients is an integrated system composed of numerous, complex psychological processes. In the second section, an extended case study illustrates how this model can be used to guide treatment plans and intervention strategies.

A CONCEPTUAL MODEL

This section presents a model for conceptualizing how client conflicts are expressed, maintained, and resolved. This discussion does not suggest how therapists can intervene with their clients but instead gives therapists a framework for conceptualizing their clients' conflicts and adaptation to them. Much of the discussion that follows is derived from the interpersonal theory of Karen Horney (1966, 1970). The five components to this model are schematized in Figure 7–1. We begin by examining how enduring personality problems result when one or more of a child's basic developmental needs go unmet.

The Child's Need Is Blocked

This conceptual model begins with a child's basic needs for secure relational ties. Part 1 of Figure 7–1 refers in the broadest sense to young children's dependency needs on their parents and, in particular, to children's need for attachment. If parenting figures are consistently responsive to the children's bids for affection and attention, children will be able to freely experience and express this need. Of course, as children develop they will have to learn to accept limitations on parents' ability to respond and to tolerate delay in parental response. If the parent is not responsive, however, anxiety will soon become associated with the child's need.

To illustrate, suppose that a young child's need for warmth and affection goes unmet from authoritarian parents. When the preschool-aged child approaches his parents for comfort or "emotional refueling," his need is re-

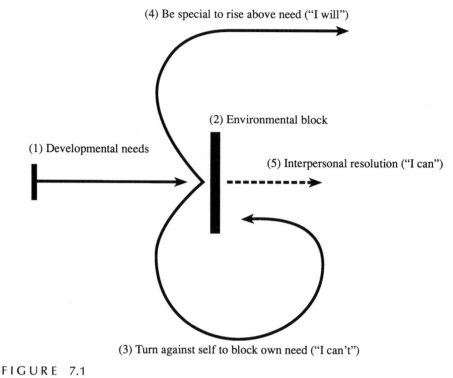

(4) Be special to rise above need ("I will")

(2) Environmental block

(1) Developmental needs

(5) Interpersonal resolution ("I can")

(3) Turn against self to block own need ("I can't")

FIGURE   7.1
The author wishes to thank Dr. Robert Hilton for this schematization.

jected (for example, "What do you want now? Leave me alone!") or rebuffed (for example, "You don't need to kiss and hug other people like that; that's sissy stuff."). If this type of interchange occurs repeatedly, the child will soon learn to anticipate rejection and feel anxious whenever his need for affection is aroused. As indicated when the arrow hits the perpendicular line in part 2 of Figure 7–1, the child still experiences the need, but the expression of it is blocked by the parents' cold response.

Most enduring psychological problems begin when a basic childhood need such as this is blocked. Although clients may struggle with many different unmet needs, the source of most generic conflicts involves a failure to provide children with nurturance, clear communication, and consistent emotional access on the one hand, and firm discipline and a predictable home environment on the other. Once the need is blocked, however, the child constructs a *compromise solution* that is designed to prevent him or her from continuing to experience anxiety over the unmet need. At the same time, however, the child will also find indirect ways to express and partially gratify the need. Parts 3 and 4 of this model will elaborate on how this compromise solution works both to block the need and, simultaneously, to rise above and indirectly gratify it. The rest of this section discusses the complex psychological maneuvers that individuals adopt to cope with this unmet need and the generic conflict engendered.

Compromise Solutions

Clients employ two psychological mechanisms in order to defend against the anxiety associated with expressing, or even experiencing, their blocked needs. First, we will examine three ways in which clients defend against their unmet developmental needs by responding to themselves in the same way that others originally responded to them. Second, we will examine three ways in which clients adopt a general *interpersonal coping style* to try and rise above their unmet need. Taken together, these two mechanisms of *blocking* and *rising above* are clients' compromise solution to their generic conflict. We will see below how this complex defensive system works.

Clients Block Their Own Need. Consider the child in the beginning of this discussion who was unsuccessful in getting his parents to respond to his emotional needs. The child tried desperately with the limited skills and means that are available to a child, but he was unable to stop the parental rejection and elicit the nurturing and support he needed. In order to gain some active mastery over his helplessness and to ward off the anxiety-arousing need, *the child began blocking his own need in the same way that the environment originally blocked it.* That is, clients turn against themselves and block their own needs by adopting the same hurtful responses toward themselves of others in their original environment. This attempt at mastery may be referred to as identification with the aggressor or, as some clinicians colloquially refer to it, "using the devil's tools to fight the devil." Part 3 of Figure 7–1 reflects how children begin to do to themselves what was originally done to them. There are three ways that this can occur.

First, clients block their own need *intrapsychically* and respond to themselves in the same hurtful, rejecting ways that others have responded to them. That is, when the child in our example feels a need for reassurance or affection, he will block his need by feeling critical or contemptuous of himself and his own need. For example, when his own unacceptable dependency needs are aroused as an adult, he will often say to himself the same critical things he heard from others years ago. Furthermore, *the critical, shaming, or rejecting affect that clients feel toward themselves is the same affect that parenting figures originally expressed toward the child's need years ago.*

Second, clients also block their anxiety-arousing need by reenacting in current relationships the same conflict that was originally experienced in earlier, formative relationships. That is, on an *interpersonal* level, clients will say and do to others what was originally done to them. For example, the child in our example will likely grow up to be a parent who similarly disparages dependency needs in one of his own children. Especially in the arena of parenting, clients will reenact the same conflicts and hurtful messages that they received in their own childhoods. As parents, many clients feel helplessly dismayed as they watch themselves respond to their children in the same hurtful ways that their parents responded to them. Despite sincere pledges that "I will never do to my children what my parents did to me," this occurs with clocklike regularity. Here again, adult offspring gain some mastery and defend against their own conflicts by reenacting what was originally done to them, rather than allowing themselves to reexperience the original hurt, deprivation, or powerlessness.

Third, clients block the experience and expression of their own conflicted need by *eliciting* the same unsatisfying response from others in current relationships that they originally received in the past. For example, the child in our example is likely to grow up and select a marital partner who cannot respond to his needs for affection, closeness, or intimacy. Or, if the spouse is capable of responding to this need, he will not be able to accept her emotional responsiveness. Why? The possibility of having a response to his old, unmet need will arouse too much anxiety. The spouse's affection will arouse the pain of the original deprivation, and the client will anticipate that his spouse will reject his need as others have in the past. Thus, this client may simultaneously elicit and reject nurturance from his spouse, which will certainly frustrate and confuse her.

In sum, clients defend against their unmet needs by (1) intrapsychically responding to themselves in the same rejecting ways that parenting figures did, (2) identifying with the rejecting parent and responding to others in the same hurtful way that they were responded to, and (3) selecting to become involved with others who provide the same hurtful response to them that they originally received as children. Although one of these three modes may be predominant for a particular client, most clients will employ all three mechanisms at different times in order to defend against their anxiety-arousing need.

At the same time as clients are blocking their needs on each of these levels, they are simultaneously trying to get them met in an indirect way. Next, we will turn to the top half of Figure 7–1 (part 4) and see how clients make a lifestyle out of rising above their unmet need and turning this defensive adaptation into a virtue.

Rising Above the Unmet Need. Parts 1 through 3 of Figure 7–1 show that when clients have had a primary need blocked throughout their development they employ three strategies to defend against it. Clients do to themselves what others originally did to them, and they try to master this conflict by turning a passive experience that originally happened to them into an active experience over which they now have some control. The key element is how the same hurtful affect that was originally expressed toward the child is taken up by individuals and actively turned against themselves to block their own unmet need. This is only half of the conflict, however. Paradoxically, just as the client defends against the anxiety of reexperiencing the unmet need, the client simultaneously tries to rise above it and have it met indirectly. Part 4 of Figure 7–1 shows the other side of the client's compromise solution—the client's attempts not to block the need but to rise above and indirectly gratify it.

The client's unmet childhood need does not dissipate or go away as he grows up. The need may be repressed or defended against, but it continues to seek expression. As a result, clients do not give up trying to have the need met. At the same time, the unmet need remains too anxiety-arousing to be expressed directly. So clients try to rise above the unmet need and indirectly fulfill it by adopting one of three interpersonal coping styles. Horney has labeled these lifestyle adaptations *moving toward, moving away,* and *moving against* others.

Moving Toward, Moving Away, and Moving Against. Clients adopt a fixed interpersonal style both to reduce the anxiety associated with the unmet need and to find some partial, indirect gratification of it. For example, in their families of origin some clients learned to cope with their conflict by *moving toward* or pleasing people. These clients could earn some needed approval and diminish the threat of further rejection by complying with their parents and being unfailingly nice or good. Their primary mode of relating to others became one of submitting, accommodating, or pleasing others and never asserting their own wishes. Thus, these clients have learned to defend against their unmet need, and to win some needed approval to indirectly gratify the need, by consistently moving toward others in a pleasing, servile way.

Other clients have learned that aggressiveness and resistance to parental wishes, if pursued long enough, will ward off the pain of an unmet need. These individuals *move against* others and expansively seek to be in control of themselves and others. They approach life and relationships with the attitude that they will win what they deserve. Thus, a repetitive interpersonal style of moving against others has been adopted in order to protect these clients from their generic conflict.

The third interpersonal style is to *move away* from others. These clients have learned that the best way to reduce their anxiety and defend against their unmet needs is through physical avoidance, withdrawal, and self-sufficiency. Although clients may employ all three of these interpersonal coping styles at different times, one style usually becomes predominant or characterological.

To review, we have seen that clients use three ways to defend against the unmet need that are similar to the ways the need was originally blocked by parents or others in the environment. Next, we turned to the top half of Figure 7–1 to see how clients also try to rise above their blocked need and indirectly have it met. First, we introduced the interpersonal styles of moving toward, against, or away from others that clients adopt to cope with their generic conflict. Now we are ready to examine how clients use their characterological interpersonal style to try to rise above their unmet need and gratify it. As we will see below, however, even though clients earn many rewards from their interpersonal coping style, it remains a defensive adaptation that does not resolve their real conflict or meet their original unmet need.

Being "Special" to Rise Above the Need. Most clients will adopt one of the three interpersonal styles as a general lifestyle to cope with their generic conflict. Clients turn this defensive coping style into a virtue and use it to feel special and rise above their need. That is, clients do not experience their interpersonal strategy as a defensive coping system but as a virtuous way of relating to others that makes them feel superior. However, this unrealistic sense of being special actually reflects the low self-esteem and damaged sense of self that results from the original unmet need and environmental block. Often, clients' only sense of worth or value comes from their ability to rise above their unmet need and either please others, achieve and succeed, or withdraw and feel cynically superior. The following discussion shows how clients convert their defensive, interpersonal coping style into a virtue.

Although moving-toward clients are compliant and submissive, they will not experience themselves as servile. Instead, these clients will convert this defensive coping strategy into a virtue that makes them special or secretly better than others. How is this done? The moving-toward client will become a selflessly and endlessly loving person. This person will become someone who is always sensitive to the needs of others and committed to the ideals of peace and harmony. In this way, the defensive interpersonal style becomes a source of self-esteem—a virtuous quality that wins needed approval from others.

Similarly, moving-against clients do not see themselves as angry, competitive, self-centered, or demanding although they frequently behave this way. Instead, they see themselves as heroes or heroines—strong leaders entitled to direct others who are inferior and less capable. Or, the moving-away client rises above the need through aloofness and glorifies this stance by feeling self-righteously self-sufficient. The moving-away client is cynical and feels better than the ordinary masses, who are so mundane as to be caught up in everyday happenings.

What was originally a way to lessen anxiety has become a fixed and pervasive interpersonal style for these clients. This broad interpersonal style has also become a way for clients to become special, gain a sense of identity and self-esteem, and rise above their unmet needs. The process of turning their defensive coping style into a virtue, gift, or talent that is prized as evidence of their specialness is part of Horney's *neurotic pride system*. The client's self-esteem is brittle and vulnerable, however, since it is based on being special and rising above rather than on valuing one's own feelings that have been valued by significant others.

We now have the two sides of the client's conflict. On the one hand, clients block their own needs and respond to themselves in the same critical or rejecting ways that adult caregivers originally responded to them. Clients will internalize and feel toward themselves the same affect that the parent originally communicated toward their need (for example, disappointment, contempt, resentment, indifference, and so on). This affect will usually be evidenced as low self-esteem when clients enter therapy. Clients are often seeking treatment to be rid of this intrapunitive feeling.

In contrast to the blocking response, the side of clients' conflict that leaves them feeling special is usually more covert and is harder for the therapist to work with. Yet the therapist must address this side of clients' conflict as well. Clients are reluctant to let go of their attempts to rise above their need by being special. Why? The interpersonal coping style they have adopted has provided them with relief from the anxiety of the unmet need. It has allowed them to earn some indirect gratification of the original need and has become the primary source of their self-esteem. For example, moving-toward clients have often been able to make others like them. In like fashion, moving-against clients have often been able to achieve a great deal of success and power, and moving-away clients have often been able to become safely aloof.

Thus, the manner in which clients have turned their defensive interpersonal adaptation into a sense of being special provides tremendous secondary gains. No wonder then that clients will be reluctant to explore this rising-above adaptation with the therapist. It has become the basis of their identity, the primary source of their self-esteem, and the only way they have of defending against their seemingly unresolvable conflict.

Once therapists understand all that this rising-above defense provides, they become more patient and accepting when clients cling to symptoms and are threatened by change. Understandably, clients will not want to risk giving all of this up without having something better to replace it with. As we will see below, however, clients never really succeed in rising above the original conflict through these compensatory lifestyle adaptations.

"Shoulds" for the Self, "Entitlement" from Others. Clients both gain something and lose something by their compromise solutions. As a result of their feeling special and virtuous, clients gain what Horney terms *false pride* and a sense of *entitlement* from others. For example, the self-effacing, moving-toward client expects unrealistic adulation and approval from others and often demands constant reassurances. The expansive, moving-against client claims leadership, respect, and allegiance from others. And, although it may look as if detached, moving-away clients have no claims, they demand that others never criticize them or make requests of them. These neurotic claims leave clients exposed to continuing frustration and conflict, however, as others frequently do not accept these unrealistic demands and expectations.

Just as the sense of being special entitles clients to make unrealistic claims or demands of others, clients also have to demand a lot of themselves in order to maintain their specialness. Accompanying clients' excessive demands on others is a harsh and uncompromising set of "shoulds" they place on themselves. For example, moving-toward clients suffer under the self-imposed demands that they should be the perfect lover, teacher, spouse, and so forth. They must always be calm, caring, sensitive, and responsive to the needs of others and never feel angry, be critical, or act selfishly. Moving-against clients demand of themselves that they should be able to quickly overcome all difficulties and obstacles. They must be able to control all of their feelings at all times and overcome bad moods simply by an act of will. Moving-away clients pay for their specialness by believing that they should be able to work tirelessly and always be productive. They demand that they should be able to endure anything without becoming ruffled or upset and that they should never need help or reassurance from anyone.

Thus the *tyranny of the should* is an exacting price to pay for the client's sense of specialness. The therapist must keep in mind, however, that the "shoulds" clients place on themselves and the neurotic claims they place on others reflect their damaged self-esteem and impoverished sense of self.

Resolving the Generic Conflict

Part 5 of Figure 7–1 illustrates how the client's generic conflict can be resolved. Ultimately, the client's compromise solution to the original conflict will never succeed. The client can block the anxiety-arousing need and try to rise above it in the ways described above. However, these compensatory maneuvers will not release the client from the conflict. Furthermore, not only will the lifestyle adaptation of moving toward, away, or against others never allow the client to resolve the original conflict, this defensive adaptation will expose the client to continual frustration. First, we will examine three reasons why the client's compromise solution will not succeed, and then explore what can be done to help the client successfully resolve the generic conflict.

First, the tyranny of the should places unrealistic and unrelenting demands on the client. These can be heard, for example, when clients enter therapy exclaiming, "I can't do all of this anymore! I can't be a giving mother, a loving wife, and successful professional. I can't be everything to everybody anymore." The quality of life is diminished by these harsh and fatiguing expectations on self, even if they do not lead to a crisis that brings the client to therapy.

Second, the client's sense of entitlement and being special will usually fail as well. That is, self-effacing clients will not be able to win the love of everyone they need. Expansive clients will not always succeed or be able to make others defer to their demands, and others will criticize detached clients or force them to compete. Inevitably, clients' attempts to become special and rise above their conflict will lead to repeated interpersonal conflicts, failure, and frustration. *Clients usually enter therapy when situational life stressors, developmental transitions in adulthood, or aging have caused their interpersonal coping strategies to fail.*

The therapist must be empathetic to the narcissistic wound that clients suffer when their attempts to be special and rise above their conflict fail. Even though the demands that clients place on themselves and others are unrealistic, it is excruciatingly painful when their interpersonal adaptation fails. In fact, a few people will even attempt suicide in response to this failure experience, and many others will contemplate it without acting. Why such an extreme response? As emphasized earlier, the interpersonal coping style that many clients have adopted is the basis of their identity and their primary source of self-worth—a brittle substitute for the genuine self-esteem they lack. From these clients' point of view, they *are* their ability to please, to achieve, or to remain superior and aloof. Clients such as this overreact to certain seemingly insignificant events because their entire sense of self is threatened when their interpersonal coping strategy fails. Therapists will become extremely important to their clients when they can accurately articulate and genuinely empathize with the full impact of this "defeat" for their clients.

Furthermore, it is shattering for clients when their interpersonal coping style fails because it arouses the original helplessness, vulnerability, and shame that accompany their unmet need. Eventually, the therapist must respond to the unmet need beneath clients' compensatory attempt to obtain security through winning other's approval, achieving power and success, or withdrawing and going away. Before the therapist can do this, however, the therapist must first respond to the intense anxiety or depression aroused by clients' beliefs that they are of no value if they can no longer successfully please, achieve, or remain aloof.

Third, the most important reason the client's compromise solution cannot succeed is because the client can never rise above the original conflict or unmet need. No matter how saintlike or loving, how successful or accomplished, or how self-contained and independent, the client is still defending against the original conflict. All of these interpersonal maneuvers are attempts to avoid the problem by blocking and trying to rise above it rather than addressing it directly.

Let us review this sequence and take it one step further to show how the client's generic conflict can be resolved. If the child's developmental need is blocked by the environment, the individual will adopt a compromise solution that temporarily relieves the anxiety of the unmet need but does not resolve the underlying conflict. On the one hand, clients try to block their own needs just as they were originally blocked by significant others. The arrow turning back against the block in part 3 of Figure 7–1 illustrates how clients turn against themselves. The arrow turning back refers to the client's intrapunitive feelings, belief that "I can't," and sense of helplessness and hopelessness.

At the same time, however, clients also try to rise above the old unmet need by becoming special, turning their defensive lifestyle adaptation into a virtue, and obtaining some indirect gratification of the original need. *All clients will be intensely invested in trying to overcome and rise above their generic conflict, as it will feel like defeat to have to come to terms with the original need or conflict.* Thus, the arrow moving out over the block in part 4 of Figure 7–1 refers to the client's grandiose sense of being special and defiant attempt to rise above the conflict (for example, "I will never let them hurt me again."). This rigid, defensive stance reflects an act of will to overcome the client's need and rise above the conflict rather than to try and resolve it by addressing it directly.

In order to resolve the generic conflict, clients must relinquish their compromise solutions. Clients must stop trying to block the original need and to rise above it. Instead of avoiding the conflict in these two ways, clients must approach it by allowing themselves to experience the original unmet need and integrate the reactive feelings that accompany it. It is more adaptive now as an adult to incorporate the original hurt and vulnerability—by reexperiencing what was once dreaded—than it is to continue to try to defend against it. Said differently, the client must allow the unmet need to come through the old block and allow the therapist to help contain the feelings and memories that emerge, as shown in part 5 of Figure 7–1. Once the original hurt or need begins to emerge in therapy, the therapist must provide a more satisfying response than the client has received in the past. The therapist does this, in part, by holding the client's pain, as discussed in Chapter 5. As we will see more fully later, this is one of the most important ways in which the corrective emotional experience that produces change occurs.

If clients receive a more effective response from the therapist than they have received from others in the past, they will not need to block their need or attempt to rise above it anymore. The therapist's more accepting and understanding response to the old need and the conflicted feelings that accompany it will alleviate the anxiety that the original need aroused. Once this occurs, clients will be able to adopt new and more effective behavioral alternatives, and expand the limited interpersonal style that they have adopted to cope with their conflict. In Chapter 9 we will examine more fully how the therapeutic relationship can be utilized to help clients resolve their generic conflict. For now, an extended case study will help therapists apply this conceptual model to therapeutic interventions.

CASE STUDY OF PETER: MOVING TOWARD OTHERS
Developmental History and Precipitating Crisis

In order to illustrate this model, we will return to the child in the beginning of this chapter and call him Peter. Throughout his childhood, Peter's authoritarian parents left his age-appropriate dependency needs for affection, warmth, and caring profoundly unmet. In addition, Peter's parents divorced when he was 6 years of age, and his father did not take an active parenting role after the divorce. Peter saw his father infrequently, and their contacts were superficial and inconsequential when they were together.

Peter's mother was overburdened by the demands of raising three children on her own, working full time, and trying to make some kind of personal life for herself. She was involved with several men in the years following the divorce, but she was never able to establish an enduring love relationship. Frustrated by the many demands and few pleasures in her life, she often made Peter the target of her resentment. She was often irritable toward Peter, criticized him when things went wrong in her life, and felt resentful of his needs. Although she tried her best to be fair to the children and give them a good home, she could not provide Peter with a consistent source of love and affection.

After his father left, Peter quickly learned that taking care of his mother was the best way to ward off her anger and disapproval and to win whatever affection he could. By 10 years of age, Peter had adopted a pervasive personality style of moving toward people. His teachers described him as an especially responsible and well-behaved boy who was a pleasure to have in class. We will now turn the clock ahead 15 years to see how these developmental conflicts are expressed in Peter's early adulthood.

Peter is now a graduate student in psychology. Becoming a therapist felt like a perfect career choice to Peter. He prided himself on his sensitivity and concern for others and took pleasure in being able to help those in need. And now that he was carrying his own client caseload, it was great to find that he enjoyed being a therapist as much as he thought he would. Best of all, Peter was finding that he was often able to help his new clients. At least all of his clients seemed to like him, and they kept returning to their therapy sessions each week. As his second semester practicum got underway, Peter felt that he was hitting his stride and on his way.

Later that semester, though, Peter's good feeling about himself as a therapist took a hard blow. After presenting a videotaped recording of one of his therapy sessions in group supervision, Peter received some unexpected feedback. The practicum instructor confronted Peter and said that he was being too nice to be helpful to his clients and that he seemed to need his clients' approval too much. The instructor went on to say that Peter was afraid of confrontations and was avoiding conflicts in the therapist-client relationship that should be addressed.

Peter was shocked by this unexpected feedback. He had no idea what the instructor was talking about, and he felt hurt and confused by the criticism. It was important to Peter that his supervisor like him and approve of his clinical work. Peter tried to explain to the instructor that he did not understand the close relationship that Peter was developing with his clients or recognize all of the important personal issues that his clients had been revealing. The instructor did not agree with Peter, however, and continued to confront him with these critical observations. To make matters worse, two students in the practicum group chimed in and agreed with the instructor's comments. With that, Peter's anxiety became so high that he could no longer even try to defend or explain himself, let alone try to understand or learn from their comments. Peter finally stopped arguing with them and quietly nodded agreement throughout the rest of the supervision session.

The next few days Peter felt sickened. He was confused and dismayed by the criticism that he was too nice and always trying to make people like him. His thoughts and feelings raced uncontrollably. For awhile, he thought that he should drop out of the practicum group, but then he decided that if he only tried hard enough he could make the instructor see that his critical comments were inaccurate. Peter's mind kept racing to find a way to discount the feedback and stop the anxiety that was churning inside.

When it rains, it pours. One week later, Peter found out that his girlfriend was having an affair with another student in the program. Although he tried to be understanding at first, he felt shocked and betrayed. Peter alternated between angrily telling her that their relationship was over and desperately trying to win her back. Peter felt shattered. He became so anxious that he was unable to eat or sleep, let alone study. It felt as if a motor were racing inside of him—accelerating out of control. Peter began hyperventilating and having anxiety attacks. By the end of the week, he was so anxious that he was unable to drive his car.

To make matters worse, Peter tried to keep all of this to himself. He thought he should remain calm and together, and he was afraid that his supervisors would not want him to see clients if he was "so messed up" that he was having anxiety attacks himself. But despite his attempts to cover up his distress, his individual supervisor soon asked him what was wrong.

Although he could not ask for it, Peter desperately wanted his individual supervisor's support, and he was greatly relieved to receive it. Peter explained how his practicum group was becoming one of the worst failure experiences of his life, and how hard it was to accept what his girlfriend had done. The supervisor was supportive, but he did say that the practicum instructor's comments fit with some of his own observations. Because he knew that the individual supervisor liked him, Peter was able to consider the feedback this time. The supervisor suggested that these were important issues for Peter to work with, but that they were more than they could handle in supervision. They both agreed that Peter should begin seeing his own therapist at the student counseling center.

It helped that his supervisor knew about his anxiety attacks and still thought he could be a fine therapist, but Peter's anxiety was paralyzing as he began his own treatment. Fortunately, Peter was assigned to a skilled therapist who quickly recognized the generic conflict that precipitated his crisis. Peter's coping strategy of moving toward people in an accommodating and pleasing manner had worked well for him up to this point. However, both of the crises that Peter had just experienced ran headlong into the heart of his generic conflict. As Peter's ability to rise above his old unmet need by pleasing others failed, the anxiety associated with his developmental conflict broke through, and anxiety attacks resulted. We must examine closely why Peter developed these symptoms.

Precipitating Crises, Generic Conflicts, and Symptom Development

Many people would have coped with the two stressful events that Peter experienced without developing such significant symptoms. We will use Peter to illustrate how symptoms develop when situational stressors tap into the client's generic conflict.

The first stressor for Peter was his practicum instructor's critical feedback. In general, criticism from a respected authority figure would be unsettling for most people but something they could cope with. For someone like Peter, however, such disapproval carries far more weight. Because of Peter's strong unmet needs for approval, his history of receiving excessive criticism, and his lifestyle adaptation of trying to win approval by being helpful and responsive, the supervisor's criticism was devastating.

Second, the practicum instructor specifically challenged Peter's interpersonal coping style of moving toward others. This confrontation not only aroused the anxiety of receiving criticism, but also undermined Peter's primary means of warding off this anxiety (for example, pleasing others and accommodating himself to their needs). Thus, the instructor's feedback intensified Peter's generic conflict and, simultaneously, weakened his defenses against it.

If not for the subsequent crisis with his girlfriend, Peter probably could have recovered from the first setback without developing symptoms. Most likely, he would have reconstituted his interpersonal coping style and been successful in winning the approval he needed from others in his life—such as other instructors, friends, and perhaps clients. As we will see below, however, the subsequent stressor with his girlfriend also struck at the same generic conflict. At that point, his moving-toward coping style failed. The anxiety associated with his old, unmet need became too intense to be blocked and broke through in anxiety attacks and symptom formation.

A partner's infidelity will be highly stressful for almost everyone. Here again, though, this particular stressor held far greater significance for Peter when viewed within the context of his generic conflict. Peter had to cope with far more than just the loss of trust with his girlfriend. He also suffered a blow to his identity and basic sense of self-worth. As in Horney's *neurotic pride system*, Peter's coping style of moving toward entitled him to be special, so that others would love and prize him inordinately. Although Peter was hardly aware of these unrealistic claims, he expected his girlfriend to idealize him as the most sensitive and loving man there possibly could be. It was impossible for Peter to believe that his girlfriend could actually be interested in someone else. Peter's neurotic pride system was painfully shattered when he found that he was not the commanding center of his girlfriend's life that he felt entitled to be.

Multiple stressors occurred for Peter in a short period of time. In and of themselves, these would precipitate a crisis for many people and lead them to therapy. If these situational stressors do not tap into a preexisting generic conflict in the client's personality, however, such strong symptoms as anxiety attacks usually will not develop. The client will often be able to recover in a relatively short time with crisis intervention or short-term supportive therapy. In contrast, when life stresses tap into a preexisting generic conflict, a client such as Peter has to cope with far more than just the demands of the current situational stressors.

Thus, when Peter's girlfriend became sexually involved with another man, he had to cope with much more than just the pain of this loss or betrayal. He also had to cope with his old unmet dependency needs that were aroused by her loss, and with the wound to his vulnerable self-esteem when his sense of being special was shattered. Clients such as Peter do not have a secure sense of self-esteem to act as a safety net to fall back on in times of crisis. As unrealistic as it is, the sense of being special and the secondary gains clients can earn by rising above their need is all that many clients have for a sense of self-worth. It is understandable, then, that Peter's anxiety became overwhelming and broke through in anxiety attacks. Both of the situational stressors intensified Peter's old unmet need, and they both took away his lifestyle adaptation for defending against his generic conflict. In this way, *clients' presenting symptoms will make sense once they are conceptualized in the context of the client's generic conflict.*

The Course of Treatment

Peter's therapist was skilled and experienced. He was empathetic to the pain that these situational crises brought on for Peter, but he also understood the generic conflict that constituted the real problem. The therapist recognized that the current crisis provided an opportunity to resolve the more important, developmental conflict that left Peter prone to reexperience crises such as these whenever others rejected or disapproved of him. In the months that followed, Peter was able to resolve the precipitating crisis and, for the first time, come to terms with his generic conflict and defenses against it. As a result, Peter was able to step back somewhat from his rigid moving-toward coping style and adopt a more flexible and varied interpersonal repertoire. Below, we will review the course of therapeutic events that allowed Peter to make these far-reaching changes.

Peter entered therapy in crisis, and the therapist was able to respond effectively to his anxiety and hurt. From the first session, Peter felt understood and cared for by the therapist. In just a few weeks, his anxiety became manageable and the anxiety attacks stopped. Although Peter remained anxious and upset, the shock and confusion that had been so disorganizing for him subsided as the therapist continued to understand his experience and respond to his feelings. As the initial crisis ended and Peter began to feel better, however, Peter began to be resistant to the feelings he had been sharing with the therapist and talked about ending treatment.

The therapist observed that as Peter felt understood and supported by him, Peter's unmet need for emotional contact was assuaged and its attendant anxiety diminished. As that occurred, Peter began to reconstitute his old defenses against his generic conflict and reemploy his interpersonal style of moving toward others. Rather than terminate therapy at this point, however, the therapist was able to help Peter identify this habitual coping pattern and understand how it served to keep him from resolving his underlying conflict. The therapist continued to focus Peter inward and to explore the feelings that accompanied his generic conflict and defensive adaptation to it. Gradually, Peter began to experience and share with the therapist the deprivation he had suffered as a child. He also began to understand how he had coped with his emotional needs by taking care of and pleasing first his mother, and then others as well. As this progress occurred, therapy moved into a new phase in which Peter again felt anxious and insecure.

A host of contradictory feelings emerged for Peter in the next few months. Peter began to recognize how unloved and alone he had felt as a child, and how he had always believed that he was not loved because he was somehow lacking or unworthy. As Peter continued to feel the therapist's support, his long-withheld feelings of sadness and longing came through the old block and were shared with the therapist.

As Peter began to mourn his childhood loss, two reactive feelings followed closely behind. Peter found himself feeling furious at his father for abandoning him and angry at his mother for forcing him to try to earn her love and approval. As soon as this anger emerged, however, the third feeling in Peter's affective constellation was aroused. Peter also became exceedingly anxious—afraid of being left helplessly on his own by the therapist, his girlfriend, and his father. Each of these three feelings in Peter's affective constellation was repeatedly aroused, and the therapist was gradually able to help Peter experience, express, and contain them. This was not a smooth or even process, however. As the primary feeling of sadness emerged, Peter's own internal blocking defenses were also activated (see part 3 of Figure 7–1). First, we will examine how the blocking side of Peter's compromise solution was expressed in therapy.

The rising-above defense was broken for Peter by his situational crises. He could no longer be special and win the approval he needed from either his practicum supervisor or his girlfriend. As his coping system failed, it opened the way for his original unmet need—and its accompanying emotional reactions—to come through the block and be expressed to the therapist. In addition to trying to rise above their generic conflict, however, clients also block their own experience of the original need. That is, the block that was originally imposed by the environment is taken up by the individual to defend against the painful feelings associated with the unmet need. Thus, Peter still blocked his own need with the therapist in both the intrapsychic and interpersonal ways discussed earlier. This side of Peter's compromise solution still needed to be worked through in therapy.

Peter tried to block the subjective experience and the interpersonal expression of his conflict by resisting each feeling in his affective constellation. For example, as the sadness of his emotional deprivation as a child emerged, Peter thought the therapist would be critical and rejecting of him. Peter was afraid that the therapist would want him to "stop crying, grow up, and act like a man." This transference reaction again served to block his sadness until Peter and the therapist were able to talk through Peter's misperception of the therapist.

Next, as Peter's anger toward his girlfriend, and then his parents, emerged, Peter felt guilty; he felt that he *should* be understanding, accepting, and forgiving of them. This intrapsychic defense also reflected his moving-toward character and served to block his unmet need again. With the therapist's support, however, Peter was finally able to experience the anger that had always been taboo for him. Why was it so threatening for Peter to experience his anger or share it with the therapist? While growing up in his family, Peter had learned that relationships were not resilient, his anger was unacceptable, and, because of his mother's propensity toward love withdrawal, he could easily destroy the little emotional support that he had won. Thus, Peter's anger threatened to break the already insecure emotional attachments he had and this, in turn, further aggravated his generic conflict. As a result, Peter's anger aroused his anxiety, which he tried to block by telling himself that he should be calm and together—especially if he were going to be a therapist.

Fortunately, the therapist was able to approach each of these feelings and work with Peter's resistance to them. Over the course of that school year, Peter was able to accept the reality and pain of his childhood loss, and allow the therapist to respond to the conflicted feelings that accompanied his generic conflict. As a result, Peter no longer needed to ward off his unmet need and its attendant anxiety so strongly. Peter felt less urgent about making others like him, more comfortable with interpersonal conflict, and more confident as his obsessive concern about pleasing others diminished. Finally, Peter was also able to keep the best parts of his moving-toward style. That is, he remained a sensitive, caring, and responsive person, although this was no longer the compulsive, unidimensional response pattern that it had been in the past.

Peter will certainly have further crises in his life, especially when life circumstances again tap into his old generic conflict. Peter has grown through this crisis, however, and therapy has helped immunize him against his predisposing vulnerability to rejection, criticism, and loss. By coming to terms with his generic conflict, the therapist helped Peter to stop carrying emotional baggage from his past into his present relationships. The internal changes that occurred for Peter will enable him to respond to future problems in a more adult, present-centered manner.

CLOSING

In this chapter, we studied a model for conceptualizing clients' dynamics. An extended case study of a moving-toward client illustrated how this model can be applied to treatment. We will also look at case studies of moving-against and moving-away clients after discussing additional information about conceptualizing clients and the process of change. At this point, however, two issues still remain incomplete.

First, we need further guidelines to be able to conceptualize clients' dynamics and use this conceptualization to guide clinical interventions. Chapter 8 provides further information about clients' current interpersonal functioning that will help therapists conceptualize their clients.

Second, as the compromise solution fails and the client's generic conflict emerges in therapy, the relationship that the therapist provides the client determines whether the client will be able to resolve the conflict and change. This pivotal juncture was identified in this chapter but specific guidelines for negotiating this phase of treatment were not provided. In Part IV, Chapters 9 and 10 will discuss more fully how the therapist can best respond to the client's emerging conflict.

SUGGESTIONS FOR FURTHER READING

1. Very useful guidelines for conceptualizing client dynamics are found in Chapter 5 of H. Strupp and J. Binder, "Psychotherapy in a New Key" (New York: Basic Books, 1984).

2. Karen Horney's work has remained the touchstone for many interpersonally oriented clinicians throughout their careers. Her writings are essential reading, especially *Neurosis and Human Growth* (New York: Norton, 1970). The reader may also be interested in another fine book by Horney: *Our Inner Conflicts* (New York: Norton, 1966).

3. Therapists in training need to be exposed to case examples that illustrate how theory guides clinical practice. Unfortunately, such effective illustrations are not plentiful. One of the most effective examples of integrating theory with practice is James Masterson's trilogy on using a developmental, object relations approach for treating borderline disorders. Masterson's books will be illuminating for many readers. See especially *Psychotherapy of the Borderline Adult: A Developmental Approach* (New York: Brunner/Mazel, 1976) and *Treatment of the Borderline Adolescent: A Developmental Approach* (New York: Wiley, 1972).

CHAPTER EIGHT

CURRENT INTERPERSONAL FACTORS

CONCEPTUAL OVERVIEW

The conceptual formulation presented here has three components. The first includes the three basic dimensions of family life introduced in Chapter 6. Most clients who enter therapy have experienced problems along each of these dimensions. Clients have usually come from families without a primary parental coalition, are often emotionally bound in cross-generational alliances and loyalty conflicts, and/or have not had their developmental needs for nurturance and discipline met. When development goes awry along these dimensions, children are likely to develop enduring personality conflicts.

The second component of our conceptualization is the schematic model for understanding how client problems are expressed, maintained, and resolved that we built on this familial/developmental perspective in Chapter 7. One important component of this conceptual model is clients' characteristic interpersonal style for coping with their generic conflict.

Now, in the third part of this conceptual formulation, we can expand the framework for examining clients' interpersonal functioning. This chapter shows how clients' current interpersonal relations provide the most important information for conceptualizing their dynamics. Furthermore, the therapist's own feelings and reactions toward the client are the therapist's best source of data for understanding the client's generic conflict and interpersonal defenses. Thus, this chapter shows how the therapist can systematically utilize the client's current interpersonal functioning and the therapist's own experience of the client to conceptualize the client's dynamics.

CHAPTER ORGANIZATION

In the first section of this chapter, we will see how therapists can be alerted to clients' generic conflict by tracking clients' anxiety. The second section helps therapists understand clients' problems by recognizing the ambivalent nature of their conflicts. The third section examines three ways in which client conflicts are expressed in the therapeutic relationship: eliciting maneuvers, testing behavior, and transference reactions. Finally, the last interpersonal factor we will examine is the degree of separateness versus relatedness in the therapist-client relationship. This section will help therapists establish an optimum degree of interpersonal distance with their clients. Each aspect of clients' current interpersonal functioning will be used to help therapists conceptualize their clients' dynamics.

TRACKING THE CLIENT'S ANXIETY

The first interpersonal factor to help therapists conceptualize their clients is to *track the client's anxiety*. Although the subjective experience of anxiety is always uncomfortable, and may be intensely painful, anxiety is the therapist's ally. Anxiety serves as a signal to help the therapist identify and focus on the client's central conflict. The therapist does not understand the client's problem or what needs to occur in therapy to resolve it until the therapist understands what makes the client anxious. That is, in order to understand the client's generic conflict, the therapist first must be able to understand why certain situations or interactions make the client anxious and how the client has learned to defend against this anxiety.

This section provides a four-step sequence that therapists can use to track the client's anxiety to clarify the nature and source of the client's conflicts. The sequence (1) identifies manifest and covert signs of client anxiety, (2) approaches directly all signs of client anxiety, (3) observes the issues being discussed and the interpersonal process occurring between the therapist and the client that precipitate the client's anxiety, and (4) focuses the client inward to explore the source and meaning of the client's anxiety.

Identifying Signs of Client Anxiety

Clients will become anxious in the session when the material they are discussing touches on their generic conflicts. As we saw in Chapter 7, clients develop complex interpersonal coping strategies and defense mechanisms to ward off the anxiety associated with their generic conflicts. If the therapist can identify the interpersonal transactions, subjective needs, or situational demands that make the client anxious, the therapist is better prepared to recognize the underlying conflict that has triggered the client's anxiety. Thus, throughout the course of therapy, therapists are continually asking themselves "What makes this client anxious?" "When does the client become uncomfortable?" "Where do his or her insecurities lie?"

In order to conceptualize the underlying conflict that is troubling clients, the therapist must actively attend to the anxiety (or anxiety equivalents) that they manifest. For example, the therapist must be alert for signs indicating that clients are now experiencing something that is making them anxious. There are a thousand different ways for clients to express their anxiety, such as nervous laughter, nail biting, hand gesticulation, agitated movement, stuttering, hair pulling, speech blockage, and so on. These anxiety equivalents will be expressed in endlessly varied ways across clients, and therapists will have to learn how each particular client tends to express anxiety. The first step in tracking the client's anxiety, however, is simply to observe when the client becomes anxious.

Approaching the Client's Anxiety Directly

In Chapter 5, we suggested that therapists approach and draw out the feelings that emerge for clients in the session. In a similarly forthright manner, the therapist should also approach client anxiety about an issue being discussed or about what is going on between the therapist and client at that moment. As before, the therapist can focus clients on their experience in an open-ended way (for example, "What are you feeling right now?") or by labeling the anxiety more directly (for example, "Something is making you anxious right now. What do you think that is?").

By focusing clients on their anxiety *as they are experiencing it,* and inviting them to explore it further, the therapist is leading clients closer to the conflict that is the source of their problems. This is why clients are often ambivalent about the therapist's request to explore their anxiety. On the one hand, clients may welcome the opportunity to share their anxiety with the therapist—and the confusion and pain that often follows closely behind. On the other hand, clients also recognize that approaching their anxiety will bring them closer to their underlying conflict, which is threatening for them to experience. As a result, therapists can anticipate that if they approach their clients' anxiety, it may intensify their anxiety and arouse their resistance.

As we discussed in Chapter 3, the therapist must respond to the client's resistance by exploring why it is threatening or dangerous for the client to approach this anxiety. This approach will be far more effective than ignoring the client's resistance or trying to push through it and persuading the client to talk about the conflict. Before the therapist and client can address the conflict itself, they must explore why it is threatening for the client to share it with the therapist. As emphasized before, the therapist must honor the client's resistance. The therapist does this by trying to understand the original, aversive experiences with others that led the client to be resistant in this particular

way, and then providing the client with a different and more satisfying response than the client experienced in the past.

Observing What Precipitates the Client's Anxiety

To review, the therapist first observes when the client is anxious, and then
helps the client focus more directly on the experience. At the same time, the
therapist must also carry out a third task. The therapist must try to recognize
(1) what issue was just being discussed or (2) what type of interaction was
occurring with the therapist that *precipitated* the client's anxiety. If the therapist can identify what has just occurred to make the client anxious, the therapist will be better able to identify the underlying conflict that has generated
the anxiety. We must examine this precipitant closely.

Clients will be able to discuss many different issues comfortably with the
therapist. When clients enter a topic area that makes them anxious, however,
the therapist must try to identify the issue or theme that has just precipitated
the anxiety. Was the client just talking about sex, death, money, success,
divorce, inadequacy . . . ? What is the issue that seems to be disturbing for
the client? Answering this question will show the therapist what issues are
linked to the client's central conflict and need to be explored further. As we
will see below, the therapist can help the client explore this more effectively if
the therapist has already formulated working hypotheses about the possible
conflicts that may be generating the anxiety.

The second way to understand the potential meaning of the client's anxiety is to hypothesize how the interaction occurring between the therapist and
the client may have triggered the client's anxiety. That is, the interpersonal
process transpiring between the therapist and client may be reenacting a
historical conflict for the client. For example, the therapist may observe the
following therapist actions coinciding with client anxiety:

1. As the therapist was expressing confusion about what was going on in
the session at that point, the client then became anxious, perhaps because his
volatile, alcoholic father would act confused and then start insulting him and
attacking him for something that went wrong.

2. The client had just made an important insight and the therapist
acknowledged her achievement. The client then became anxious, perhaps
because she believed that she would always have to be so insightful and
perform so well, as a parent had always expected of her.

3. The therapist had just been supportive, and perhaps the client felt anxious because strings had always been attached to what he had been given in the
past. The client may have become concerned that the therapist would make
him pay for his support in some way, just as his parent always used to do.

The therapist should generate working hypotheses such as these about
how the current therapist-client interaction may have aroused a historical

conflict for the client. These hypotheses can then be used to help the therapist and client explore the client's anxiety and understand the underlying conflict that is the source of it.

Focusing Clients Inward to Explore Their Anxiety

Restating this sequence, the therapist is alert for signs of client anxiety and approaches it whenever it occurs. Simultaneously, the therapist tries to identify what precipitated the client's anxiety and begins to generate working hypotheses about the underlying conflict that is the source of it. Finally, the therapist must focus the client inward to explore what the anxiety means. If the therapist can work through the client's resistance to approach the anxiety, and help the client express the thoughts, feelings, and memories that are associated with the anxiety, the client's internal conflict will usually emerge. The following dialogue illustrates this process.

Client:
> You know, this sounds awful to say but I don't think my mother really wants me to change very much in therapy. I don't think she's a bad person or anything, but I do think I'm getting better, and she's sort of bothered by that.

Therapist:
> How so?

Client:
> Well, I haven't been depressed for awhile now, and I've actually been pretty happy and outgoing the last month or so. Maybe it's just coincidence, but it seems that as I've gotten better, my mother has withdrawn and been harder to talk to. I think that might have gone on between us for a long time.

Therapist:
> Yes, I think so too. You know, you have been understanding some very difficult and important things in the past few weeks. It's a pleasure to see you doing so well.

Client:
> [fidgets, begins picking at her nail, and starts talking about another topic]

Therapist:
> Did something just make you feel uncomfortable?

Client:
> I don't know, how much time is left?

Therapist:
> What are we talking about, or what is going on between us right now, that is making you anxious?

Client:
> [long pause] I think I'm afraid you're going to go away or something.

Therapist:

Uh-huh. Well, we were just talking about how your mother goes away when you are feeling stronger, and I just told you that I thought you were doing very good work in here.

Client:

Yeah, but you're not going to stay with me either if I get better.

Therapist:

What do you mean?

Client:

If I get better, then we stop. I won't be able to come see you anymore, and then I won't have my mother, or you, or anybody!

Therapist:

I think the conflict that you and I are having together right now is central to many of your problems. To be strong and happy and independent, you feel you have to be alone. And if you want to be close to others, then you have learned that you have to be sad and depressed and needy. I think you have had to struggle with that awful choice all of your life.

Client:

[*crying*] Yeah, maybe I have.

In this way, tracking the client's anxiety can help the therapist conceptualize the client's generic conflict. It can also lead the therapist and client to the internal conflict that is the basis of the client's problems. We will return to this issue and explore it further in the following section.

THE AMBIVALENT NATURE OF CONFLICT
The Two-Sided Structure of Clients' Conflicts

A second interpersonal factor for conceptualizing client dynamics is to recognize the ambivalent nature of conflict. There are two sides to the client's generic conflict, and therapists must respond to both sides before problems can be resolved. What is meant by "both sides" of the client's conflict? The word *conflict* refers to two opposing impulses. Often, therapists fail to recognize both sides of the conflict that underlies clients' problems and only respond to one side of the conflict. Therapists can better understand their clients' problems when they can identify the two conflicting needs, wishes, or impulses that comprise the conflict. Recognizing the two-sided structure of conflicts will enable therapists to respond to the *ambivalence* that has immobilized the client and prevented change from occurring.

Colloquial expressions convey the two-sided nature of conflict. For example, we often say that someone is "stuck between a rock and a hard place," that someone has grabbed "both horns of the dilemma," or that a difficult relationship is "like a two-edged sword." These expressions capture the push-pull nature of conflict—that you are "damned if you do and damned if you don't." Below, two previous case studies are reexamined in order to highlight the two-sided conflict that comprises the client's problem. Once the therapist is able to recognize the structure of the conflict and articulate the ambivalent feelings that result from having this conflict, seemingly irrational and self-defeating behavior becomes understandable.

The young adult client in the sample therapist-client dialogue that ended the previous section wanted to get better—to end her chronic depression, become more outgoing and involved with friends, and find a career path that she could pursue. Until the last few weeks, however, the client had not been able to accomplish any of these goals. Although she had expressed these wishes for many years, she could not follow through and realize them. For example, she rarely initiated activities with peers and often declined the invitations she received from others. She repeatedly enrolled in college but would eventually lose interest and drop out after one or two semesters. Without recognizing the two-sided conflict that immobilized this client, her behavior seems irrational.

On the surface, it does not make sense that a client such as this will not do what she says she wants to do unless she really is just lazy, sick, masochistic, unmotivated or receiving too many secondary gains from being home and depressed. Therapists and others in clients' lives often attribute such pejorative labels to clients when their underlying conflict is not understood. Clients' contradictory behavior does make sense, however, once the two-sided, push-pull nature of their conflict is recognized.

In the preceeding dialogue, the client and therapist had just brought into focus how the client is immobilized between two aversive consequences that prevent her from resolving her problem. On the one hand, she wants to grow up and have her own life, friends, career, independence, and identity. But, at the same time, she also feels a need to be close to her mother and feel her mother's continuing support and availability. The client's conflict is that her mother will withdraw and induce guilt if she starts to pursue her own goals and succeed with friends, in school, or with life in general. Unable to break this "tie that binds," the client repeatedly fails and has to return home. Only on her return home and failure to emancipate does her mother again become available to her. Having to sacrifice her own independence to secure the support she also needs, the client becomes depressed over her inability to do what she wants and over her internalized resentment toward her mother's binding control. An informative discussion of these family dynamics is found in Jay Haley's book, *Leaving Home.*

After a few months, the same cycle will be reenacted again. That is, the frustrated client will start to act on her own need for autonomy, seek peer contacts, and reenroll in school. Just as before, however, her mother will withdraw, and the client will not be able to emancipate without her mother's support. In a few months, the client will return home again, feeling hopeless and a failure. Completing the cycle, the mother will again become comforting and supportive of the daughter in her defeat. This type of cyclic transactional pattern can continue for decades, until both sides of the client's conflict are made overt and worked through in therapy.

Another illustration of conflict was provided by Jean, the client in Chapter 5. Recall that she was the client who began to change only when she experienced her conflicted feelings with the therapist, rather than merely talking about them. Without recognizing her underlying conflict, Jean's behavior also seems irrational and self-defeating. Jean's primary symptom was her continuous involvement with selfish, demanding, and abusive men. Jean complained that she felt unhappy, used, and afraid in these destructive relationships, but she was unable to disengage from them. She remained in the relationship no matter how bad things got for her. Paradoxically, when the man decided to leave her, she would feel panicked, not relieved, and would quickly become reinvolved in a similar type of relationship. This pattern had continued throughout her twenties and thirties, and finally led her to seek help for her agitated depression.

At the time Jean entered therapy, she was applying the same pejorative labels to herself of masochistic and stupid that were noted earlier. Jean's friends also described her as crazy and hopeless for continually reinvolving herself in the same type of destructive relationship. As before, however, Jean's seemingly irrational and self-destructive behavior does make sense once the two-sided, push-pull nature of her conflict is recognized.

For years, Jean had said she wanted to be able to meet her own needs, set limits and say no sometimes, and leave relationships that were not supportive. But, year after year, she continued to meet a man's need at the expense of her own well-being. She could not say no and set self-preservative limits, even though she had learned the skills to do so in assertion training classes. Nor would she leave relationships in which she was dominated, manipulated, and exploited. Next we will examine the conflict that prevented Jean from doing what she wanted for herself and that makes her seemingly irrational behavior understandable.

A countervailing force covertly opposed all of Jean's attempts to change. As soon as Jean started to act on her own needs, set limits, or try to leave a relationship, she felt cold, small, and alone to the point of panic. In other words, she was gripped by intense separation anxieties whenever she made any movement toward her own individuation. Thus, as soon as Jean started to do what she wanted for herself these painful feelings were activated. Her only means of abating these separation anxieties and feeling related to others again was to retreat to the familiar dependent/victim role.

This paralyzing conflict developed in Jean's family of origin. Growing up, Jean was an extremely parentified child. She was expected to respond only to her parents' needs, and she was harshly rebuffed or painfully shamed for expressing her own "selfish will." Throughout her childhood, she received so much criticism from her parents, and so little emotional support, that she desperately needed whatever thin threads of approval she could earn by devoting herself to them. Whenever she tried to express her own wishes or ask for what she would like, she was told that she was selfish and demanding. As a little girl, Jean clearly was left starving for the approval she could not receive but desperately needed. Afraid of receiving further rejection from her parents, she was eager to serve them and comply with whatever they asked of her. Thus, as a child, Jean became a captive of her own need for relatedness that she could neither relinquish nor fulfill. In her book *Prisoners of Childhood*, Alice Miller elucidates this type of poignant conflict.

Ultimately, in order to maintain some minimal sense of relatedness to others, Jean *identified* with her parent's critical rejection of her. That is, she internalized her parents' contempt for her and began hating herself for being "bad" and "selfish." As an adult, she recapitulated the feelings and experiences of her childhood by selecting punitive, selfish men who confirmed and fostered her own internalized feelings of self-loathing and worthlessness.

With this developmental background in mind, it is easier to see how Jean's seemingly irrational behavior does in fact make sense. Her only sense of herself as a person, and her only means of being in a relationship, is to meet another person's need. When she finally becomes depleted by this role and begins to respond to her own needs (set limits, ask for what she wants, leave a hurtful relationship), panic results. Her separation anxieties, unmet dependency needs, and self-hatred becomes overwhelming, just as they were for her when she was a child. In order to diminish the panic, she becomes connected to others again by retreating to the abusive relationship and reenacting the same pattern. She again responds to the boyfriend's demeaning demands and suffocates her own needs, feelings, and life. The same cycle will soon start again, however, as her frustration and resentment over having her own life denied begin to reemerge. Temporarily, she will start to respond to herself and her own needs, only to be immobilized again by the same separation anxieties and guilt.

A cyclic dynamic such as this is difficult to change. As Jean illustrates, however, change is possible if two things occur. First, Jean began to change this pattern when she experienced a relationship with the therapist in which her own needs were listened to, responded to, and valued for the first time. This was difficult to provide, however, because Jean was adept at rejecting the care and concern that she desperately wanted from the therapist. Second, the therapist was also able to help Jean understand the two-sided structure of the conflict that had bewildered and immobilized her throughout her life. Understanding the conflict helped Jean change by allowing her to feel more compassionate toward herself and her own predicament, and more accepting of the choices and compromises that she had been forced to make throughout her life in order to survive. This acceptance, in turn, helped her to disengage from her own self-hatred and value herself and her own needs for the first time. Soon after this internal change occurred, Jean became involved with a supportive and responsive man for the first time.

Ambivalent Feelings

The two clients above illustrate the push-pull nature of conflict—that there are two opposing forces that the client has not been able to reconcile. Therapists cannot conceptualize the client's dynamics until they can articulate "both horns of the client's dilemma" and recognize its two-sided structure. In addition to framing the client's problem as a conflict, therapists must be able to *respond to the opposing feelings that accompany both sides of the client's conflict.* Too often, therapists are ineffective because they only respond to one-half of the client's ambivalent feelings. The case vignette that follows illustrates that the client cannot change unless the therapist acknowledges both sides of the client's ambivalent feelings.

Marie is a 25-year-old female client. During the course of therapy Marie discovered how angry she was at her mother. To this day, her mother expected Marie to be perfect, insisted that Marie never had any problems, and always needed Marie to be happy. In therapy, Marie began to realize how much she resented her mother for denying so many of her true feelings and for having so many expectations of how she *should* be. Marie's therapist resonated with her new awareness and actively supported her anger.

At first, it was liberating for Marie to be able to express her long-suppressed anger. She was both excited and relieved to realize that she no longer needed to fulfill her mother's unrealistic expectations. This good feeling was short-lived, however. In the following weeks, Marie's new-found freedom gave way to a growing sense of futility and pessimism. The therapist thought that Marie must be guilty about defying her mother's expectations and was depressed because she was defensively turning the anger she felt toward her mother back on herself.

While repeatedly offering this interpretation, the therapist continued to draw out and encourage Marie's anger. Moving in a different direction than the therapist, however, Marie began to share fond memories about her mother and recalled with longing special times they had spent together making cookies after school. The therapist was not very responsive to Marie's positive feelings toward her mother, however. The therapist thought that Marie's positive feelings were part of denying her anger toward her mother, avoiding the conflicts in their relationship, continuing to idealize her mother and thereby remaining committed to meeting her mother's expectations.

Marie's therapist only recognized one side of her ambivalence and failed to respond to the feelings on both sides of her conflict. Yes, Marie was angry at her mother, and these suppressed feelings needed to be explored, expressed, and validated. But, at the same time, Marie also knew that her mother had offered her many fine things as a parent and she did not want to forego the good things they had shared. Marie's conflict was not knowing how she could keep the good things she had experienced with her mother without having to internalize the problematic aspects of their relationship as well. Thus, on the one hand, Marie wanted to reject the unrealistic demands to be perfect and happy that her mother placed on her. But, at the same time, Marie became depressed when it seemed like the only way to do this was to give up her identification with her mother altogether. Rightly so, Marie did not want to lose her most important female role model and risk losing the feminine parts of herself as well.

Therapy stagnated as Marie remained depressed, so her therapist sought consultation from a colleague. The colleague quickly recognized both sides of Marie's conflict and encouraged the therapist to allow Marie to simultaneously have contradictory feelings of appreciation and anger toward her mother. As a result of this consultation, the therapist began responding to the other side of Marie's feelings as well. For example, the therapist soon responded, "You feel two different ways toward your mother at the same time. You're angry at her for expecting you to be perfect, but you also treasure many of the fond times you've had together. Tell me about both your angry and your loving feelings toward her."

As the therapist encouraged Marie to explore and express both sides of her feelings, her depression lifted. Marie began to clarify what parts of her mother she wanted to keep and make a part of herself and what parts of her mother and her mother's expectations she wanted to discard. This process of differentiation also allowed Marie to clarify which issues she wanted to confront and try to change in her current relationship with her mother and which issues she preferred to let go of and simply accommodate herself to. Marie spurted forward in therapy as soon as the therapist helped her come to terms with both sides of her ambivalent feelings. Therapy was soon successfully terminated as Marie better integrated parts of her own identity as a woman and initiated a rapprochement with her mother.

In sum, clients change when the therapist recognizes the two-sided structure of their conflicts and responds to both sides of their ambivalent feelings.

WAYS CLIENTS BRING THEIR CONFLICTS INTO THE THERAPEUTIC RELATIONSHIP

This section examines three important ways in which clients bring their conflicts into the therapeutic relationship: eliciting maneuvers, testing behavior, and transference reactions. Sometimes clients will employ certain interpersonal operations—such as eliciting maneuvers—with the therapist in order to avoid and defend against their conflicts. At other times, clients will employ different interpersonal mechanisms—such as testing behavior—to approach and try to resolve their conflicts. Testing behavior reflects a healthy, growth-oriented attempt to master conflicts. One of the most interesting aspects of psychotherapy is working with these complex and often contradictory inter-personal maneuvers within the therapeutic relationship. The third way clients bring their conflicts into the therapeutic relationship and reenact them with the therapist is through transference reactions—the client's systematic mis-perceptions of the therapist. These three interrelated concepts reflect funda-mental aspects of interpersonal psychotherapy and are presented below.

Eliciting Maneuvers Allow Clients to Avoid Conflicts

Sullivan (1968), Horney (1970), Fromm (1982), and other interpersonal theo-rists have described how clients develop fixed interpersonal styles to avoid anxi-ety and defend against their conflicts. The rigidly fixed interpersonal coping styles of moving toward, moving away, or moving against others are examples of ways in which most clients are inflexible in their perception of others, con-stricted in their range of emotions, and limited in their range of interpersonal responses. In part, clients systematically employ these interpersonal styles to (1) *elicit* certain desired responses that will avoid their conflicts and diminish anxi-ety and (2) preclude responses from others that will arouse their generic con-flicts. To illustrate how eliciting maneuvers serve to defend against conflicts, we will return to the case study of Peter, the moving-toward client in Chapter 7.

Peter's moving-toward interpersonal style tended to elicit approval, ac-ceptance, kindness, and trust from others. As a general lifestyle, Peter was helpful—he sympathized, agreed, and cooperated with people. For example, Peter tried to understand his girlfriend's infidelity and win his supervisor's approval. Even in therapy, he tried to enact this same interpersonal style by trying to please his therapist and elicit his approval.

In contrast, Peter was never appropriately critical, forthright, assertive, angry, or skeptical. These types of responses, which are necessary for a well-functioning person to employ at times, were not part of Peter's interpersonal repertoire. For example, he did not communicate (or even experience) how angry he was with his girlfriend, nor did he assertively set limits with his practicum instructor regarding how much critical feedback Peter could incor-porate at one time. In addition to avoiding these anxiety-arousing behaviors, his pleasing interpersonal style also discouraged angry, confrontive responses from others that would also arouse further anxiety for him.

If Peter's therapist had reflexively responded to what Peter's interper-sonal style elicited, Peter would not have changed in therapy. That is, if the therapist had merely supported Peter and met his need for approval—as

Peter had always elicited from others—Peter would have only reenacted in therapy the same rising-above defense that he had used throughout his life. Instead, Peter's therapist used process comments to make Peter's moving-toward style overt in their relationship. Instead of automatically responding to what Peter elicited, the therapist focused on it as part of Peter's problems that needed to be addressed in therapy.

Over the course of several months, the therapist gradually helped Peter understand how his fixed interpersonal style of moving toward others served to protect him from his generic conflict. Peter began to observe how this fixed interpersonal style elicited from others the approval, support, and nurturance he had missed as a child. In addition, he began to recognize how his pleasing style discouraged the critical, angry, or rejecting responses from others that were so threatening for him. As Peter made progress in mastering his developmental conflicts in therapy, he became less needful of compulsively winning others' approval and was able to expand his interpersonal repertoire. As he no longer needed others to regard him as ever kind, loving, and gentle, Peter began to be appropriately assertive, direct, and more confident for the first time in his life.

Moving-toward clients like Peter use eliciting maneuvers that are familiar but not especially difficult for beginning therapists to work with. In contrast, moving-against clients employ different eliciting maneuvers that are often challenging for beginning therapists. These clients often do something in the first few minutes of the first session to take command of the relationship or make the therapist feel insecure in some way. For example, the client may insist on sitting in the therapist's chair, question the therapist's adequacy, or criticize one of the therapist's early responses. This provocative presentation elicits fear and withdrawal in many beginning therapists, competition in some, and for a few, counterhostility. If the moving-against client succeeds in eliciting one of these responses from the therapist, therapy will not progress. The client will have successfully neutralized the therapist's effectiveness and defended against his or her anxieties surrounding having problems, asking for help, entering a new relationship that will require relinquishing some control, and so forth. In this way, the client's eliciting maneuvers have acted to successfully protect the client from conflicts, but at the price of change.

Therapists do not want to respond reflexively to these eliciting maneuvers with their own characteristic tendencies toward flight or fight. What can therapists do instead? First, they can begin to formulate hypotheses about (1) the impact this behavior might have on others in these clients' lives and (2) what conflicts these clients might be avoiding by these maneuvers. Next, on an interpersonal level, therapists can try to find some other way to engage these clients in which the usual relational patterns of domination, intimidation, or competition are not enacted. There are many ways to do this, and several possibilities are discussed next.

One way for the therapist to find another way to relate is simply by not being "undone" by the client's criticism, as for example, when the therapist calmly responds: "Your previous therapist was a psychiatrist, and you're not sure that a younger social worker such as myself can help you. Let's talk about that. Tell me more about your concern."

Another alternative is for the therapist to make a process comment and describe or ask about the current interaction. For example, the therapist might say: "You're speaking in a loud and angry voice right now. Are you aware that you are doing that?" With some clients, the therapist may wish to take this approach one step further and begin to explore the effects of this interpersonal presentation on others. For example, the therapist might say: "Here again you're criticizing me. How do others usually respond when you do this?" Many of these clients will be unaware of the impact they character- istically have on others, and this interpersonal feedback can provide a pro- ductive new starting point. However, the purpose here is not to find a vehicle for winning the control battle and getting "one up" with the client. This would only continue the problematic interpersonal process. Rather, this approach is intended to help the therapist engage in a neutral way with the client rather than reflexively responding to the eliciting defenses.

Or, still another possibility is for the therapist to focus on how the client's eliciting maneuvers affect the client. For example, the therapist might say: "You have insisted on sitting in my chair even though I asked you not to. Now that you are there, how does it feel?" Clients often become aware of feeling alone, empty, or anxious at these moments, which also provides a new point of departure.

Some of these responses will work well with a particular client, and not at all with another. Therapists' goals in such situations are (1) to attend to their own reactions and observe what the client is eliciting in them, (2) formulate working hypotheses and try to conceptualize how this may serve to help the client avoid the generic conflicts, and (3) try to find another way to respond (for example, via process comments) that does not reenact the same relational scenario that the client usually elicits.

Although moving-against clients often intimidate beginning therapists, this usually does not last very long. With a little more experience and a supportive supervisor, beginning therapists learn not to charge so readily at a waving red flag. Beginning therapists learn to appreciate the fact that the intensity and rigidity of clients' eliciting maneuvers are commensurate with their degree of anxiety and conflict. Although different tactics may need to be tried, therapists can usually find other ways to engage with these clients and avoid reenacting the intimidated, competitive, or hostile responses these cli- ents usually elicit from others. All in all, however, moving-away clients often pose the most challenging eliciting behaviors for therapists.

Most people who select counseling careers have strong relational needs. However, when moving-away clients continue to maintain emotional distance, many therapists will give up and disengage. When this occurs, these clients' eliciting behaviors have successfully defended them against relating to the therapist and thereby allowed them to avoid the threats entailed by closer involvement. When this happens, clients' conflicts will not be activated, but the therapist's only real vehicle for resolving conflicts is closed as well. Rather than reflexively turning off, as these clients' aloofness elicits, the therapist may use process comments to try and find other avenues for relationship. Beginning therapists must be patient with themselves and their clients, however, since it will be threatening for clients to relate in a different way.

In sum, therapists must be aware of what clients systematically tend to elicit in others and hypothesize how this interpersonal strategy protects them from their central conflict. More important, *therapists must also attend to their own feelings and reactions that are elicited by the client.* This self-awareness is one of the therapist's most important sources of information about the client. If therapists can observe what clients elicit, it will inform therapists about the nature of clients' conflicts, interpersonal defenses against their conflicts, and how their conflicts are being played out in the therapeutic relationship.

We have already seen how therapists must generate working hypotheses to understand why clients elicit certain responses in them, such as reassurance, disinterest, competition, confusion, irritability, nurturance, and so forth. The therapist's task is to keep from responding reflexively to what the client is eliciting and, if possible, to try to respond in a way that does not reenact the client's conflict. Over time, the therapist can begin to help clients recognize their eliciting mechanisms and understand how they have served as a protection from clients' generic conflicts. It does take courage, however, for beginning therapists to tolerate their own "bad" or unacceptable feelings long enough to consider how they may be used to foster an understanding of clients' dynamics.

Finally, beginning therapists must understand one further aspect of clients' eliciting behaviors. We have seen how clients use eliciting maneuvers to hold therapists away from their conflicts and the vulnerable feelings that accompany them. Problems arise, however, when their eliciting behaviors tap into the therapist's own dynamics and immobilize the therapist's effectiveness. An example of this occurs in interpersonal sequences in which the client acts helpless and escalates her or his distress; the therapist tries to help but fails at each attempt; and then the therapist feels responsible and inadequate, becomes angry or critical of the client, and emotionally withdraws.

Such scenarios are commonplace. When they occur, *clients often switch to the other side of their ambivalence and try to reengage the therapist,* perhaps by reassuring the therapist about how helpful the sessions are. That is, the client does not really want to succeed in immobilizing the therapist or ending the relationship and will often try to get the disengaged therapist involved in the relationship again. *Premature terminations often occur when the therapist fails to hear the client's renewed bids for relationship because the disengaged therapist has "given up" on the client.* Thus, therapists must keep clients' ambivalence in mind. Just as clients may use eliciting behaviors to try to push the therapist away, they may subsequently try to reengage if they are successful in distancing/immobilizing the therapist. Especially with more troubled clients, therapists must keep both of these engaging and disengaging maneuvers in mind.

Testing Behavior Enables Clients to Resolve Conflicts

We have seen above how clients employ their fixed interpersonal style to systematically elicit responses from others that avoid anxiety. These eliciting phenomena, or "security operations" as Sullivan called them, are interpersonal defenses. As contradictory as it sounds, however, at other times, clients will use interpersonal strategies to approach and try to resolve problems. Clients often carry out this side of their ambivalence about treatment—their healthy attempts at mastering their conflicts—by "testing behavior." That is, clients systematically bring their conflicts into the therapeutic relationship by reenacting them in some direct or metaphorical way with the therapist. Unconsciously, clients then "test" to see if the therapist responds in the same problematic way that others have in the past or if the therapist can provide a new, more facilitating response that allows them to resolve their conflicts and progress in therapy. Most of the discussion that follows is based on aspects of control/mastery theory by Weiss and Sampson (1986).

In a healthy attempt to master conflicts, clients actively (but not consciously) elicit from the therapist the same conflicts they have had and are having with others in their lives. Clients test to see if they can change old relational patterns and disconfirm the pathogenic beliefs that stem from these patterns (for example, "If I get stronger and do what I want with my life, my parent will be hurt and will withdraw.") Parallel to the concept of providing a "corrective emotional experience," the therapist can fail this test by responding in a way that reenacts old relational patterns, or the therapist can pass the test by behaviorally demonstrating that relationships can be different.

Many of these "transference tests" are easy to recognize, and therapists can readily pass them and thereby allow clients to progress in treatment and move on to other issues. For example, suppose a compliant, dependent housewife says to her male therapist, "Where should we start today?" On the one hand, the therapist will fail the test and confirm the client's pathogenic relational patterns if he says, "Tell me about _____." On the other hand, the therapist will pass the test and demonstrate that he is capable of engaging in a more egalitarian way than the client has been able to do with her husband and father when the therapist says, "I'd like to hear about what is most important to you. Let's begin with something that you would like to tell me about."

However, beginning therapists are more likely to struggle with tests that involve issues of power and control. Clients are often unconsciously testing the strength of the therapist to assess whether it is safe to go on to more threatening issues. For example, when clients push limits with the therapist, they are often testing to see if the therapist will respond ineffectively, as did the parent. That is, they are testing to see if they can control or manipulate the therapist as they could their parent, or whether the therapist is able to be stronger, set limits, and thereby provide the safety they did not receive before. The following case example illustrates this point.

Graduate students in Carl's clinical training program were supposed to videotape all therapy sessions. Early in treatment, however, Carl's client Lucy complained that the videotaping made her "self-conscious." She said it was hard for her to talk about what was really important as it was and that the videotaping made an already difficult situation "impossible." She continued to stress this concern for several weeks and finally told Carl that he was not helping her because there were too many things that she could not talk about when the tape was on.

Carl was torn and did not know what to do. He knew the clinic rules, and that his supervisor would abide by them, but he also felt that he should be flexible enough to do what his client needed. Without consulting his supervisor, he reached a compromise with Lucy and agreed to turn the videotape off for the last five minutes of each session. Lucy was appreciative and did indeed disclose new material to Carl during those last five minutes. Carl felt badly about doing this without his supervisor's permission but also thought it was the only way to help his client and keep her in treatment.

Carl soon observed, however, that the therapy was not going well. Lucy became scattered and started jumping from topic to topic. Carl tried to "pin her down" and focus on her escalating feelings, but she "squirted away" each time. In an emotionally distraught manner, Lucy communicated that she was very upset and needed more guidance from Carl, but whatever he did failed to help. Realizing that things were getting out of control, Carl decided to talk with his supervisor about his dilemma.

First, Carl and his supervisor spent some time resolving what Carl's decision meant for their relationship, and then his supervisor began helping Carl hypothesize what this "test" might mean about Lucy's dynamics. Armed with some new ways of thinking about what was going on in the client-therapist relationship, Carl accepted his supervisor's firm insistence that the videotape remain on throughout every session. When Carl reinstated this limit at the beginning of the next session with Lucy, she protested strongly. She accused Carl of being "untrustworthy" because he broke their agreement, informed him that she could no longer talk about certain important things, and told him that she would have to "think about" whether she wanted to remain in treatment with him.

Carl felt badly about her threats, but he tolerated his discomfort and stuck to the rules. Although she continued to blame and complain, Lucy did return. In fact, despite her protests, she became calmer, more contained, and began to focus more productively in therapy. Over the next few weeks, Lucy went on to recall how threatening it had been for her to be able to "boss my father around."

It is adaptive for clients like Lucy to elicit their conflicts and test whether the therapist will reenact or resolve them. Clients cannot progress to more conflicted, vulnerable material if the current therapeutic relationship is not safer than past relationships have been. There is little value, however, in merely reassuring clients or trying to convince them that the therapeutic relationship is safer. Also, clients are not consciously aware of testing therapists in these ways, and it is rarely useful to point out testing behavior to them. Instead, as in all human relations, it is what the therapist does, not says, that counts. Therapists pass tests and provide a corrective emotional experience when they consistently respond in ways that behaviorally disconfirm problematic relational patterns.

In order to know what kind of response the client needs, therapists must (1) consider client response specificity and (2) learn how to assess client reactions to therapeutic interventions. These important guidelines for passing client tests are addressed in the following subsections.

Client Response Specificity. As discussed in Chapter 1, therapists must respond differently to different clients. Depending on clients' developmental backgrounds, the same therapeutic response that passes the test for one client may fail the test and reenact conflicts for another. For example, in response to pressure from her client, Beverly agreed to reduce her fee substantially. Almost immediately, her client began wearing expensive jewelry, delighted in telling Beverly about expensive shopping trips, and described how "wonderful" it was to fly first class on her vacation. Realizing that she was allowing the client to take advantage, as she had been able to do with her doting mother, Beverly renegotiated the reduced fee. Later that same session, the client brought up important new material and entered a productive new phase of treatment. When the client responded to the reinstated limits by making therapeutic progress, Beverly knew that by being firm she had passed the client's test. The client could only feel safe and move on to other more threatening issues when she was sure that she could not manipulate Beverly as she could her mother and others.

Although lowering the fee failed the test for the above client, in the following example this action was a helpful response. Another client, recently divorced, was coping with a diminished income and having trouble making ends meet. Knowing that this client grew up accommodating to demanding, witholding parents, the therapist realized the added significance it would hold if he extended himself to the client and offered a more flexible fee arrangement. The client could not ask the therapist for this directly and was initially reluctant to accept any of the alternative fee arrangements that the therapist suggested. When the therapist asked about her reluctance to even consider his offer, the client burst into tears. His response disconfirmed the client's belief about herself that she "didn't matter" and evoked the longing she had felt for her parents to reach out to her. Changing the payment schedule with this client disconfirmed certain pathogenic beliefs about herself and relationships and moved the treatment into more intensive work about her deprivation. Thus, the same response by the therapist will often have very different effects on different clients.

Client response specificity puts substantial demands on the therapist, however. It takes away the security of having a "cookbook" or rule-bound approach to therapy and requires the therapist to remain close to the personal experience of every client. However, within this highly idiographic context, some guidelines are available to help therapists respond more accurately to the specific needs of differing clients. As we have seen, therapists learn what clients need by inquiring about repetitive transactional patterns in their families of origin and by conceptualizing clients' current interpersonal functioning. In addition, therapists also learn how to pass tests and provide clients with the interpersonal experiences they need by assessing client reactions to therapeutic interventions.

Assessing Client Reactions. As beginning therapists get better at conceptualizing their clients' dynamics, it will become easier to anticipate the responses clients need in order to be able to change. But how do therapists know if they have passed or failed the client's test? What guidelines exist to assess whether the therapist has successfully provided a corrective emotional experience or merely reenacted the conflict? If beginning therapists rely completely on their supervisor's advice, they will remain dependent and insecure. If they rely solely on a particular theoretical approach, they will be more secure but run the risk of becoming rigid and dogmatic. Do better alternatives exist? Although supervisors and theories are of great assistance, beginning therapists must also learn how to independently assess client responses to therapeutic interventions to determine their effectiveness.

It can be reassuring for beginning therapists to realize that the client will often teach them what they need to do. That is, clients often inform the therapist of the responses they need. Clients do not usually verbalize this in so many words, but they predictably guide the therapist by their behavioral responses to the therapist's interventions. We will closely examine how clients help the therapist in this way.

When the therapist responds effectively to a client's test and disconfirms problematic relational patterns, the client gets stronger, which can manifest in many different ways. For example, in the minutes following the therapist passing the test, the client may begin to talk more directly about personal experience rather than continuing to talk about others. Or, the next vignette the client relates may have more richness, clarity, or express more meaning than has been typical before. In general, the therapeutic process may acquire more immediacy or relevancy and become less intellectualized or repetitive. Clients may engage more directly with the therapist just after a test has been passed. That is, whether the client brings up a conflict with the therapist or expresses warm feelings toward the therapist, a stronger, more direct interpersonal contact is often initiated. Further, if the therapist has just provided the client with a needed response, the client's affect may also emerge or intensify. Clients may become sad, happy, calm, or angry, but their feelings about what has happened become more accessible to them and/or can be shared more fully with the therapist.

Therapists also know they have responded correctly and passed the test when the client brings up new material and enters new conflict areas. In the important moments following the therapist's passing the test, the client may also make meaningful historical insights. On their own, clients often make meaningful connections between their current behavior and past relationships. They do not just passively consider interpretations from the therapist; instead, they generate their own insights that are enlivening and meaningful for them. Although it is usually unproductive to lead clients back to historical connections, significant changes result when clients spontaneously make these bridges.

To put it simply, when the client responds to the therapist's intervention by getting stronger and engaging more directly in the work, the therapist has usually passed the client's test. For example, when Carl turned the videotape on for the full session, Lucy complained and even threatened to terminate. But by maintaining appropriate professional boundaries, Carl demonstrated that he was different than Lucy's father and was therefore safer. Carl could tolerate Lucy's disapproval and do what she actually needed rather than what she demanded. As a result, Lucy began to work more productively and introduced important new material into her treatment.

Finally, it is essential for therapists to conceptualize what they have done to pass (or fail) clients' tests and allow them to progress in treatment. This conceptualization can then be used to guide subsequent interventions and to continue providing clients with the interpersonal experience they need in order to change. For example, in different ways and at other anxiety-arousing points in treatment, Lucy will again push the limits with Carl. If Carl has learned from their previous interaction, however, he will be better prepared next time to provide the response Lucy needs.

In their behavioral responses to therapeutic interventions, clients also tell therapists when they have failed to provide the experiences they need. On having failed a test, the therapist will often observe that the client becomes weaker—more anxious, dependent, confused, or distant. These reactions are often evident almost immediately and may continue into subsequent sessions. Therapists should formulate working hypotheses about how their recent interaction may have reenacted the client's conflict when (1) clients begin talking about others rather than themselves; (2) the therapeutic process becomes repetitive or intellectualized; or (3) clients become compliant, lose their initiative, or cannot find meaningful material to talk about. In addition to these signs, we will examine another fascinating way clients inform therapists that they are failing tests.

When therapists pass tests (for example, take pleasure in the client's success rather than being threatened by the success as significant others have been), clients usually acknowledge the therapist's achievement by acting stronger and progressing in treatment. When a therapist repeatedly fails a specific test (for example, not taking into account the potential validity of a client's criticism of the therapist, just as the client's parent always needed to be "right"), clients may inform the therapist that something is awry by recalling other relationships in which the same conflict was enacted. That is, when the therapist keeps responding in a problematic way that confirms clients' conflicts, clients may begin to tell the therapist stories about their past, other people they know, or characters in books or movies who are enacting the same problematic relational pattern. *Therapists should always consider the possibility that whenever clients are talking about another relationship, they may be using this as a metaphor to describe what is going on between the therapist and the client.*

Therapists must listen for the relational themes that characterize the vignettes clients choose to relay. If clients repetitively tell stories in which trust is betrayed, someone is left, control battles are being enacted, and so forth, clients are often unconsciously expressing how these same conflicts are currently being enacted in the therapist-client relationship. When this occurs, the therapist can use a process comment to make this relational theme overt and bring the conflict back into the therapeutic relationship, where something can be done to resolve it. For example, the therapist might say: "Both of these people you have been telling me about failed to hear something important that others were trying to tell them. I wonder if something like that could be going on between you and me? Maybe you told me something earlier that was important to you that I didn't hear very well. Do any possibilities come to mind?"

In sum, just as clients use eliciting behaviors to avoid and defend against their conflicts, they also use "transference tests" to try and resolve conflicts in the therapeutic relationship. By tracking the therapeutic process in the ways suggested here, therapists can learn whether they are providing clients with the needed interpersonal experiences. This approach refines therapists' conceptualizations of their clients' dynamics and gives therapists the flexibility they need to respond to the varying conflicts that clients present. We turn now to the traditional concept of "transference," a third way in which client conflicts are expressed in the therapeutic relationship.

Transference Reactions Reveal Client Conflicts

Another interpersonal factor for conceptualizing clients is *transference reactions*. Transference is one of the most important concepts in psychotherapy. Therapists use this term in different ways, however, and over the years competing definitions have evolved. For some, transference has come to refer to all of the thoughts, feelings, and perceptions that the client has toward the therapist. For others, transference just refers to those reactions that have been inappropriately displaced onto the therapist from someone in the client's past. In other words, transference occurs when emotional reactions that actually belong to a person in the client's past are inaccurately *transferred* to the present relationship with the therapist. Such transference reactions systematically distort the client's perceptions of and reactions to the therapist. Therapists can use transference reactions both to conceptualize client dynamics and to help clients resolve their conflicts within the therapeutic relationship.

Transference Is an Everyday Occurrence. To some degree, everybody transfers in their daily lives and everyday interactions. That is, everyone systematically misperceives others based on previous learning that is overgeneralized to the present situation. For example, imagine that a university professor is standing in front of a large lecture hall about to convene the first class meeting of Psych. 100. Before he has even begun to lecture, many students will be transferring expectations from significant male authority figures in their own lives onto the professor. Thus, 18-year-old Mary sits in the first row of the lecture hall and looks up to the professor admiringly. Just as she still somewhat idealizes her father, Mary similarly respects the middle-aged professor, even though she actually knows little about him.

In contrast, from high up and far away in the last row of seats, Joe looks down on the professor disparagingly. Joe anticipates that the professor does not know as much as he thinks he does and that he will not be very well prepared for class. Just like his own father, who always had to be right and on top, this professor will probably try to get away with putting a lot over on them in class. Joe has already decided that this "know-it-all" professor is not going to get away with much if Joe can help it.

Hopefully, the professor will be aware of the fact that people tend to transfer expectations onto authority figures who hold power and onto those who have high public visibility (movie *stars*, sports *heroes*, and political *leaders*). If the professor is not sensitized to transference reactions, however, his self-confidence as a teacher will take a roller-coaster ride. One day, Mary will follow him out of class and tell him what an interesting lecture he gave, whereas the next day, Joe will drop his books when the professor starts to speak and demand that he defend half of what he says.

Transference reactions such as Mary and Joe have toward the professor are everyday occurrences. The more conflicted or disturbed one is, however, the more one distorts the current reality by inaccurately displacing reactions from the past onto the present. For example, Joe and Mary have strong initial reactions to the professor that are based on little real-life experience with him. If Joe and Mary function fairly well psychologically, they will become more realistic in their assessment of the professor as they have more exposure to his teaching. In contrast, the more Mary idealizes her father and the more Joe disparages his father, the more likely it is that they will not be able to perceive the strengths and limitations of the professor accurately. Instead, they will maintain their initial perceptions and expectations despite the fact that they are inaccurate or overdetermined.

Just as transference reactions are more intense and pervasive the more disturbed one is, transference reactions are also more likely to occur in emotion-laden situations. For example, transference reactions are especially pronounced when two people are falling in love. In this regard, many married couples recall their courtship as the happiest time in their lives. The couple is so elated during this time because each member systematically misperceives the partner as someone who can fulfill unmet developmental needs and make one feel lovable, capable, or worthy when one has not felt this way before. This romantic period is usually short-lived, however. The transference projections soon break down as they both realize that the partner cannot satisfy all of their original needs as they had hoped. If the underlying unmet needs and resulting transference distortions have been especially strong, the result can be dashed dreams and angry feelings of betrayal. In contrast, if the transference distortions of the partner have not been extreme, they can readily be shed to allow a more realistic and enduring relationship to develop. Relinquishing these transference distortions of the new spouse is the major psychological task of early marriage.

In therapy, the therapist can systematically utilize the client's transference reactions to better understand the client's conflicts. In fact, *one of the most effective ways to learn about the client's central conflicts is to note how the client perceives and reacts to the therapist.* Almost without exception, the client's conflicts will be reenacted in the therapeutic relationship. If the therapist is alert when these transference reactions occur, they provide an invaluable tool for conceptualizing the client's conflicts.

Utilizing Transference Reactions to Conceptualize Clients. Some therapists are uninterested in the client's transference reactions because they do not see them occurring in therapy. The therapist will often miss the client's transference reactions, and the important information they provide, unless the therapist actively attempts to draw them out. How can the therapist elicit the client's transference reactions so they can be utilized in therapy? Two ways of accomplishing this are suggested in the following discussion.

First, the therapist should find tactful but direct ways to inquire about the client's feelings and reactions toward the therapist. For example, we have already seen that it is important for both therapists and clients to learn about the client's reactions to being a client and seeking help. It is even more important to learn about the client's perceptions of and feelings toward the therapist when dynamically laden issues are being addressed. Although the sample questions that follow will not be productive if they come out of the blue, they can provide a wealth of new information if they are well-timed and integrated into the ongoing discussion:

> As you were driving to our session today, how did you feel about coming to see me?
> When you find yourself thinking about therapy, what kind of thoughts do you have about me?
> What are you feeling toward me right now as we talk about this sensitive issue?

Second, the therapist should also explore what the client projects onto the therapist. That is, the therapist should ask:

> What do you think I am feeling toward you as you tell me that?
> How do you think I am going to respond to you if you do that?
> What do you think I expect you to do in that situation?

It is threatening for most beginning therapists to break the social norms they grew up with and address the client's feelings about the therapist so forthrightly. But feelings can be addressed sensitively and respectfully, yet still directly. If therapists take this risk and use these lines of questioning, clients' transference reactions will be made overt, and the therapist will be able to work with clients in an immediate, powerful way.

It is often difficult for beginning therapists to believe that clients have many significant feelings toward them that have little to do with the reality of who they are. However, important unspoken fears, concerns, and wishes are operating. If these issues are not addressed, they will influence the therapeutic relationship in significant but covert ways. If beginning therapists try to elicit the client's subjective reactions toward and projections of the therapist, important new information about the client's central conflicts will be revealed.

In Chapter 4, we discussed how adopting an internal focus will uncover new conflicts that would not have surfaced otherwise. In the same way, exploring clients' reactions toward the therapist will also reveal new issues that need to be dealt with in treatment. Furthermore, this approach will also show how the same problems that clients are having with others, and that they originally experienced in formative family relationships, are being recapitulated in the therapeutic relationship. Thus, transference reactions reveal clients' generic conflicts and, as we will see in the following chapters, provide an opportunity to resolve them in the therapeutic relationship.

In addition to clarifying conflicts, transference reactions also reflect the fact that the client's feelings are trustworthy. The client's emotional reactions may not make sense at first because they often do not fit the current situation in which they are aroused. As a result, many clients experience their emotions as irrational and do not trust their own internal processes. This is especially likely to occur in the therapeutic relationship in which clients have many emotional reactions toward the therapist that seem uncalled for, exaggerated, inappropriate, or unrealistic.

The client's emotional reactions in general, and toward the therapist in particular, are not irrational. Many times they do not fit the present circumstances, but they do make sense when they can be placed within their original learning context. That is, real-life events have legitimately caused clients to feel the way they do. If the therapist helps clients trace back their feelings to the original learning source, they will prove to be an *appropriate* reaction to someone else in another time and place. Although this may seem paradoxical at first, *transference reactions ultimately reveal that the client's feelings always make sense.*

In sum, clients transfer emotional reactions from past formative relationships onto the current relationship with the therapist. Helping clients understand where their emotional reactions originally stem from is a powerful intervention that leaves clients feeling in control of themselves. Finding that their feelings do make sense, even though in another time and place, is validating and empowers clients. Furthermore, making this connection between the past and the present is one way to leave the past behind so that new ways of responding can emerge.

OPTIMUM INTERPERSONAL DISTANCE

Finally, to examine the last aspect of clients' current interpersonal functioning, we draw on the separateness-relatedness dialectic presented in Chapter 6 and apply it to the therapeutic relationship. In order to establish a relationship that is capable of producing change, therapists must have an effective degree of involvement with their clients. If the therapist is inappropriately close, it will not be safe for clients to take the risk of letting the therapist influence them. Similarly, if the therapist is too distant or removed, the relationship will not be significant enough to effect change. Thus, one of the most important process dimensions for therapists to monitor is the balance of separateness versus relatedness in the therapeutic relationship. We will see in what follows that at times, all therapists will have difficulty maintaining an optimum interpersonal distance with some clients. However, the single biggest problem facing most beginning therapists is finding an effective degree of closeness or involvement with their clients.

Enmeshment

At times, all therapists will become inappropriately overidentified with certain clients who hold particular symbolic meaning for them and who tap into the therapists' own issues and dynamics. Because of their own personality dynamics, however, some therapists will consistently become overinvolved with many of their clients. How can therapists recognize when they have become inappropriately overinvolved with a client rather than being appropriately involved in a concerned and available way? Whenever therapists find that they are angry or critical of a client for not changing, they are overly invested in the client. Therapists are also enmeshed when they have dreams about a client, often think about a client outside of the therapy session, feel depressed when a client is not changing, see the client as being just like themselves, or become envious or elated over positive changes in the client's life. This overinvolvement is different from care and concern for the client, which is appropriate and necessary. When enmeshment occurs, therapists usually need the client to change in order to meet their own needs, such as to shore up their own feelings of adequacy as a therapist or to manage their own internal conflicts that have been aroused by the client.

Substantial problems occur when therapists become overinvolved with a client. They tend to become controlling of the client and to inappropriately project their own personal conflicts onto the client. It is easy to see how this tends to recapitulate the client's conflict in the therapeutic relationship. For example, many clients have grown up in families with overly controlling or intrusive parents. When the therapist's own experiential range is too limited to encourage clients' own autonomy and allow them to experience their own controls and personal boundaries, the therapist is responding in the same problematic way as the parents. This reenactment with the therapist will prevent clients from being able to resolve their conflicts around intimacy and control.

Furthermore, when therapists become too close or overidentified they lose their ability to think objectively about the client. Therapists will have a heightened emotional reactivity to the client that will cloud their understanding of the client. When this occurs, the therapists' accurate empathy will be lost to a global, undifferentiated sympathy. Most important, therapists will not be able to discriminate the differences between themselves and the client that inevitably exist, and therapists will begin to see the client as being just like themselves. Although this closeness or sameness may be reassuring to clients at first, enduring change will not occur in an enmeshed relationship.

Disengagement

At times, all therapists will also hold themselves too far away from certain clients. This usually occurs when the client arouses the therapist's own personality conflicts. Also, some therapists will consistently err on the side of being too removed from most of their clients. This distance, which renders therapy ineffective, occurs because of the therapist's own enduring personality conflicts. When the therapist is not emotionally available to the client, therapy loses its intensity and becomes intellectualized. Therapists do not "feel with" the client, and they lose their intuition, empathy, and creativity. When this occurs, the client does not have the supportive relationship necessary to explore conflicted emotions. Psychotherapy is more than an intellectual discourse, and enduring personality change will not occur in an emotionally disengaged relationship. Without the impetus provided by genuine personal involvement, a corrective emotional experience will not occur.

Client conflicts will also be recapitulated in the therapeutic relationship when the therapist is too distant or uninvolved. For example, many clients had aloof, self-centered, or authoritarian parents who could not meet their childhood needs for emotional contact and support. A distant therapist will be safe for these clients because their anxieties over their unmet dependency needs—and their conflicts associated with being close to others—will not be aroused in the therapeutic relationship. Unfortunately, however, just as the client's conflicts are not aroused in a disengaged relationship, the opportunity to resolve these conflicts is lost as well. Thus, when therapists defend themselves against their own anxieties that are aroused by closer involvement with clients, many clients will not be able to change.

An Effective Middle Ground of Involvement

In order to be effective, the therapist must find an optimum middle ground of involvement. For several reasons, maintaining this effective middle ground of involvement throughout the course of therapy is one of the most challenging aspects of psychotherapy. First, therapists are repeatedly confronted with anxiety-arousing issues *in their own lives* by the affect-laden material that clients present. All therapists must become aware of how they tend to respond when clients arouse their own anxieties. For example, some therapists will become passive or withdraw from the client. Some therapists will distance themselves by intellectualizing the relationship, as in interpreting the client's affect before the client fully experiences it. Other therapists become controlling and overly directive, telling clients what they should do in a particular situation. Therapists must examine how they tend to respond when their own anxieties are aroused by the material that clients present and learn to hold these propensities in check.

In this regard, a useful exercise for beginning therapists is to write down or role play their initial reaction propensities in different anxiety-arousing situations. Some of these situations might include an angry client being critical of the therapist, a needy client asking to sit on the therapist's lap, or a competitive client questioning if the therapist is really bright enough to be of help. In small discussion groups of three or four, trainees can provide each other with feedback and share their observations of the other therapists' responses in these challenging situations.

Second, the balance between overinvolvement and underinvolvement is also difficult because clients often try to move their therapists along this continuum of involvement. Clients do this as an interpersonal strategy to defend against their conflicts. That is, when the therapist has been responding effectively, clients may become threatened by the anxiety-arousing material that begins to emerge for them. Clients will often defend against their own difficult emotions that are being aroused by creating either distance or enmeshment in the therapeutic relationship. For example, clients may try to bore the therapist or push the therapist away by talking about issues they are not really concerned about. Or clients may try to elicit too much involvement from the therapist, such as by exaggerating their distress and escalating their demands for help. Thus, forces both from within the therapist's own dynamics and from the client's defensive eliciting behaviors will pressure the therapist away from an effective middle ground of involvement.

Therapists who are able to maintain their own middle ground of involvement are more dependable and provide a more even therapy. There are no stormy ups and downs or lengthy impasses of emotional disengagement. It is also safer for the client to be vulnerable and trust when the therapist is consistently concerned and available without becoming controlling, unresponsive, or overreactive. Furthermore, if the therapist maintains an optimum interpersonal distance, the client does not have to be concerned about disappointing an overinvolved therapist. Nor, on the other hand, does the client have to elicit the attention or concern of an uninvolved therapist, which often recapitulates the client's generic conflict as well.

The important balance is for therapists to maintain their own objectivity and separateness while at the same time being available and responsive to the client. *Therapy is usually successful when the therapist can maintain this optimum interpersonal involvement throughout the course of therapy.* Conversely, therapy usually reaches an impasse and ends prematurely when the therapist and client become enmeshed or cannot emotionally connect with each other.

One exercise to help therapists recognize the process they are enacting with their clients is to consider the following questions after every session:

1. What are my feelings/reactions toward this client?
2. How do my feelings/reactions parallel those of significant others in the client's life?
3. What is the client doing to arouse such feelings/reactions in me, and how do these behaviors tie into my conceptualization of the client's generic conflict and interpersonal defenses?
4. Do my feelings/reactions typify my feelings/reactions to other clients and/or significant others in my life?

If therapists write answers to these questions after each session, it will ensure that they are attending to the process dimension. Asking themselves such questions will also help therapists discriminate their own countertransference reactions toward the client from the client's eliciting behaviors and interpersonal coping style.

In sum, all therapists will sometimes become locked in one of the extremes of over- or underinvolvement. However, beginning therapists are especially prone to become overidentified with their clients and see their clients' problems and lives as being too similar to their own. This is the most common way in which clients' conflicts come to be reenacted in the therapeutic process. It is discouraging for beginning therapists when their supervisors repeatedly point out how they are metaphorically reenacting the client's conflict in the way they are interacting. Beginning therapists must be patient with themselves and accept the fact that it is difficult to maintain this effective middle ground of involvement that safeguards against recapitulating the client's conflict. By gaining more clinical experience, examining one's own experiential range, and tracking the separateness-relatedness dialectic in the therapeutic relationship, beginning therapists will become increasingly capable of maintaining an optimum interpersonal distance.

When therapists do become over- or underinvolved, however, they must reestablish an effective middle ground with their clients. When therapists cannot realign the relationship on their own, they must consult with a colleague or supervisor. In fact, *the most productive use of supervision is to help therapists regain control of their own emotional reactions so that they can reestablish an effective degree of involvement.* Maintaining this optimum interpersonal distance is the best way to keep from recapitulating the client's conflict in the therapeutic relationship.

CLOSING

In this chapter, we examined four dimensions of clients' current interpersonal functioning: tracking clients' anxiety; the two-sided structure of clients' conflicts; how clients' conflicts are brought into the therapeutic relationship through eliciting maneuvers, testing behaviors, and transference reactions; and establishing an optimum interpersonal distance. This discussion may help therapists better understand their clients' self-defeating or contradictory behavior and their seemingly irrational feelings. In turn, this greater understanding may enable therapists to be more patient and compassionate toward the conflicts with which clients struggle. These interpersonal factors, together with the familial perspective and conceptual model presented in the previous two chapters, will enable therapists to better understand and intervene with the problems clients present.

With these conceptual guidelines in mind, we now return to intervention issues. The next chapter examines how the therapist can use a process approach in the therapeutic relationship to resolve clients' problems. However, in order to utilize the process dimension, transference reactions, or other interpersonal avenues, therapists must be able to talk directly with clients about what is going on in the client-therapist interaction. Because discussing this relationship is essential to interpersonal psychotherapy, and because doing so is threatening for many beginning therapists, Chapter 9 also explores therapists' fears about using process comments and addressing clients' conflicts in the therapeutic relationship.

SUGGESTIONS FOR FURTHER READING

1. Sullivan originally emphasized how clients' anxiety served to inform the therapist about their conflicts. His classic primer on interviewing, *The Psychiatric Interview* (New York: Norton, 1970), is still an illuminating clinical guide. Sullivan's interpersonal theory is presented in his book, *An Interpersonal Theory of Psychiatry* (New York: Norton, 1968). Both of these works are recommended to interpersonally oriented therapists.

2. Alice Miller's book, *Prisoners of Childhood* (New York: Basic Books, 1981), is also highly recommended. It will sensitize therapists to the developmental arrests and internalized conflicts that interfere with adult functioning.

3. Chapter 2 of Jay Haley's book, *Leaving Home* (New York: McGraw-Hill, 1980), elucidates the family dynamics and structural family relationships that impede individuation and emancipation for certain adult clients.

4. Readers are encouraged to learn more about clients' testing behavior (and the interesting theory of control/mastery) by reading Chapters 4 through 6 of "The Psychoanalytic Process" by J. Weiss and H. Sampson (New York: Guilford Press, 1986). Control/mastery theory is also clearly explicated in a popular press book, *Imaginary Crimes*, by L. Engel and T. Ferguson (Boston: Houghton Mifflin, 1990).

5. Margaret Mahler's developmental theory provides an invaluable

conceptual model for helping therapists establish an optimum interpersonal distance with their clients. The reader is strongly encouraged to read Chapter 6, "Rapprochement," of M. Mahler, F. Pine, and A. Bergman, *The Psychological Birth of the Human Infant: Symbiosis and Individuation* (New York: Basic Books, 1975).

6. Family systems concepts of cohesion and adaptability can also be used to describe an optimal interpersonal distance. Interested readers may examine D. H. Olson, et al., "Families: What Makes Them Work" (Newbury Park, CA: Sage, 1983).

RESOLUTION AND CHANGE

CHAPTER NINE

AN INTERPERSONAL SOLUTION

CONCEPTUAL OVERVIEW

Once the therapist has conceptualized the client's dynamics, how does change occur? Is the client's generic conflict resolved through an emotional catharsis of childhood traumas, from having unmet needs from different developmental stages fulfilled, or from delving into illuminating insights about the past? No. Although valuable information about client dynamics can be obtained from familial experience, a consistent focus on past experiences will not produce change. Understanding the past shows how and why the present is being approached and shaped the way it is. Resolution must be found in the current interchange with the therapist, however, not in reconstruction of the past. The primary reason for encouraging clients to explore the past at times is to illuminate their current ways of feeling and dealing with life. Further, a historical focus often serves only to defend clients against the anxiety of confronting current conflicts. Thus, the past can be brought to bear on current problems, but for change to occur, clients must enact a resolution of their conflicts in their current relationship with the therapist.

If the fulcrum of change is the current relationship with the therapist, what must the therapist do to help clients change? Does the therapist need to provide clients with "the love they never received?" Is the therapist's role to "reparent" the client? No. The therapist cannot satisfy clients' unmet developmental needs, although this fantasy will be activated for many clients. Instead, the therapist has a more modest, but attainable, goal. The therapist must provide a relationship that allows the client to undergo as an adult those feelings, needs, and experiences that were too threatening to confront as a child. We will see that when this occurs, and therapists provide clients with a more satisfying response to their conflicts than they have received in the past, enduring change occurs.

Furthermore, the client's developmental conflicts are not just talked about abstractly in therapy—they are brought into the present by being reenacted in the therapeutic relationship. In order to change, the therapist and client must not recapitulate the client's conflict in their interpersonal process, as so commonly occurs. Instead, they must mutually work out a resolution to the client's conflict in their real-life relationship. If this *corrective emotional experience* occurs, the therapist will be able to help the client generalize this emotional relearning to other arenas in the client's life in which the same conflicts are being enacted. Conversely, if the therapist and client only talk about issues and dynamics, but their interpersonal process does not enact a resolution of the conflicts they are discussing, change will not occur. The purpose of this chapter is to clarify this process dimension and show how the therapeutic relationship can be used to resolve client conflicts.

CHAPTER ORGANIZATION

The first section of this chapter addresses how the interpersonal process that therapists enact with clients can be used to resolve clients' conflicts. The first part of this section reviews the course of therapy up to this point in treatment and summarizes three ways in which client conflicts are brought into the treatment setting and reenacted with the therapist. The primary focus of this chapter then shows how therapists can use the process dimension to help clients resolve these conflicts. Five case studies illustrate this approach.

The second section examines why therapists are often reluctant to use process comments and address clients' conflicts in the therapeutic relationship. Therapists must be able to metacommunicate and work with the process dimension to provide a corrective emotional experience, but this approach is anxiety arousing for many beginning therapists. Six reasons why therapists avoid these direct interpersonal interventions are discussed, along with guidelines to help therapists do this more effectively.

THE INTERPERSONAL PROCESS MUST ENACT A RESOLUTION OF THE CLIENT'S CONFLICT
Client Conflicts Are Reenacted in the Therapeutic Relationship

Whereas the previous chapters in Part III focused on conceptualizing client dynamics, we now return to intervention strategies. Before going on to examine how therapists can use the process dimension to resolve conflicts, we will look at a brief overview of the course of therapy. This review serves to introduce the next stage of therapy and to place it within the overall context of the developmentally unfolding course of therapy.

Clients have unmet developmental needs that result in feelings that are too painful to be tolerated and integrated. Symptoms and problems develop as clients try to gain control of these emotions by manipulating or controlling their environment. The therapist's task is to identify these underlying conflicts and draw clients' attention to the compromise solutions they have adopted to avoid their internal conflicts. The therapist must then provide a supportive holding environment that allows clients to reexperience and integrate these threatening emotions rather than continuing to defend against them.

During the course of therapy, the therapist encourages clients to bring up for discussion the issues they feel are most important. The therapist's primary role is not to give advice, explain, reassure, self-disclose, or focus on the behavior or motives of others. Instead, the therapist follows the client's lead and listens for patterns, themes, and feelings that recur throughout the material the client presents. The therapist continues to focus the client inward, responds to the client's affect, and works to keep the client an active participant in the change process. As the therapist learns more about each client, the therapist will be able to conceptualize the generic conflicts and interpersonal coping styles that are expressed in the different issues and concerns that each client presents.

The therapist will be able to use this conceptual formulation to provide structure and direction to the course of therapy. For example, the therapist will be able to point out when and how clients employ their interpersonal coping strategy to rise above their conflicts. The therapist will also be able to help clients become aware of how they block their own needs and feelings by responding to themselves in the same way that others originally responded to them. The therapist will also be able to help clients explore why they become anxious at a particular time, what types of responses they tend to elicit from others, and how they systematically avoid a particular interpersonal mode or affect. In these ways, the therapist helps clients become aware of their underlying conflicts and the maladaptive ways they have learned to cope with them. Although this conceptual awareness will be an important part of helping clients change, something more is needed.

At the same time the therapist and client explore the *content* of the client's dynamics, the therapist and client will also play out these same dynamics in their *interpersonal process*. As stated before, the client and therapist do not just talk about conflicts in therapy, they actually relive them in the therapeutic relationship. This occurs in three ways.

First, *transference reactions* bring the client's generic conflict into the current relationship with the therapist. As the client's unmet developmental needs begin to emerge in therapy, the client will become concerned that the therapist has been responding, or is going to respond, in the same frustrating way that significant others have in the past. These fears and misperceptions of the therapist predictably occur, and therapy will reach an impasse until the therapist can differentiate her or his own current response from the frustrating responses that the client has received in the past.

Second, clients will systematically *elicit* responses from the therapist that recapitulate their conflict. That is, clients do not merely misperceive the therapist, they actually elicit responses from the therapist that metaphorically reenact their generic conflict. When therapy fails, clients have usually recapitulated their generic conflict in the therapeutic relationship by eliciting responses from the therapist that are dynamically similar to responses they have received from significant others in the past. These include responses from the therapist that may be rejecting, idealizing, sexualizing, competitive, controlling, abandoning, critical, hopeless, and so forth. Clients elicit these old problematic responses from the therapist for different reasons. At times, clients may do this for defensive reasons, to avoid their internal conflicts and maintain object ties. At other times, clients do this for more adaptive reasons, attempting to master their conflicts by testing to see if they can obtain a new and more satisfying response than they have received before.

Third, the *process* or manner in which therapists respond to clients may unwittingly reenact their conflicts in the therapeutic relationship. The relationship with the therapist must provide a more satisfying response to the client's conflict than the client has received in the past. It is difficult to provide this corrective emotional experience, however. Clients will expect, and often successfully elicit, the same hurtful responses from the therapist that they have received in the past. The task for therapists, then, is to identify how their interpersonal process may be reenacting the client's conflict and to use a process comment to make this interaction overt and a topic for discussion. The therapist and client can then work together to establish a different pattern of interaction that does not recapitulate the client's conflict. As stated before, however, it is far easier to understand this intellectually than it is to enact with clients.

Thus, if it is to lead to change, the therapeutic process must enact a resolution of the client's conflict rather than a repetition of it. When this occurs, clients have received far more than just an explanation for their problems. They have *experienced* a meaningful relationship in which their old conflicts have been aroused, but they have received a more satisfying response from the therapist that provides a resolution of their conflict.

Once the client has the real-life experience that change can occur, the therapist can help the client generalize this corrective emotional experience to other arenas in which similar conflicts are being enacted. This final *working through* phase of treatment will be discussed in the next chapter. With this overview of the change process in mind, we will now examine more closely how therapists can use the interpersonal process they enact with their clients to resolve conflicts.

Using the Process Dimension to Resolve Conflicts

Clients must experience a new and more satisfying response to their conflicts in their relationship with the therapist. To provide this, it is not enough for therapists to listen empathically, give interpretations, or facilitate client insights about the historical roots of problems. Nor is it enough to train and direct clients to try out new, more adaptive responses in their environment. Although these and other interventions are certainly useful, they are often insufficient to produce enduring change.

In addition, clients must experience a relationship with the therapist in which their old conflicts are aroused but the therapist does not respond in the same problematic way that others have in the past. This is easy to say but deceptively difficult to do. Therapists commonly fail to recognize how they are reenacting the client's conflict in their interpersonal process. In the three ways noted above, clients do not just talk about their problems in the abstract, they actually reenact the same conflicts they are discussing with the therapist in their interpersonal process. When therapy fails, the therapeutic process has usually reenacted the same conflict that the client has been struggling with in other relationships and that originally brought the client to therapy.

Through transference reactions, testing behavior and eliciting phenomenon, there is a strong propensity for the therapeutic process to recapitulate the client's generic conflict. As we will see below, it challenges the therapist's own personhood to enact a solution to the client's conflict rather than a repetition of it. Below, five different case examples highlight the process dimension.

Example 1: It Is Difficult for Therapists to Recognize the Process When They Are Participating in It. The first example below summarizes an ineffective therapeutic relationship. This brief case summary illustrates how difficult it can be for therapists to recognize the interpersonal process they enact with their own clients. It is easy for therapists to understand the process dimension conceptually and relatively easy to identify when a client's conflict is being reenacted with another therapist. However, with their own clients, it is far more difficult for therapists to recognize how the interpersonal process is recapitulating the conflict.

An alcoholic client began therapy by expressing how much pain he was in as a result of his drinking problem. His wife was threatening to leave him, and he was on probation at work. His 8-year-old son had recently seen him in an embarrassing situation while intoxicated and had asked him not to drink anymore. The client was distraught that even though the structure of his life was collapsing, he could not stop drinking. During their first session the client sobbed, "Nothing ever works out; everything I try to do falls apart in the end."

The therapist was moved by the client's plight, but unfortunately, she became overinvested in helping him change. The therapist found it difficult to listen to how hopeless he sounded, and she kept reassuring him that things would get better. The therapist disclosed that she had had a serious drinking problem of her own many years ago and that she knew just what he needed to do in order to stop drinking. The therapist and client quickly established a friendly relationship in which the client successfully elicited a great deal of nurturance from the responsive therapist. The client enjoyed this support immensely and sincerely tried to follow the therapist's advice and suggestions.

Things went better for about a month, but then the client fell off the wagon and began drinking heavily again. When he started arriving late for his therapy sessions, and then missing several of them, the therapist began to feel let down. It was the final straw for the therapist when the client arrived for therapy intoxicated. The therapist felt angry and betrayed because she had extended herself to him more than she usually did with other clients. She felt that he was letting them both down and told him so. In this way, the therapist became punitive toward the client, and she also induced guilt over the impact of his "irresponsible" drinking on his family. The client was contrite and tried, unsuccessfully, to elicit her sympathy and support again. The client did not show up for his next appointment, however, and did not return to therapy.

This interaction recapitulated the client's conflict in two ways. First, the client initially elicited a promise of love and support from the therapist, but the therapist eventually turned to criticism and control. This confirmed the client's disillusionment that "nothing ever works out; relationships all go bad," about which he had forewarned the therapist during their first session. Second, the therapist benevolently tried to rescue this client, who was behaving as a victim. The caretaking, advice-giving response from the therapist inadvertently defined the client as being incapable of managing his own life. Unfortunately, this response paralleled a similarly diminishing attitude that the client had received from his indulgent, but belittling, parent. The rescuer-victim process that was enacted in therapy prevented the client from addressing his real conflicts over adequacy, achievement, and commitment, which he defended against, in part, through drinking.

In reviewing this case several weeks later, the therapist reported that "the client just wasn't ready to stop drinking yet. He's going to have to get worse and really hit bottom before he'll be able to admit there's a problem and do something about it." The well-intentioned therapist did not recognize that the interpersonal process they had enacted in their relationship unwittingly recapitulated the client's conflict and prevented change from occurring. As often occurs when therapy fails, the therapist only attended to the content of what they talked about and not to how their process might be recapitulating the client's conflicts.

From an emotionally neutral vantage point—such as that of supervising a student or looking at a colleague's therapy session on videotape—it is relatively easy to see how the client's conflicts have been reenacted in the interpersonal process. In humbling contrast, it can be exasperatingly difficult to see one's own interpersonal process while engaged in an intense, affect-laden relationship. This is true for the well-seasoned expert and especially apt for the novice clinician. Beginning therapists will repeatedly reenact the client's conflict in their interpersonal process without realizing that this reenactment is occurring. It is difficult to learn to shift one's perceptions from the content level to the process level. Beginning therapists must be patient with themselves and know that the ability to recognize and respond to the process level is acquired slowly. Further reading on this topic is critical in helping therapists learn a process-oriented approach. In "Suggestions for Further Reading," at the end of this chapter, two readings dealing with how therapists can metacommunicate with clients and work with the process dimension are included.

Example 2: Process Comments Can Keep Therapists from Recapitulating the Conflict. In the previous example, the therapeutic process recapitulated the client's conflict. In the next example, a similar dynamic begins. Initially, a depressed client elicits the same critical and rejecting responses from the therapist that he has received in earlier formative relationships. In this case, however, the therapist recognizes their interpersonal process. By using a process comment to describe their current interaction, the therapist effectively realigns this maladaptive pattern of interaction.

Many clients enter therapy because of depression. These clients feel sad, believe they are bad, and act powerless to change their circumstances. In many cases, these clients communicate their very real suffering to the therapist with emotional pleas for help. Yet whatever the therapist tries to do or suggest does not work. Often, the therapist's efforts to meet the client's request for help are met with "Yes, but . . . " A problematic cycle begins in which the client feels increasingly desperate and intensifies his emotional pleas for help. For example, the client might exclaim, "I can't go on living if things don't change soon!" In response to the client's escalating distress, the concerned therapist becomes more active and tries even harder to respond in some helpful way. However, nothing the therapist does has any impact or provides any relief for the client.

As the client rejects the help elicited, the therapist's own needs to help are frustrated. In some cases, the therapist's own sense of adequacy as a helping person will be threatened. When this occurs, *the client's eliciting behavior has tapped into the therapist's own issues and dynamics.* In response to this, some therapists will become punitive and critical toward the client, whereas others will withdraw and emotionally disengage. When this occurs, the therapeutic process thematically repeats similar conflicted interactions that the client has experienced in the past and has not been able to resolve in other current relationships.

When therapy is unsuccessful, the therapist usually remains critical toward or disengaged from this "impossible" client. The depressed client's conflict is recapitulated as the client again feels dependent on a relationship with someone who is critical, inconsistently available, or threatening to terminate the relationship and abandon him or her. What is the alternative? In successful therapy, the therapist is able to make a process comment and describe or inquire about what is going on between them in their present interaction. Rather than focus on the *content* of what they are talking about (for example, depression), the therapist can point out *how* they are responding to each other. This is a very effective way to see and change the maladaptive, repetitive pattern of interaction. For example, the therapist might respond:

> Let's talk about what is going on between us right now and see if we can understand what's happening in our relationship. It seems to me that you keep asking me for help, but keep saying "Yes, but . . . " and don't ever allow me to help you. I think that I get frustrated with you then and become more demanding of you. What do you see going on between us?

With a process comment of this type, the therapist is joining with the client in trying to understand their mutual interaction. The therapist is responding to the client's need by helping the client look at the depression and how it is expressed to others. The process comment has also allowed the therapist to break the cycle of escalating client need and therapist frustration, at least temporarily.

How does this help clients change? In this example, the client is *experiencing* a relationship with the therapist that provides a new and different solution to an old and problematic pattern of interaction. The client is not rejected or abandoned, as has happened in the past, but remains engaged in a relationship with someone who consistently responds to the client's concerns. The client has not experienced this consistency, availability, or acceptance in past relationships. If this *corrective emotional experience* is repeated in many other big and small ways throughout the course of treatment, the client is experiencing a resolution of the conflict in the relationship with the therapist. When clients have the *experience* of change, rather than being advised what to do, being reassured, or having their behavior interpreted, they are better prepared to make enduring changes.

A key concept in the interpersonal process approach is that the capacity for change is fueled by the personal significance that the therapeutic relationship holds for the client. When an interpersonal solution is enacted in a meaningful relationship with the therapist, change is facilitated in two ways. First, in the context of this new type of relationship, clients can now approach the conflicted feelings that accompany their original unmet needs. In other words, clients have the supportive relationship necessary to undergo those experiences that were too threatening to be dealt with in childhood, rather than having to continue to defend against them. Second, the experience of change with the therapist *shows* clients, rather than merely telling them, that current relationships can be different and more satisfying than formative relationships have been in the past.

An example is provided by continuing the previous dialogue with the depressed client:

Client:
Yeah, I do keep saying "Yes, but . . . " to you. That's terrible—if I'm doing that with you too, then there's no way I can get better. Should we just stop now?

Therapist:
Oh no! It makes sense that you are having the same problems in here with me that you have with other people. In a way, it is a problem, but in another way, it gives us the opportunity to resolve your problem right here in our relationship.

Client:
How?

Therapist:
If you and I can work out a different kind of relationship than you have had in the past, one that doesn't repeat this same old pattern, I think it will go a long way toward helping you change.

Client:
Do you think we can do that now if we haven't been able to up to this point?

Therapist:
Yes, I think it's very possible. In fact, I think we are breaking that pattern right now, just by talking about the way we interact together. Tell me, how is it to be talking with me about our relationship and the way we respond to each other?

Client:
I like it. It's different.

Therapist:
I like it too. I feel like I'm working with you, rather than being pushed away as I was feeling before.

In this example, the therapist has used a process comment to effectively alter the current interaction with the client. For the moment, the process comment has kept their interaction from recapitulating the client's conflict.

Some variation on the old "Yes, but . . . " pattern will probably soon reappear, and the therapist will have to make another process comment and work through a similar cycle again. In this way, however, the therapist is temporarily providing the client with a different response that does not recapitulate the client's conflict. If the therapist continues to find ways to provide this response throughout the course of treatment, the client will experience a corrective relationship and change will occur. The next example shifts from this single, time-limited interaction to a macroperspective that tracks the process dimension over the course of therapy.

Example 3: The Process Dimension Bridges Differing Theoretical Orientations.

Therapists with different personalities and therapists working from different theoretical orientations can all help clients change. Every theoretical approach clarifies some important aspects of client problems. The greater component of change, therefore, is less the personality and theoretical orientation of the therapist than the nature of the relationship that the therapist provides the client. Change is likely to occur whenever the way in which the therapist and client interact provides a resolution of the client's conflicts rather than a repetition of them.

After two years in analytically oriented therapy, Mrs. Jones still could not take charge of her life. She was always complying with her husband's demands, and it was impossible for her to tell her children what to do and have them obey her. She also complained of her stultifying daily routine as a housewife, yet she was never able to do anything to improve it. At her husband's behest, she would periodically enroll in a class or interview for an office job, but she was never able to follow through on any of his suggestions.

In therapy, Mrs. Jones had spent many hours reviewing her childhood. Her therapist had an uncanny ability to see the same unifying themes in many of the memories and recollections she shared with him. For example, her therapist repeatedly observed how she was subtly discouraged from initiating activities on her own or was not allowed to feel good about a success experience during childhood. Anytime she did something well as a child, her parents did not notice it or seem very happy about it if they did.

Mrs. Jones's therapist once explained to her, in a sensitive and informative way, that she had a passive-dependent personality style. Mrs. Jones was impressed that her therapist seemed to understand her so well. He knew so many things about her without her even having to tell him. Although her problems had not changed much yet, she still believed her therapist would cure her. He was so bright and insightful, and he genuinely seemed to care about her as well. And even though he did not like to tell her what to do, when things became too much, he could usually help by explaining what the problem really meant. It was so comforting to be with him; Mrs. Jones did not know what she would do without him.

It was Mrs. Jones's husband who finally ran out of patience with the slow course of treatment. After two years, he was fed up with the big therapy bills and his wife's unremitting discontent. His wife's helpless dissatisfaction felt like a subtle but unending demand for him to love her more, give her more, or somehow fill up her life. He was tired of these subtle, nagging demands, and he wanted a change now.

Mr. Jones was a man of action in his work, and he was not going to acquiesce to this way of life any longer. He obtained the name of a behaviorally oriented therapist on the faculty of a nearby college. A friend had told Mr. Jones that this therapist was a "problem-solving realist" who could make things happen fast. This sounded like just the right approach to him. Mr. Jones insisted that his wife stop treatment with her present therapist and begin immediately with the new therapist. Mrs. Jones was panicked at the thought of leaving her therapist, but she sensed that her husband was truly at the end of his rope. Although she still believed in her therapist and felt very close to him, she was afraid that her husband might actually leave her if she did not do what he said.

After her first few sessions with the new therapist, Mrs. Jones was surprised to think that perhaps her husband had been right after all. The new therapist wasted no time in taking charge of the situation. It was exciting to have the therapist outline specific steps for her to follow, and it was sensible to have a specific plan laid out for how she was going to change. The therapist discussed a list of treatment goals with her, and they planned a set of graduated steps for meeting these goals on a scheduled timetable.

In their first hour together, the therapist had Mrs. Jones role play how she responded to her children when they disobeyed her. Then, with the therapist serving as a model and coach, they rehearsed more assertive responses that Mrs. Jones could try with her children. The therapist also had Mrs. Jones enroll in an assertion training class the therapist was running for some of her other female clients. Each week Mrs. Jones was also to complete a homework assignment. For the first week, she was to call up one new person she might like to develop a friendship with and ask her to lunch. She was supposed to report back to the therapist on this assignment at the beginning of their next appointment.

Mr. Jones was encouraged by this practical, problem-solving approach to his wife's problems. He began to think that something might change after all. Mrs. Jones was hopeful too. She felt reassured by her new therapist's goal-oriented, problem-solving approach. In fact, Mrs. Jones became determined to be the best client her therapist ever had and promised herself that she was going to do *everything* the therapist asked her to do.

Therapy progressed well for the first few weeks, but then things started to slow down again. Although she did not really know why, Mrs. Jones began to find it hard to muster the energy to attend the new class she had signed up for. She knew her therapist would be disappointed in her for not doing what she was "supposed to do," but she just could not help it. Although she felt guilty about it, Mrs. Jones began missing her therapy sessions.

Although both of these therapists were capable of helping Mrs. Jones, they both failed to have a significant impact on her problems. They were both unsuccessful even though they used seemingly very different treatment approaches. Theoretically, the analytically oriented therapist might attribute the unsuccessful outcome to the great difficulty in restructuring the passive dependency needs of a basic oral character. The behaviorist might note that Mrs. Jones was not sufficiently motivated to change because she was receiving too many secondary gains from her help-seeking behavior. If we look at the interpersonal process that transpired between both therapists and the client, however, a very different picture emerges. These two therapists actually responded in a very similar (and problematic) way to Mrs. Jones.

We must look carefully at what Mrs. Jones *experienced* in therapy. With both therapists, Mrs. Jones reenacted the same maladaptive pattern that she had with her children and with her husband. Her presenting problem was that her children ran over her and she could not make them listen to her or obey her. Her compliance with her take-charge husband was a profound example of the same problem. Therapy failed in this case because her pattern of being passive and compliant recurred in the process that was enacted with both therapists. Unwittingly, both therapists provided a relationship in which she remained the passive helpee vis-à-vis the leader-helper. This interpersonal process reinforced her feeling that the source of strength and problem resolution did not reside in her but in the therapist.

In order for Mrs. Jones to change, she would need to experience a therapeutic relationship in which she did not feel one down to a benevolent authority who held the power to solve her problems. Rather, she had to feel that the ability rested within herself to initiate, gain control over her own life, and resolve conflicts. Then her own strengths and resources could be utilized, along with the therapist's skill, in a more collaborative relationship.

Unfortunately, both of her therapists were comfortable with the helper-helpee relational process and did not bring it up as a focus for treatment. Neither therapist made the process comment that, in certain ways, their interaction repeated the same conflict and interpersonal style that was problematic for Mrs. Jones in other relationships. A process comment like this would have allowed Mrs. Jones to look at her problematic behavior in a supportive environment. More important, it would have given her permission to change her passive/compliant style and become more forceful and autonomous *in her relationship with the therapist.*

As long as the therapists were telling her what to do, Mrs. Jones could not set limits with her children, take a more assertive stance with her husband, or follow through and do what she wanted to do for herself. That is, the content of what she discussed with both therapists (issues about autonomy, independence, assertiveness) was not matched by the interpersonal process they enacted. Unless Mrs. Jones has the actual experience of behaving as an active, strong participant in her relationship with the therapist, she will not be able to adopt this healthy, stronger stance in other areas of her life. *That is, the process must be congruent with the content.*

This is not a simple task for the therapist, however. To enact a more egalitarian, collaborative relationship with someone like Mrs. Jones requires therapeutic skill and careful monitoring of the process. Mrs. Jones is an accomplished master at getting therapists, husbands, children, and others to lead, direct, and control her. Both the behaviorally and analytically oriented therapists could have been helpful to Mrs. Jones if they had enacted a different process in their relationship. If they had encouraged her to initiate and lead—rather than directing her—Mrs. Jones's central conflict would have emerged in the therapeutic relationship. That is, Mrs. Jones would have become anxious as soon as either of the therapists encouraged her to behave more assertively and competently *in the therapeutic relationship*. Either therapist then could have focused her inward on this anxiety and examined why it was threatening for her to step out of her dependent/compliant mode. Simultaneously, either therapist could have given her permission to act more assertively and competently within the therapeutic relationship and worked with her in a way that facilitated this new behavior in the sessions. Instead, Mrs. Jones continued to defend against her anxiety over being assertive/effective by retreating to her dependent help-seeking role, and both therapists reenacted this conflict with her.

In most therapeutic relationships, the therapist and client will temporarily reenact the client's generic conflict in their interpersonal process. In successful therapy of every theoretical orientation, however, the therapist and client do not continue to reenact the old pattern. Instead, they are able to identify this process and work out a different type of relationship that resolves, rather than reenacts, the client's conflict. Once clients find that their old conflicts can be confronted but that they do not have to result in the same hurtful or frustrating outcomes, clients are able to generalize this relearning to other relationships as well.

Example 4: Working with Process Allows Conflicts to Be Resolved in the Therapeutic Relationship.

Beginning therapists often feel pressured to "do" something to help their clients. This urgency may lead therapists to a premature emphasis on intervention techniques before they understand the interpersonal process that is occurring. Without first conceptualizing what is transpiring between the therapist and client in terms of the client's broader dynamics, intervention techniques will often fail. In contrast, when the therapist understands what is occurring in the therapeutic relationship, it is usually relatively easy to find effective ways to intervene. When therapists understand the corrective interpersonal experiences that clients need to undergo in therapy, they can readily intervene with a variety of techniques from different theoretical approaches (see Wachtel, 1982). Therapists can employ a diversity of techniques from different modalities, evaluate their effectiveness, and modify them to better fit the particular client. Thus, beginning therapists should repeatedly ask themselves "What does this mean?" rather than "What should I do?" As we will see below, the second question is readily answered by the first.

In the following example, two critical incidents are summarized from the treatment of an incest victim. In both incidents, the therapist uses intervention techniques that have a highly significant impact on the client. It is not the intervention techniques per se (validating the resistance and role play) that facilitate change, however. Both interventions are effective because they follow from the therapist's understanding of how the client's dynamics are being expressed in the current interaction and because the therapist is able to work with these dynamics in the here-and-now immediacy of the client-therapist relationship.

Based on her presenting symptoms, Sandy's male therapist hypothesized that she was probably an incest victim and anticipated that trust would be a central issue in their relationship. Therapy had gotten off to a good start, but several months into treatment, progress began to slow down. The material that Sandy presented was becoming repetitious, and therapy was not progressing as well as it had been. About this same time, Sandy recounted two different stories in which the relational theme was feeling unsafe with men. The therapist hypothesized that Sandy was using these stories to talk indirectly to him about trust in their relationship, and that her profound concerns about safety, betrayal, and vulnerability were now being activated with him.

The therapist began to talk with Sandy about trust in their relationship and asked about the different feelings she was having toward him. Sandy genuinely liked the therapist and was finding him very helpful. However, when the therapist pursued the trust issue further and asked specifically whether she felt "safe" with him, her affirmative response seemed distant and unconnected. It soon became clear to both of them that Sandy was emotionally removing herself from the therapist as they talked more directly about safety in their relationship.

The therapist responded to Sandy's concern by accepting both sides of her feelings and tieing her concerns directly to their relationship by saying: "I know that one part of you likes and trusts me, but another part of you doesn't feel safe at all. I think that both sides of your feelings toward me make sense and are important for us to work with." Sandy sheepishly nodded and gestured vaguely to indicate that this was true.

Rather than trying to talk her out of these concerns or convince her of his trustworthiness, however, the therapist validated her distrust and went on to expand it more fully: "If I violated your trust in some way after you had taken the risk to ask me to help you, it would be very bad for you. If I tried to approach you sexually or foster any other kind of relationship between us, it would hurt you very much. In fact, I think it would hurt you so much that you would not be able to risk trusting or asking for help again."

Sandy began tearing, looked at the therapist, and slowly nodded in agreement. The therapist continued to elaborate her concern in terms of their relationship: "If I took advantage of our relationship, you would be without hope. I think you would again get very depressed, enter into other relationships that would be destructive for you, and start thinking seriously again that you do not want to be alive."

As the therapist spoke and made Sandy's concern overt in terms of their relationship, her whole demeanor changed. She remained tearful but became alert and present with him, agreeing with what he was saying. As they continued to talk together about this, the therapist went on to say: "I understand how much it would hurt you if I betrayed your trust, and no part of me wants you to have that terrible experience again. In fact, I *like* the part of you that doesn't trust me. That distrustful, removed part of you is your friend and ally. We need her—because she is committed to not letting you get hurt again. That's why it's so important that we go at your speed in here, that you have control over what we talk about, and that you can say no to me and know that I will honor your limits."

After responding affirmingly to her "resistance" and working with this conflict in terms of their relationship, important changes occurred. Over the next six weeks, Sandy began to recall her childhood abuse. In the past she had only alluded to it vaguely. Now, for the first time, she recalled in vivid detail and with strong emotions how she had been repeatedly sexually abused over a period of years by her stepbrother, who was twelve years older. When she went to her mother for help, she was punitive, denied that the abuse was occurring, and told Sandy never to talk about anything like that again. Sandy did not even consider seeking protection from her stepfather, who had always been distant and unresponsive. After failing to receive help, Sandy poignantly recalled spending much time sitting alone on the floor of her closet with the door closed, feeling afraid, ashamed, and deeply alone. In response to this deep sharing, the therapist was comforting, validated her experience, and began to help her with the many significant connections she began to make between this family pathology and her current life.

During one of these sessions when Sandy was recapturing the experience of her childhood abuse, the therapist used a role-playing technique to provide a different response to the trauma she had suffered. The therapist said: "I wish someone could have been there to stop him and protect you. No one was there for you, but if I had been there, I would have walked into your bedroom when he was there, turned on the light, and in a loud voice commanded: 'Stop it! Get away from her and leave her alone right now! I see what you're doing and it's not fair. You're hurting her and I won't allow it.' "

After speaking this loudly and forcefully, as if he were actually saying it to the perpetrator, the therapist stood up and rolled Sandy's coat into a ball. Using it as a little Sandy doll, he held it close and said reassuringly: "You're safe now, and he's gone for good. I'm going to call the police now, and keep protecting you so that you'll never have to worry about him hurting you again."

By symbolically giving Sandy the response that she desperately longed for—but did not get—as a little girl, the full intensity of her pain and rage was evoked. When these powerful feelings ran their course, Sandy became more composed and said, "I'm going to be all right." The therapist, still holding the rolled-up jacket tenderly, carefully tucked it in Sandy's arms and said: "This is the little girl you were. She needs you to open up your heart to her and give her a home. You need to take care of her—and not push her away anymore like they did and you have done. You need to hold her, talk to her, and listen carefully to what she tells you. I want you to join me in taking care of this part of you, so this little girl is no longer hurt and alone behind the closet door."

Sandy readily accepted this responsibility, and later bought a doll that she used to represent the part of her that needed to be cared for but had not been protected. Although all of Sandy's problems did not go away, significant, long-standing symptoms disappeared and did not return.

Sandy had been anxious, withdrawn, and depressed in her early 20s, but now in her late 30s she had been increasingly anxious, dependent, and almost incapable of leaving home alone. However, two weeks after this session, Sandy got her driver's license and began driving for the first time in six years. Soon afterward, she got a job as a waitress—her first paid employment in over ten years. Although she had always foiled any type of success for herself, she enrolled in a local college and began receiving predominantly A's in all of her classes. Whereas Sandy felt helpless, characteristically acted as a victim, and was repeatedly taken advantage of by others, she now became more assertive, forthright, and independent.

What allowed Sandy to get stronger in these very significant ways? Several factors made this therapeutic intervention effective. By using a role-playing technique, the therapist brought Sandy's conflict into the therapeutic relationship and provided her with the corrective interpersonal responses she needed. In sharp contrast to what occurred in her family, this time Sandy experienced protection, validation, appropriate boundaries, and a supportive holding environment. The therapist's compassionate and protective response also helped Sandy shift from an identification with her parent's rejection of her and her own resulting shame and self-hatred to an identification with the therapist and his compassion for her predicament, which eventually led her to be able to care for herself and feel that she did matter for the first time in her life. These far-reaching consequences were set in motion by the therapist's confirming and comforting response to Sandy's vulnerability. By providing this experience in the immediacy of their relationship, even though it was just enacted in fantasy, Sandy received a corrective emotional experience that allowed her to become stronger and capable of protecting herself for the first time.

Example 5: The Process Dimension Shapes All Interpersonal Relations. As we have seen, the most likely reason for therapy to fail is because the therapist and client reenact the client's conflict in their interpersonal process. Because beginning therapists are not used to tracking the process dimension, it is difficult to recognize how the process may be reenacting the client's conflict. In order to highlight the process dimension and help discriminate the process that is enacted from the content that is discussed, the next illustration utilizes an example from outside of the arena of psychotherapy. The following example is taken from an athletic event that actually occurred. In this very different setting, however, we will see that the interpersonal process dimension can still be observed.

It is the championship game and two basketball teams are competing fiercely for the league title. One team is the defending champion from last year—a mature and confident team. The opposing team is the underdog—a team made up of talented but younger players who are far less experienced. The defending champions are heavily favored to win this game and repeat as champions. They have been here before and have already proven that they can withstand the pressure necessary to win championship games.

It is late in the fourth quarter, and the game is tied. The fans are on their feet, cheering at the prospect of an upset. The coach of the young team can feel that the game is about to slip away, however. His players are becoming rattled by the screaming fans, the advancing clock that now makes every mistake critical, and the unrelenting play of the opponents. To help compose his inexperienced players, the coach calls a two-minute time-out. His team has played well up to this point, but the seasoned coach knows that in these closing, pressure-packed minutes, the other team's experience is likely to make the difference.

Crouched on the sideline, the coach positions his five players in a semi-circle in front of him. With the roaring crowd only a few feet away, the coach quietly makes eye contact with the first player on his left. Without speaking, he calmly holds the first player's gaze for about 12 to 15 seconds (a very long time amidst such pandemonium). Having compelled the first player's attention, the coach turns to the second player and maintains eye contact with him for another 12 to 15 seconds, and so on with each of the five players. Each time, as he turns to engage the next player, the previous player's attention remains riveted on the coach. Finally, after making contact with each player in this way, the coach holds up a chalkboard with one word written on it: "POISE."

The players and coach sit together silently for the remaining seconds of the time-out. The referee blows his whistle, the players return to the court, and the underdogs defeat the defending champions. The players did not make mental or emotional errors in the closing minutes of the game: they did not turn the ball over to the other team, they made clutch free throws in the final seconds of the game, and they smoothly executed the plays they had practiced all year. In a word, they played with "poise."

This coach astutely identified the central issue that could defeat his team in the final minutes—being intimidated by a more confident and experienced team, losing their composure, and making mental mistakes that would cost them the game. Having recognized the central issue, however, the coach did not just *tell* his team that they had to remain poised in the final minutes in order to win. Instead of telling them what they should feel, he gave them the *experience* of composure during the time-out. The players were able to finish the game with such composure because the coach used the relationship he had developed with each of his players to give them the experience of composure during the final tense minutes. Having felt composed during the time-out, the players were able to generalize this experience to their performance on the court and play with "poise."

Similarly, it is far more effective if the therapist-client interaction provides an experience of change than if the therapist merely tells the client what to do or explains what something means. It is often difficult to provide a relationship that enacts a resolution of clients' conflicts, however, and there are no easy formulas that tell the therapist how to enact this with different clients, all of whom are unique. Thus, the therapist must take the personal risk of entering into a significant emotional relationship with each client and have the flexibility to provide the interpersonal experience that each client needs in order to change.

THERAPISTS MUST WORK WITH CLIENTS' CONFLICTS IN THE THERAPEUTIC RELATIONSHIP

So far, this text has presented numerous interpersonal processes to help therapists conceptualize and intervene with clients' problems. The purpose of this section is to highlight more fully one central feature underlying all these interpersonal processes. An essential element of interpersonal psychotherapy is to address how clients' conflicts are expressed in the therapist-client interaction. These conflicts can then be resolved, in part, by working together to find new ways to relate that resolve, rather than reenact, clients' problematic relational patterns that originated in the past. For example, the therapist begins this process by asking the client to explore how his extratherapeutic problems may be occurring in their relationship: "How does this control battle you have been describing with your wife go on between us? Where do you see the control issue in our relationship?"

By bringing the client's conflicts directly into the therapeutic relationship in this way, the therapist creates the opportunity for a corrective emotional experience. For this client to change, he must find that the therapist is neither trying to control him nor able to be controlled by him, as occurs in the client's other relationships. Only if the client has this real-life experience of change can he resolve his conflict, find that control can be shared in close relationships, and learn that some relationships can be different than those in the past. Although this immediate, real-life experience of change is a powerful way to intervene, it is threatening for most beginning therapists to "talk about you and me." Thus, the purpose of this section is to help therapists take this risk and judiciously use their real-life client-therapist relationships to help clients change.

The first part of this section reviews how therapists have already been asked to bring clients' problems into the therapeutic relationship and work with them in terms of the current client-therapist interaction. The second section examines why this process is anxiety arousing for therapists and offers guidelines to help therapists do this more effectively.

Intervening Within the Therapeutic Relationship

To some extent, most of the interventions discussed so far have asked the therapist to work on the client's issues within the context of the therapist-client relationship. To review, at the beginning of treatment therapists were encouraged to speak directly to clients about their current interaction when they were trying to establish a collaborative relationship (for example, "Am I understanding what is most important to you here?"). Talking about what is going on between the therapist and client was even more salient in working with resistances to treatment (for example, "What's it been like for you to talk with me today?"). With an internal focus, further demands to work directly with the current interaction were made (for example, "You keep talking about others, and I keep asking about you. What do you see going on between us?"). Therapists were also encouraged to work with the client's affect in a way that brought the full intensity of whatever feelings the client was experiencing into the here-and-now immediacy of the therapist-client relationship (for example, "I can see how much this has hurt you and how sad you are feeling right now."). Finally, this focus on the interaction between the therapist and the client was especially highlighted in working with transference reactions (for example, "How do you think I am going to react if you do that?").

Thus, a significant aspect of all of these interventions was to bring issues into the therapeutic relationship, where they could be dealt with in terms of what was currently going on between the therapist and the client. Although many beginning therapists find it threatening to work so directly with clients, they also find it powerfully effective when they can do so. Next, to provide an interpersonal solution to the client's problems, the therapist is again asked to work with clients in this forthright and personally engaging way.

The client's generic conflicts are not just talked about in abstract discussions about others, they are reexperienced in the real-life relationship with the therapist. The most effective means the therapist has of resolving these conflicts is to clarify how they are reoccurring with the therapist and try to work out a different relationship that resolves, rather than reenacts, the conflicts. Returning to the previous example, suppose the client has just described two recent interactions with others in which the basic relational theme was a control battle. Although doing so may seem a dreadful prospect to some beginning therapists, the best way to resolve the conflict is to make it overt and address it directly in the client-therapist relationship. As suggested above, the therapist does this by saying something like: "Does that control battle go on between us? Do you ever feel like you and I are fighting over control of our relationship?"

By taking this risk and inviting clients to discuss their conflicts vis-à-vis the therapist, the therapist can bring real-life immediacy to the therapist-client interaction. Problems with others are now not just being talked about intellectually but, perhaps for the first time, are being addressed directly as they occur. In this process, the potential for change is at hand. Below, we will examine further how the therapist can best respond at this critical point, and we will look more closely at the opportunity for change such an approach provides.

Suppose the client says, "No, I don't feel like we are in a control battle." The therapist can use this response to begin exploring what is different about their relationship (for example, "Good, I'm glad that's not a problem for us—any ideas about what makes our relationship different?"). At times, clients may say something positive, such as "You treat me with respect—that's what's different." This comment can provide an important entrée into the client's concerns in other relationships and can serve as the basis for establishing the fact that other kinds of relationships can exist.

Or, the client may respond, "We're not in a control battle because this isn't a real relationship—you're just my therapist." Clients routinely avoid the immediacy of their conflicts by discounting the therapist. Clients cannot make significant gains in therapy until this defense is resolved, however. By clarifying how they really are two people that have been having a relationship for some time, even though there are constraints on it, the therapist can begin to explore the threats aroused for the client by more meaningful involvement. The therapist and client can then agree to watch for these concerns and address them as they arise in their relationship. It is usually most effective if therapists do not bring up these relational patterns in the abstract, but rather wait until they think the client is experiencing them in the current interaction before addressing them.

One thing the beginning therapist fears is that the client will respond to the therapist's question affirmatively (for example, "Of course you're in control. You insist that we stop at ten 'til—whether I'm finished or not. And you're subtle about it, but you often take control by making things go where you want."). Although beginning therapists may fear this response, it is not problematic. On the contrary, now that it is openly acknowledged that the same conflict the client has with others also exists with the therapist, there exists the opportunity to talk about this issue and try to resolve it. The therapist can do this by:

1. Accepting the validity of the client's concerns whenever possible (for example, "Yes, we do have to stop at ten 'til, and that is an unnatural ending for you. I can see how you would feel controlled by those time constraints.").

2. Exploring the client's perceptions further and mutually trying to understand them better (for example, "What do you think is going on for me when I try to take things somewhere? What am I trying to do at those times?").

3. Differentiating from other figures in the client's life (for example, "Yes, I have had ideas about where we should go, but I have also been interested in following your lead. In fact, I may be different than some other people in your life because I genuinely liked it when you disagreed with me last week and told me what you thought instead. I like it when neither of us feel controlled and we can both say what we want. It makes our relationship feel more alive to me.").

4. Offering to be sensitive to this concern in their relationship, expressing a willingness to handle the issue differently in the future, and inviting the client to join in making their relationship different by telling the therapist whenever this conflict occurs between them (for example, "I don't want you to be controlled in our relationship the way you have been in others. That's no good for you or anybody else. So let's try to do something about it. From now on, I will watch the clock and let you know when it's five minutes before we have to stop. And any time you feel like I am directing you away from where you want to go, tell me and we'll stop right then and talk about it. How does that sound to you?").

Taking the above approaches will not be easy, as clients repeatedly will insist on reestablishing the same constricted relational patterns and complementary roles. If the therapist is willing to tolerate personal anxieties and sustain this effort, however, clients often become intensely engaged with the therapist and highly motivated to explore this and other conflicts more deeply. As clients find that a relationship can exist in another way with the therapist, new issues emerge in therapy, and clients begin to respond in new and more effective ways with others.

This affectively immediate, real-life experience of change is powerful but anxiety arousing for many clinicians. Below, we will explore why being an agent of change in this way can be threatening for therapists, and we will provide some practical guidelines to more effectively enhance this process.

Addressing Therapists' Fear of Working with Process

Although the best vehicle for effecting change is the therapeutic relationship, it is often anxiety arousing for therapists to say, "How does that problem go on between us here in therapy?" This direct intervention often breaks the social norms and family rules that therapists grew up with and seemingly places great performance demands on the therapist. Because of this, beginning therapists often will not make process comments and will be reticent about addressing conflicts in the therapeutic relationship. We will see in the discussion below that although a few beginning therapists can do this readily, most find it interesting but anxiety arousing, and a few find it highly threatening.

Initially, beginning therapists have a range of different reactions to working with clients using a process approach. For some, it is easy. They have always been able to talk forthrightly with others about problems in their relationships, and it makes sense to them that the client's conflicts will be replayed with the therapist. For these therapists, it is enlivening to bring issues into the therapeutic relationship, and they are comfortable responding in this direct way. The process approach simply gives them the permission they may need to work with clients this way.

However, for most beginning therapists the process approach is problematic. Bringing clients' conflicts into the therapeutic relationship is an interesting possibility but is also very threatening. Because beginning therapists have had so little clinical experience, their confidence is low, and they are understandably not eager to have what little confidence they may possess shaken by stepping outside of familiar bounds. Further, even if they see that this approach could be effective, they are not sure when the client's conflict is being reenacted and what to do if they did make the reenactment overt.

For some therapists, it is highly threatening to be direct with others, and it may even feel "dangerous" to do so. Below, we will examine six of the most common concerns that beginning therapists have about working with conflicts in the therapeutic relationship and suggest some possible solutions.

First, beginning therapists are often afraid to bring the client's conflicts into the open because they are unsure when or if the client's conflicts are being reenacted in the therapeutic relationship. This concern is a realistic one, since beginning therapists have not had much experience conceptualizing clients' dynamics or systematically tracking the process dimension. As beginning therapists become more skilled and more comfortable with the tremendous amount of new information they are assimilating, they will become more confident and better able to attempt process interventions. It is certainly anxiety arousing to say "This is what I see going on between us . . . ", and beginning therapists will probably initially have some successes and some failures with this approach. However, novice clinicians should not feel pressured to make these interventions until they are ready to do so. Responding out of a sense of pressure will cause the very process the therapist is trying to create with the client to go awry. That is, if the therapist is disempowered by feeling that there is no choice about when or how to intervene, the therapist will be incapable of empowering the client.

How can the beginning therapist know when the client's conflicts are being enacted between them? The best way to find out is to consult with a supportive supervisor who can help the supervisee recognize these processes. Once he or she has conceptualized how some aspect of the client's conflict is being replayed in the therapist-client interaction, the supervisee can explore personal fears about trying to make this interaction overt with the client and rehearse alternative responses with the supervisor. As noted before, beginning therapists can learn how to work in this way, but it will often take two or three years before these responses feel natural and come effortlessly. Again, good advice for the beginning therapist is "Be patient."

A second fear for many beginning therapists is that clients will feel that the therapist is being too blunt or personal if he or she directly addresses what is going on in the relationship. Therapists fear that the client will feel hurt, not like them, or, worse yet, just stare blankly back at them! Of course, process interventions can be made in a blunt, intrusive—and ineffective— way. Warmth, tact, a sense of humor, and good social graces will go a long way toward making every intervention more effective.

Beginning therapists may also be worried about trespassing social norms and expectations. Speaking directly about what is going on between two people does go against unspoken social rules, and clients may be surprised by this. To help ease the transition, therapists can offer contextual remarks that facilitate the bid for more open communication. For example, the first few times the therapist addresses the process dimension with a client, the therapist can provide an introductory remark that acknowledges the shift to another level of discourse:

> Can we be forthright with each other and speak directly about something? Let me break the social rules for a minute and ask about something that might be going on between us.
> I know that people don't usually talk together this way, but I think it would help if we could talk about . . .

Therapists will not be too blunt or direct for the client if they respond respectfully and provide transition comments to help client's make the shift from the socially correct to the direct, interpersonal approach. Rather than being threatened by this invitation for more forthright communication, most clients welcome it and find it reassuring.

A third concern for some beginning therapists is that it does not feel safe to be so "real" with the client. This fear is aroused when therapists stop talking solely about the client, or others in the client's life, and begin talking about what is going on between them as well. At this point, therapists are "stepping off the podium," or out of the "role" of therapist, and becoming more present with clients. As a result, sessions become more intense but therapists' availability makes them more vulnerable and this will be anxiety arousing for therapists at times. We have already seen that the power to effect change derives from the meaning the therapeutic relationship has come to hold for both participants. A corrective emotional experience cannot occur when the relationship is not important to both the therapist and the client. Greater emotional contact creates meaning in relationships, and this occurs when the therapist and client talk honestly about their relationship. This greater closeness, however, is likely to activate the therapist's own conflicts. For example, therapists must relinquish some control in order to become closer, and this will be anxiety arousing at times. Therapists may also be concerned that genuine emotional contact with the client will lead to a loss of appropriate therapeutic boundaries and result in some form of overinvolvement or acting out on the client's or therapist's part. Clearly, connecting with clients in this more direct, immediate way arouses countertransference issues. The guidelines given in Chapter 6 for finding an "optimum interpersonal distance" will help therapists recognize when, owing to their own issues, they are becoming too close to or too distant from the client.

Further, in making process comments, how do therapists know if what is going on is due to their own countertransference issues or to the client's dynamics? The beginning therapist has two methods of differentiating whether the client's dynamics or the therapist's own issues are operating. A supportive but forthright supervisor who closely tracks the therapeutic process with the supervisee is a primary necessity for separating therapist from client dynamics. It is too much to ask trainees to all on their own maintain a balance of emotional relatedness and objectivity.

Another way beginning therapists can safeguard against confusing their own and clients' issues is by not jumping in and making observations about the therapist-client relationship as soon as they see something significant occurring. Instead, it is safer and more effective for the therapist to generate working hypotheses and then gather more data by waiting to see whether the hypothesis fits a second or third time. If the issue is relevant for the client, it will systematically recur. If it does not, then it is likely that the therapist's own issues are involved. Thus, the therapist should not be cavalier about making process comments. When in doubt about whether an issue is the therapist's or the client's, it is best for the beginning therapist to wait, gather additional information about the therapeutic process, and/or consult with a supervisor before commenting to the client.

Psychotherapy is an all-too-human enterprise. On the one hand, the therapist's relationship with the client is the most significant means of effecting change. On the other hand, the therapist's own countertransference issues are the most common factor in recapitulating the client's conflict. This two-sided circumstance should not keep therapists from working with clients in the personally engaging ways suggested here. However, the complex nature of the therapeutic venture requires that beginning and experienced therapists alike (1) make a lifelong commitment to being open to their own countertransference propensities, (2) consult with supervisors and colleagues as a regular ongoing career activity, and (3) seek their own personal therapy when countertransference issues persist. Countertransference issues are most likely to occur when therapists are not readily receptive to this possibility. Beginning therapists who are open to countertransference possibilities and discuss them with supervisors as they arise should feel free to work with clients in a process manner.

Fourth, for some therapists, making issues overt with clients connotes a hostile, intimidating confrontation. Such a confrontive stance is not the intent and needs never to occur. Process interventions can be presented in an aggressive manner—as can any intervention—but there is nothing intrinsically hostile about communicating directly. If therapists think these interventions will be hostile, demeaning, intrusive, or have any other negative impact on the client, they should not use them. Therapists should either wait until it feels as if they can use these interventions constructively or simply respond in other ways.

Similarly, for some therapists, being more direct in therapy arouses the fear of "hurting" the client. These expectations of client vulnerability are usually inaccurate. As noted above, most clients will actually welcome the opportunity for a more straightforward dialogue. As clients find that it is safe and productive to speak with the therapist about what goes on between them, this will also reassure the therapist that it is possible to be sensitive and direct at the same time.

For a few therapists, the concern about therapist hostility and client vulnerability takes on more personal significance. Some therapists who grew up with the highly authoritarian parenting described in Chapter 6 may have been exposed to "double-binding" family communications. That is, there was a great discrepancy between what was being done (the child routinely being threatened, humiliated, screamed at, or hit) and what was being said ("We are a loving family and everyone is happy."). The essential element in the double bind is the clearly understood but unspoken family rule that the child cannot speak about or acknowledge the incongruency in any way. For example, the double-bound child cannot make these contradictory messages overt and say, "You're yelling at me and telling me I'm disgusting and bad. Stop it, you're hurting me!" Among other reasons, children who have grown up with these double binds are terrified to make them overt because rejection and abandonment have been routinely threatened.

Such double-binding communications occur in many severely authoritarian families and are generic in emotionally, physically, and sexually abusive families. Therapists having abuse in their backgrounds may find it frightening to use process comments and to metacommunicate about what is occurring. These therapists often fear that if they speak directly about what is going on, the client will be damaged by them and their inherent destructiveness (the reason they have always believed that they deserved the abuse they received from their parent) will be revealed. Thus, intense anxieties can be generated by breaking double binds and violating family rules about how directly people should communicate. These dynamics are most appropriately resolved in the therapist's own therapy, not in the supervisory relationship.

A fifth concern for many beginning therapists is that their own inadequacies will be revealed. If therapists bring out how the client's conflict is being replayed between them, therapists often fear that they will be "painted into a corner with no way out." Rather than seeming like a productive way to intervene, this approach may seem like the last thing in the world the therapist would want to attempt. For example, the beginning therapist may think: "Yes, there it is, the same conflict that he has with his wife is going on between us right now. And it sure is getting in our way, but I don't have any idea what to do about it."

Whether the therapist chooses to address them or not, such reenactments will usually occur. By making them overt, however, therapists do not assume responsibility for causing the conflicts or changing them—as they often feel they do. Instead, therapists are simply clarifying what is occurring in the relationship and proposing that both work together to try to change the problematic pattern. As outlined above, therapists can do this in several steps. First, therapists must clarify the unfolding interpersonal sequence that usually goes on in the client's interactions with others at this point. Then therapists must differentiate that they have not been responding to the client in this way—or if they have, acknowledge their own participation in this conflict and express their willingness to change. Following this, therapists can offer to work together with the client to find a different way to relate so that the client is not invalidated, controlled, aggrandized, rejected, needed, and so forth, as before.

The client will often feel discouraged (or may feel blamed) when the therapist makes the process observation that with the therapist too, the client's conflict has come into play. Initially, the client may feel hopeless, discouraged, or blameworthy because this reenactment confirms the client's pathogenic belief that relationships cannot be different or better than they have been in the past. The client may recognize intellectually that other ways of relating are possible, but this possibility holds little meaning experientially when the current enactment with the therapist follows the only relational pattern ever experienced. However, the therapist is already responding to the client's conflict in a more effective way by recognizing that this is how relationships have always gone in the past, empathically understanding that this has been an unsolvable and painful problem, and accepting the (historical) validity of the hopeless feelings based on past experiences. By simply providing such validation and empathy and offering to work with the client to try to make their interaction different, the therapist demonstrates to the client that their relationship is no longer following the same well-worn, problematic pattern. When therapists provide this, they give clients the corrective relationship they need for change to occur.

Preparation will also help therapists overcome inadequacy concerns. As mentioned above, beginning therapists must be prepared if they are to successfully bring the client's conflicts into the therapeutic relationship. Beginning therapists should observe an issue occurring several times and feel that they understand what is transpiring before they make an observation in the therapy setting. Even if the client does not agree with the observation, such groundwork will make the therapist feel in command and able to comfortably wait for another opportunity to reintroduce the topic. As beginning therapists become more confident, it will be easier for them to explore more open endedly what may be occurring in the client-therapist relationship. For example, an experienced therapist, when feeling confused, may inquire, "How did we get into this anyway?" In the beginning, however, therapists should bide their time and wait until they understand what is being enacted before addressing it with the client. Further, beginning therapists should wait to intervene until they have regained control of whatever internal responses have been elicited by the client. For example, if the client successfully elicits anger in the therapist, the beginning therapist should not respond while angry but wait until neutrality has been regained.

Finally, many beginning therapists feel conflicted about owning their own personal power. The interpersonal processes suggested here have a strong impact on clients, and many therapists feel conflicted about wielding such a powerful tool. It is threatening to make strong interventions that can have a lifelong effect and to accept the responsibility that comes with having such power.

There are many different reasons why the therapist's own potency can be anxiety arousing. As discussed in Chapter 6, some therapists were parentified or aggrandized as children. For such therapists, legitimate competencies can be readily exaggerated into unrealistic all-powerful or all-responsible grandiosities. Initially, it may be exciting to be specially powerful in this way, but it soon becomes lonely, scary, or burdensome. As a result, these therapists may eschew or quickly retreat from strong interventions.

A more common source of therapists' reluctance to assume an impactful role with clients is therapists' own separation anxiety or separation guilt. For these therapists, emotional ties to parental caregivers were threatened by their competent or independent functioning. For example, as the young child began to explore and make independent movements toward greater autonomy, parents may have looked sad, acted indifferently, demanded more, ridiculed attempts at mastery, or otherwise paired anxiety with competence strivings. Therapists with these developmental experiences may retreat from strong interventions by repeatedly saying, "I don't know what to do," "I'm afraid of hurting the client," or "I'm so screwed up myself that I have no right to try and help somebody else." All therapists have their own personal problems and limitations. When these types of comments persist, however, it may indicate that the therapist wants to avoid the responsibility for the impact on the client of clearly and directly addressing the client's conflicts.

What can help trainees with these concerns? The supervisory relationship is crucial in enabling therapists to embrace their own personal power and be as effective as possible. The supervisee must feel empowered with clients through the supervisor-supervisee relationship. Such empowerment occurs when the supervisee feels personally supported by the supervisor, receives conceptual information and practical guidelines when needed, and is able to address and resolve conflicts that may arise in their relationship. It is crucial that the beginning therapist not feel required to do whatever the supervisor wants. If the supervisee feels that the supervisor is solely directing, rather than mutually collaborating, on the case, the supervisor-supervisee interpersonal process is problematic. Even though the supervisor is ultimately responsible for the client, supervisor and supervisee should be consulting together in a way that allows the supervisee to feel primary investment in the case. For this to occur, the supervisee must have primary responsibility for what occurs in sessions and be free to act on his or her own ideas as well as the supervisor's. If this is not the situation, the supervisee will not be able to experience his or her own successes and failures and thus will not learn from them.

Ideally, the supervisor will help supervisees evaluate the effectiveness of their interventions and consider alternatives without taking away the supervisees' own initiative. When the supervisor and supervisee become "stuck" on a conflict in their relationship, the same issues often carry over to the supervisee-client relationship and are reenacted in that interpersonal process. Often, the therapeutic relationship will not progress until the conflicts in the supervisory relationship are resolved. In contrast, when the supervisor and supervisee can maintain a collaborative relationship, the supervisee will be able to make strong, effective interventions that have a significant impact on the client.

Finally, although same-sex supervisor-supervisee relationships can be preferable at times, they are not essential for supervisees to develop their own personal power. Positive interpersonal processes, as described above, are possible with supervisors of either sex and enable beginning therapists to overcome developmental hurdles and shoulder the responsibility of being effective therapists. As emphasized before, however, the developmental process to becoming as effective with clients as possible is gradual. It may take several years before therapists can allow themselves to have as meaningful an impact on clients as possible and to fully possess their own personal power. If beginning therapists do not progress along this feeling-of-adequacy dimension as they move through training, they should discuss this issue with their supervisors and/or seek treatment for themselves.

CLOSING

The underlying assumption in all interpersonal therapies is that the therapeutic relationship will come to resemble other prototypic relationships in the client's life. Clients' conflicts will emerge in the therapeutic relationship, especially if the therapist tracks the process dimension and attends to what reactions clients elicit from the therapist and others. Therapists should not artificially construct situations to recreate clients' conflicts; rather, it is essential that therapists respond to clients in genuine ways. Therapists should not contrive or manipulate events in the therapeutic relationship in order to strategically create experiences for clients. If therapists try to artificially construct situations, the therapeutic relationship may become duplicitous, lose its integrity, and recapitulate problematic familial interactions for clients. In contrast, however, if therapists are willing to work with the natural expression of clients' conflicts in the here-and-now immediacy of the therapeutic relationship, therapists can offer clients a meaningful, real-life experience of change.

SUGGESTIONS FOR FURTHER READING

1. Practical guidelines to help therapists learn how to metacommunicate and when to intervene with the process dimension are found in Chapter 15 of J. Anchin and D. Kiesler, (Eds.), *Handbook of Interpersonal Psychotherapy* (New York: Pergamon, 1982). See especially pages 285–294.

2. S. Cashdan's book, *Object Relations Therapy* (New York: Norton, 1988), helps explain and apply object relations theory. More important, this text provides superb clinical illustrations of interpersonal process, helps therapists recognize and respond to metacommunicative messages, and demonstrates how the therapeutic relationship can be used to effect change. See especially Chapters 3 and 5.

3. The film *Ordinary People* (directed by R. Redford, 1980) provides an effective illustration of the corrective emotional experience presented here and illustrates how clients can resolve their conflicts with others only after they have been able to confront and resolve them in their real-life relationship with the therapist.

4. Useful illustrations of how therapists can integrate other theoretical modalities with the interpersonal approach are provided by P. Wachtel in Chapter 3 of J. Anchin and D. Kiesler (Eds.), *Handbook of Interpersonal Psychotherapy* (New York: Pergamon Press, 1982) and *Psychoanalysis and Behavior Therapy: Toward an Integration* (New York: Basic Books, 1982).

CHAPTER TEN

WORKING THROUGH AND TERMINATION

CONCEPTUAL OVERVIEW

Working through and *termination* are two distinct phases of therapy. Once clients have experienced a more satisfying response to their generic conflict from the therapist, the task is to generalize this experience of change beyond the therapy setting. That is, the central conflict that has just been resolved in the therapeutic relationship must now be worked through in other relationships as well. Although this may be the longest phase of therapy for some clients, it is a period of growth and change. During this phase, clients are assimilating and applying the emotional relearning that has occurred with the therapist. As clients now go on to address and resolve with others the same conflicts that they have been able to resolve with the therapist, therapy evolves to a natural close. The final termination phase then provides one last opportunity to reexperience and master old generic conflicts, to internalize the helping relationship with the therapist, and to successfully emancipate from therapy.

CHAPTER ORGANIZATION

The first section of this chapter describes the working-through process. First, it provides an overview of client change that places the working-through phase within the context of the overall course of therapy. Following this overview of client change is a description of the working-through process. Sample therapist-client dialogues illustrate how the emotional relearning that has occurred with the therapist can be generalized to other conflict areas. The third part of this section highlights the client's transition from concerns about problems and conflicts to future plans that reflect life-enhancing aspirations and goals. This transition from conflict- to growth-oriented concerns is often marked by the emergence of the client's Dream.

In the second section, we discuss the critically important phase of termination. The section offers specific guidelines for effecting successful terminations and highlights common pitfalls that occur around termination. Finally, in the third section, we provide two case studies of a moving-against and a moving-away client. These two case summaries provide an overview of the change process with different types of clients and show how a corrective emotional experience with the therapist can lead to broad-based personality and behavioral change.

WORKING THROUGH
The Course of Client Change: An Overview

Beginning therapists usually lack a conceptual overview of how client change comes about. Because they have not worked with many clients, or may not have experienced their own effective therapy, most beginning therapists do not have a sense of the ordered sequence in which change often occurs. In the previous chapter, the sequence of therapist activities over the course of therapy was reviewed. The first part of this section extends this framework for conceptualizing the course of therapy. This section offers an overview of the change process by outlining when and how clients resolve their conflicts and adopt new, more adaptive responses. Clients usually change in a predictable sequence of steps, and this unfolding course of change is reviewed from the beginning of therapy up to the final working-through and termination phases.

Some change occurs for some clients as soon as they decide to enter therapy. The decision to enter therapy involves acknowledging that there really is a problem that the client is no longer going to deny or avoid. This decision is also an acknowledgment that clients recognize they cannot resolve the problem alone and that they accept their need for help. Most clients recognize that their resolution to seek help is a healthy step forward, and they feel good about making this decision. As a result, some clients will feel more in control of themselves—which may precipitate some initial change. Although this internal commitment to work on their problems usually produces little relief initially, it is a crucial step that will allow change to occur later in the course of treatment.

Some small changes in feeling and behavior may also occur during clients' initial sessions with the therapist. Clients are reassured when the therapist invites them to express their concerns directly, listens intently and nonjudgmentally to them, and articulates the subjective meaning that their concerns hold for them. Clients' anxiety often diminishes as they find that the therapist can understand their experience and respond compassionately to them. This validation and support does not resolve clients' conflicts, but it does engender hope and help to relieve their distress—which may in turn diminish their symptoms.

More substantial changes begin to occur when the therapist succeeds in focusing clients inward on their own thoughts and feelings and away from their preoccupation with the problematic behavior of others. When clients examine their own internal and interpersonal reactions, they often recognize how their behavior contributes to an interpersonal conflict—and may be able to change their participation in it. Adopting an internal focus for change is also one important way to reframe how clients think about their problems. Redefining the conflict with the other person as being, in part, an internal problem usually reveals new and more adaptive alternatives that clients can adopt.

Next, as the therapist focuses clients inward on their own experience, their conflicted emotions will emerge. These conflicted emotions are the basis of clients' problems. The pace of change accelerates as clients begin to experience and express the emotions that accompany their problems, and as the therapist responds to each sequential feeling in clients' affective constellation. Clients have the opportunity to resolve their problems when they stop defending against their recurring conflicted emotions and instead start experiencing, expressing, and understanding them. Far-reaching changes are set in motion when clients begin to master their affective constellation in this way. For the first time, clients will then be able to change maladaptive, repetitive responses that are integrally linked to their generic conflicts and interpersonal coping styles.

As clients' conflicted emotions emerge, the therapist is also better able to conceptualize clients' generic conflicts and interpersonal coping styles. The therapist then focuses treatment along these conceptual lines and clarifies how clients are reenacting the same dynamic patterns throughout the various issues and concerns they present. Some further change may occur as the therapist helps clients recognize these dynamics and as clients further reframe their definition of their problems. In and of itself, this intellectual awareness may not lead to significant behavioral change, but it does facilitate the next and most significant point of change.

The same conflicts that originally led clients to seek therapy, and that they have been discussing with the therapist, will usually be reenacted in the therapeutic relationship. This reenactment in the therapeutic relationship provides both an opportunity for therapy to fail—by recapitulating the client's conflict—and an opportunity for therapy to succeed—by resolving the conflict that has emerged in the therapeutic relationship. A critical incident often occurs when clients feel the therapist is responding in the same problematic ways that significant others have in the past. This usually occurs in one of three ways. First, although the therapist actually may not have responded in this problematic way, the client has a transference reaction and systematically

misperceives what the therapist has said or done. Second, the client's interpersonal style or testing behavior may actually elicit the same problematic
response from the therapist that the client has received in the past. Third, the
client's conflict may be brought into the therapeutic relationship when
countertransference reactions are stimulated in the therapist that recapitulate
the client's conflict.

Although therapists often fail to recognize it at first, this type of reenactment predictably occurs in most therapeutic relationships. Clients cannot resolve their conflicts unless this reenactment is resolved, however, and the
therapist and client can work out a different and more satisfying solution to the
client's conflict in their real-life relationship. Only when the therapist and client
can resolve this conflict in their relationship does the client have a real-life
experience of change. This interpersonal resolution in the therapeutic relationship is the pivotal step that determines whether enduring change will occur.

Finally, in order to change, clients must reenact these types of corrective
emotional experiences with the therapist many times and generalize this emotional relearning to other relationships. This working-through phase of therapy
in which client change is integrated and generalized is described next.

The Working-Through Process

Change first occurs with the therapist. With just the therapist's encouragement and advice, some clients who function well can successfully adopt new
behavior. When the new behavior is integrally linked to the client's generic
conflict and interpersonal coping style, however, most clients will need to
practice this new response in the therapeutic relationship. Thus, therapists
must give clients permission to try out new ways of responding within their
relationship and clarify that they do not wish to respond in the same problematic ways that others have in the past. If the therapist gives this permission
and encouragement repeatedly, clients will eventually test the therapist and
try out anxiety-arousing new responses. If the therapist responds positively,
rather than metaphorically recapitulating unsatisfying responses that clients
have received in the past, clients can resolve their conflicts and change.

This corrective emotional experience is a powerful agent for change, but
one-trial learning is not sufficient to effect change. The client will need to
reenact this and other dynamic themes over and over again in the therapeutic
relationship. In addition, the therapist must also help clients generalize this
new experience of change to other relationships beyond the therapy setting.
Typically, clients try out new ways of responding in the following progression.

First, change occurs in the client's relationship with the therapist. Clients
then change with acquaintances they do not know well or with others who are
not especially important to them. This is often followed by change with supportive others who are important to the client, such as caring friends, teachers, or mentors. Next, clients often change old response patterns with

historical figures with whom the conflicts originally arose, such as parents. Finally, the last arena for change is often with primary others with whom the conflict is currently being lived out, such as spouses or children.

During the working-through stage of therapy, some clients will rapidly assimilate the new ways of responding and readily apply them throughout their lives. In contrast, other clients with more pervasive conflicts will work through their conflicts slowly. These clients must repeatedly confront the same conflicts, fears, and habitual patterns of response over and over again. Each time, the therapist must patiently point out how the same dynamic issues are being played out again in this situation and help clients master this particular manifestation of their generic conflict. In this regard, the generic conflict will be repeatedly expressed in four areas of client functioning:

Current interaction with the therapist.

Reviewing crisis events that have recently occurred for the client or that originally precipitated the client seeking treatment.

Current relationships with others in which the client's emotional problems are being aroused.

Historical relationships with family members.

For many therapists, working through is the most enjoyable phase of therapy. The therapist often serves as a cheering squad who takes pleasure in clients' newly obtained mastery and encourages them as they successfully adopt new responses in progressively more challenging situations. At this late stage of therapy, the therapist can also become more actively involved in providing information, suggestions, and guidelines to help clients enact new behavior. Some therapists find that behavioral and cognitive procedures for rehearsing alternative interpersonal responses are especially helpful during this phase. The nature of the therapeutic relationship also changes during this period. As clients improve through the working-through period, they will gradually come to perceive the therapist in more realistic terms. As this occurs, the therapist can disclose more personal information to the client. That is, once the transference projections and eliciting phenomenon have been addressed and resolved, therapists are able to share more of themselves with their clients.

In working through, however, the therapist must still be prepared to respond to all of the conflicts, resistances, and defenses that have come before. Although some others in the client's life will respond positively to the client's new changes, others will not. As a result, clients will continue to have experiences with others that arouse their old developmental conflicts again. This also provides an opportunity to further work through the client's generic conflict, however. Through each setback or crisis, the therapist and client again gain access to the client's conflicted affective constellation. They can recognize how the client's conflict is being expressed in this particular relationship and can observe how the same resistances, defenses, and interpersonal coping patterns are still being employed. Most important, in each successive encounter with the generic conflict, clients have the opportunity to receive a more satisfying response from the therapist. Repeatedly enacting a more satisfying interpersonal solution with the therapist will enable clients to continue to adopt more effective ways of responding with others beyond the therapy setting.

It is not always easy for therapists to provide this corrective emotional experience, however. Although clients are improving during the working-through period, they will still be struggling intensely with their central conflicts. This means that strong resistances and negative transference reactions toward the therapist will still have to be negotiated. Therapists must be able to tolerate and work patiently with clients' transference reactions, such as accusations that the therapist "doesn't really care about me," "is trying to control me," "isn't strong enough to handle me," "needs too much from me," "is afraid of a strong (or dependent) woman," "will take advantage of me," and so on.

Furthermore, at times most clients will become discouraged by the repetitious working-through process. Seeing that the same old conflict is confronting them again, clients may feel that nothing has changed, that it is futile to keep trying, and that they should consider dropping out of therapy. At these critical points in therapy, the therapist must provide clients with a relationship that offers them the promise of change. Therapists can make no guarantees of change, and they cannot assume responsibility for the client's motivation to continue. However, *therapists must actively reach out and extend their care and concern to the client.* The therapist must communicate that there can be another way and that the therapist remains committed to working with the client even though the therapist knows how discouraged the client feels at this point. It is the therapist's belief in the potential for change, and *personal commitment to helping this particular client change,* that pulls clients through these expectable crisis points in the working-through phase.

In the therapist-client dialogue below, we will see how clients first change in their relationship with the therapist and how the therapist can then help clients generalize this change to other conflict areas in their lives. As we will see later in this chapter, this *critical incident* may occur as a dramatic, transference-laden confrontation. Alternately, as in the example below, the critical incident may be so subtle as to almost go unnoticed.

A therapist has observed that her client, Tracy, has habitually responded to others in a compliant, pleasing manner. Tracy always goes along with others, believing that her wishes and feelings do not matter. Tracy said that she did not believe that others would ever be interested in listening to her or doing what she wanted to do. In therapy, the therapist repeatedly pointed out how Tracy often acted in this compliant way with others. The therapist linked this behavior to Tracy's presenting symptom of crying spells and used this issue as an entré to explore Tracy's low self-esteem and feelings of worthlessness.

In addition, the therapist encouraged Tracy to respond differently in their relationship. That is, the therapist showed that she cared about what Tracy had to say and invited Tracy to express her own opinions in therapy—even if that meant disagreeing with the therapist. After two months in therapy, this significant new behavior emerged in the therapeutic relationship:

Tracy:
You're right, I guess I never have felt very good about myself.

Therapist:
From other things you've said, it seems to me that your mother just wasn't there for you as a child. You didn't get the support you needed from her. We need to explore that further.

Tracy:
No, I don't really want to talk about her. I remember her more fondly, but my father was pretty harsh with us.

Therapist:
You just said no, you don't want to talk about your mother, and that I was wrong about her.

Tracy:
I'm sorry; sure we can talk about her. What do you want to know?

Therapist:
Forget your mother, you just disagreed with me! You just told me you didn't want to do what I wanted to do and suggested what you thought would be better. That's great!

Tracy:
What?

Therapist:
You just did what we have been talking about for so long. You expressed your own opinion, said what you thought, disagreed with me. I am so happy for you!

Tracy:
Aren't you mad at me?

Therapist:
Oh no, we can disagree and still be close. That was a brave thing you just did.

Tracy:
I guess maybe it is okay for me to say what I think sometimes?

Therapist:
Sure it is. I care about what you think. I want to know what you feel, and I want to do things your way too.

Tracy:
[*tearing*] But you're safe. It's easy to do that with you. You're not like other people.

Therapist:

Yes, I am "safe," and it is easier to do things like that with me than with other people. But you have changed to be able to do that with me, you've grown. You couldn't do that before, you know.

Tracy:

Yeah, that's right.

Therapist:

And if you can value yourself enough to express what you think in here with me, then you can begin to do that out there with other people as well.

Tracy:

Do you really think so?

Therapist:

Yes, I'm sure you can. If you can do it with me, you can do it with them.

Tracy:

Oh, I would love to be able to do this with my boyfriend.

Therapist:

What do you want to be able to say to him?

Tracy:

Well, the next time he . . .

Why is the therapist in this example so excited about such a seemingly small change? Is this single manifestation of a new behavior all that is necessary for Tracy to resolve her problems? No, but this is a highly significant event and it brings her to the working-through phase of therapy. Within the safe orbit of the therapeutic relationship, Tracy could try out a new behavior that taps into her generic conflict and arouses intense anxiety. For Tracy, adopting such a seemingly insignificant, self-assertive behavior arouses life-long feelings of worthlessness. And, simultaneously, it discards the primary means she has developed to protect herself from these painful feelings (that is, to go along with others). In order to master her conflict, Tracy will have to reexperience over and over this same sequence. This sequence involves (1) having her old conflict aroused (having to go along), (2) trying out a new and more adaptive response with the therapist (asserting her own preference), (3) receiving a different and more satisfying response from the therapist (accepting Tracy's initiative), and (4) generalizing the new behavior to others beyond the therapy setting. This repetitious reworking of the new behavior and the old conflict is called working through.

The next week when Tracy returned for her session, she made no mention of this incident with the therapist and said nothing about what went on with her boyfriend. Recognizing this as resistance, the therapist waited for the opportunity to acknowledge what had occurred between them the week before and to reassure Tracy that she was supportive of her new assertive response.

Therapist:

We haven't talked yet today about the important new way that you responded to me last week. Did you have any thoughts about that during the week?

Tracy:

No, not really.

Therapist:

Fine, but I just wanted to say again how happy I was for you. It felt very good to me to see you express your own opinion and be able to disagree with me.

Evidently, this reassurance must have given Tracy the permission she needed. The following week, Tracy was able to adopt the same type of assertive behavior with her boyfriend for the first time. This successful experience, in turn, encouraged her to confront the same issue in another more threatening relationship—with her father.

Tracy:

[beaming]: Guess what! I did it! I've been dying to tell you all week!

Therapist:

Ha! What did you do?

Tracy:

I did what we talked about with my boyfriend. He was talking about something, and I disagreed with him and told him what I thought. It felt great! I don't think he minded either.

Therapist:

Good for you! You're on your way.

Tracy:

I can't believe how easy it was. I wish it could be that easy with my father. He's always putting me down when I say something.

Therapist:

Maybe you're ready to start changing your relationship with your father as well. How do you respond to him when he puts you down?

Tracy:

I get real quiet when he does that. I feel like crying, but I don't. I wish I could just tell him that I don't like it and I want him to stop.

Therapist:

Yeah, confronting him at the time he does that and setting limits with him would certainly change your relationship. It would be saying to him, and to yourself, that you value who you are and what you have to say and you're not going to let him hurt you like that anymore.

Tracy:

But I could never do that. I'd like to, but I just couldn't.

Therapist:

You haven't been able to do that in the past, but you have been changing in here with me, and now with your boyfriend, too. So maybe you can do something different with him as well. What holds you back from setting limits with him; what are you most afraid of?

Tracy:

He wouldn't take me seriously; he'd just laugh at me.

Therapist:

How would that make you feel?

Tracy:

Worthless. *[begins crying]*

Therapist:

So that's where that awful feeling comes from.

Tracy:

Yeah. *[long pause]* It makes me mad too.

Therapist:

Of course it does. He's hurt you very much. You have every right to be angry at him for treating you like that!

Tracy:

It's not fair. I don't want to let him do that anymore. It's not good for me.

Therapist:

That's right, it's not good for you, and you don't deserve it. Now that you can see that clearly, you don't have to go along with it the way you used to.

Tracy:

What can I do?

Therapist:

What would you like to do the next time he does that?

Tracy:

Well, maybe I can tell him to stop it. Tell him that I just don't want to be treated like that anymore . . .

In ever-widening circles such as these, clients confront and work through the same dynamic conflicts in the different spheres of their lives. Unless the therapist conceptualizes the client's dynamics and hypothesizes how the client might reenact this conflict in their relationship, however, it is easy for the therapist to miss these subtle transactions. For example, at the beginning of this sequence, Tracy said she did not want to follow the therapist's suggestion of discussing her relationship with her mother. If the therapist had not anticipated that Tracy would tend to comply with her in therapy—and if the therapist had not been alert to supporting any budding sign of self-direction or assertiveness from Tracy—this change-producing sequence would have been missed. In addition, if the therapist had responded by focusing on the content (for example, "But it is important for us to look at your relationship with your mother because . . . ") rather than by focusing on the process (for example, Tracy asserting herself and disagreeing with the therapist), this opportunity for change would also have been lost. Tracy would have complied with the therapist and dutifully talked about her relationship with her mother. In the context of this interpersonal process that recapitulates her central conflict, Tracy would not be able to become more assertive or to uncover the long-standing emotional conflicts that led to her compliant interpersonal style.

Often, the therapist will eventually become discouraged about working with clients such as Tracy who are not able to try out or successfully incorporate new, more adaptive responses. The therapist may become either critical toward or disengaged from the client for not changing, without realizing that the client's generic conflict has been recapitulated in their relationship. Thus, the client is unable to change even though the therapist and client continue to talk about adopting more assertive behaviors with others, the therapist sincerely supports and encourages this, and the client learns useful skills that facilitate performing the new behavior. Generating working hypotheses about how the client's conflict may be reenacted in the therapeutic relationship will help therapists more quickly recognize and more effectively respond to these reenactments.

Client Transition from Present Conflicts, Through Family-of-Origin Work, and on to Future Plans

In the working-through phase, the therapeutic action continues to be located primarily in the present time sphere. That is, the significant events that occur are current interactions with the therapist that enact resolutions of problematic relational patterns. These corrective experiences are then generalized as clients begin to try out new ways of relating with others in their lives. As clients succeed with changes in these current relationships, two new subphases in the working-through process may emerge. Leaving the focus on current inter-actions, clients often become interested in looking back to the familial experi-ences where they learned these problematic self-other relational configurations. Below, the first section provides therapeutic guidelines to help with this "family-of-origin work." Following this retrospective inclination, clients may also begin to look ahead. That is, they may start to think more about what they want their life to be in the future and to reformulate life plans to better fit the person they are becoming. This subphase is ushered in by the emergence of "the Dream" and will be explored in the second subsection.

Family-of-Origin Work. It is usually not very productive for therapists to lead clients back in time to explore historical family relationships. Early in treat-ment, therapists can learn a great deal from this exploration about the correc-tive experiences that clients will need in treatment. Although this history will inform the therapist, most clients will not be able to make meaningful bridges between current and past relationships from this initial exploration. Too often, the beginning therapist will pressure clients to see seemingly obvious connections, but these relational patterns do not "come alive" for clients. At a later point in treatment, however, many clients will spontaneously lead the therapist back to developmental experiences. This client-initiated exploration, which often occurs during the working-through period, is usually highly productive.

As clients make their own meaningful links between formative and current relationships, they often ask the therapist what they should do about their current relationships with family members. Two broad guidelines are discussed to help clients with this family-of-origin work. First, we will see how clients must change how *they* respond to old problematic relational patterns in their current interactions with family members. Second, the concept of "grief work"—grieving for and coming to terms with what one has missed developmentally—will be introduced. Working in both these areas results in an interpersonal and internal resolution of family dynamics.

Clients who struggle with more serious, pervasive, or long-standing problems will have family-of-origin work to do. Many clients do not wish to confront parents about problems from the past, and if this is the case, therapists should not pressure these clients to do so. However, some clients will want to address past conflicts with parents and other family members and try to resolve them. It is enormously gratifying and a powerful impetus for change when such rapprochments succeed, but such present-day interpersonal solutions of historical problems do not usually occur. Occasionally, parents have grown and changed, but in most cases, and especially with more serious problems, the client will receive the same invalidating, blaming, or hurtful responses that the parent made originally. This is especially painful when the client's unconscious motivation for confronting the parent was the fantasy of getting the parental love, approval, or respect that the client had missed but always longed to receive. If the therapist has not prepared the client for this potential disappointment, the client will be setback and experience profound feelings of helplessness and hopelessness. Further, the client often will be breaking family rules by addressing conflicts with parents directly, and in many cases, punitive homeostatic mechanisms will be set in motion. For example, when Tracy confronted her father about always "putting her down," he again disparaged her. In addition, her mother later threatened to disown her for being "disrespectful" and "ungrateful," and her sister telephoned and tried to make her feel guilty for "hurting Daddy" and "stirring up trouble"! Thus, *the problem is not as simple as just the parent mistreating the child. Instead, more serious, long-term problems (such as self-hatred, bulimia, or chronic depression) can develop when the parent succeeds in making the child feel responsible or blameworthy for the parent's mistreatment.*

Clients like Tracy feel hopeless when the parent and broader family system cannot change. Although these clients often go on to act helpless in other current relationships, in actuality, they are not helpless. Their interpersonal resolution does not rest on the parent changing, but on how they change and respond in current interactions with living parents or in their internal relation to deceased parents. In order for clients to make enduring changes in deep-seated relational conflicts, they must change their own responses in these prototypic interactions. For example, Tracy's father was too limited to be able to hear her concern and talk with her about the problem. However, Tracy stopped "going along" with her father's disparagement of her as she had always done and as other family members had required her to do. Instead, Tracy began setting limits with her father, which he rudely laughed off. Nonetheless, things changed profoundly for Tracy when she metacommunicated with her father, saying: "I keep asking you to 'Stop it' when you put me down, and you laugh at me and keep on doing it. I can't make you stop, but I don't have to pretend that it's okay anymore. It hurts me and I don't like it." Although her father stayed in the same disparaging mode and again made fun of her "very sensitive feelings," things got much better for Tracy when she changed how she responded to him. As she was able to sustain this stronger stance toward him and the family system over the next few months, she felt less afraid than she had ever been, her long-standing feelings of "worthlessness" largely disappeared, and her intermittent battles with bulimia dissipated.

Clients change, in part, by changing how they respond in current problematic interactions with parents. Clients also change by doing "grief work" and coming to terms with the feelings left in them by hurtful parent-child transactions. *Clients do not need to confront parents about historical relationships, but they do need to acknowledge to themselves what was wrong, stop their own participation in any ongoing mistreatment, and grieve for what they missed.* Regardless of whether parents change and whether they are living or deceased, clients can further master their conflicts through this internal work.

Testing the reality of new possibilities with parents may or may not lead to improved relations. Often parents cannot change, and even when they do, grown offspring still need to acknowledge what was wrong in the past and mourn what they missed developmentally. Again, the therapist must provide a supportive holding environment that allows clients to fully integrate the anger and underlying sadness that was too threatening for them to experience before. The therapist must also help clients come to terms with both "the good news and the bad news" through grief work. The good news is that through this work, clients can disconfirm their pathogenic belief that they were in some way responsible or to blame for the rejection, mistreatment, or parentification that occurred. The bad news is the unwanted reality that clients' developmental needs, such as for secure affectionate ties, were not adequately met and cannot now be met in any current adult relationship, such as with spouses, friends, or therapists. Only after such losses or deprivation can be acknowledged as real and fully experienced can clients go on for the first time to get their adult needs met in other current relationships. In other words, clients have not been able to get legitimate adult needs met in current relationships if earlier developmental needs have been operating unacknowledged.

Two countertransference propensities often keep therapists from helping clients reach resolution in family-of-origin work. First, therapists sometimes fail to help the client integrate what was good as well as what was problematic in the client's development. Therapists can err by denying familial problems or by only blaming the parents. To avoid the latter, therapists in most cases should discourage the client from ending all contact with parents. When a client breaks off all communication with family members, splitting defenses are usually operating, and no internal resolution or real change can occur. In such cases, the therapist will be idealized, and clients then will be compelled to compulsively recreate the split-off "bad" side of their conflicts in other relationships.

Second, therapists often want to bypass the work of mourning. It is difficult to help clients come to terms with the painful feelings aroused by acknowledging that they missed what they needed. Clients do not want to end the hope or fantasy of getting what they missed, and this often arouses the therapist's own unfinished family business as well. If the therapist tries to bypass the work of mourning and move too quickly to a problem-solving approach of finding substitute supportive relationships, clients will not be able to internalize much from these practical interventions. Only after original losses have been grieved for can clients open up to and be sustained by new relationships in a way they have not been able to experience before. As clients improve in these very significant ways, they leave the past behind and begin to look ahead to a different future. Next, we will examine "the Dream," the second subphase of the working-through period.

The Dream. Clients make adaptive behavioral changes and feel subjectively better as they work through their conflicts. As clients improve, the therapist and client become less concerned with historical conflicts and current interpersonal problems. Instead, they often become more involved in plans for the future and issues regarding health and personal growth. This exciting transition from psychopathology/neurosis/conflict to health/growth/creativity is signaled by the emergence of the Dream.

In his book, *The Seasons of a Man's Life,* Levinson (1978) describes the profound influence of the Dream in shaping the structure of adult life and the course of personality development. As Levinson points out, the Dream does not refer to casual daydreams or night dreams but, in the largest sense, to the kind of life that one wants to lead. At first, the Dream may be poorly articulated and tenuously connected to reality, but it holds imagined possibilities of self-in-adult-world that generate excitement and vitality. It is the central issue in Martin Luther King's historic "I Have a Dream" speech or in Delmore Schwartz's story, "In Dreams Begin Responsibilities."

The Dream has roots in the grandiose and unrealistic hero fantasies of adolescence, but it is more than this. In early adulthood, the Dream still has the quality of a vision—of who and how one would like to be in the world. In this way, the Dream is both inspiring and sustaining for the individual even though it may be mundane to others. For example, individuals have Dreams to be a good husband and father, an excellent craftsman, a respected community leader, an ethical attorney, a medical doctor who relieves suffering, a good teacher who helps children grow, a successful but honest businessperson, an artist, or a spiritual leader. *In order to have purpose and a sense of aliveness, occupational and marital choices must incorporate some aspects of the Dream. When the Dream has been abandoned or is unconnected to the life structure, the life will not be infused with vitality and meaning even though the person may be successful.*

Up until the working-through phase of therapy, therapists are usually responding to the despair of broken dreams, the disillusionment of unfulfilling dreams, and the cynicism of abandoned dreams. In many cases, the life-infusing Dream that Levinson has articulated has not yet been addressed in therapy. In the working-through phase, however, clients are resolving their conflicts and emerging as healthier individuals. At this point, therapists must help clients to articulate and renew their Dreams and to find ways of incorporating aspects of their Dreams in their everyday lives. To achieve this, therapists must first be able to differentiate the Dream from the broken dreams that often underlie clients' presenting symptoms. As we will see below, the broken dreams that clients present to therapists often reflect failed attempts to rise above their conflicts and become special.

In the process of working through, clients are progressively relinquishing their interpersonal coping styles of moving toward, away, or against others. Clients gradually recognize their compensatory strivings to be special and rise above their conflicts by pleasing others, achieving success and power, or becoming safely aloof and cynically superior. As clients give up their characterological coping strategies, they stop blocking the expression of their generic conflict. This allows their conflicts to be expressed, and potentially resolved, in the therapeutic relationship. However, therapists must anticipate that it will be a devastating failure and a total loss of self-esteem for clients to relinquish these attempts to rise above their conflicts. Thus, one important component of helping clients resolve their conflicts is to replace these defensive, grandiose strivings with the client's own attainable, yet sustaining, Dream.

Arthur Miller's Pulitzer-prize-winning play, *Death of a Salesman*, poignantly illustrates how the neurotic striving to rise above the conflict inevitably fails, how it can lock clients in their generic conflict for a lifetime, and how it stifles the Dream. The protagonist, Willy Loman, has adopted a moving-toward interpersonal style to cope with his profound feelings of inadequacy and shame. With a smile and a shoe shine, Willy pathetically strives not just to be liked but to be well-liked. In a brilliant exposition of multigenerational family roles and relationships, Miller shows how Willy's grandiose strivings to rise above his conflicts by being well-liked are also acted out through his oldest son, Biff. Willy exaggerates Biff's accomplishments as magnificent, excuses or ignores his shortcomings, and never responds to the reality of his son's actual feelings, needs, or wishes.

Near the end of the play, both father's and son's defensive strivings to rise above fail. Willy is fired from his job—a crushing humiliation that shatters his myth of being well-liked and his lifelong coping strategy of winning approval. That same day, Biff fails to secure an important business opportunity that his father has encouraged. With this setback, Biff realizes that he has been living out his father's myth that he would become a fabulously successful entrepreneur. In the closing scene, however, the father and son each respond very differently to their respective crises.

Biff is able to relinquish the unrealistic script of superachievement and success that his father has demanded of him. In the last scene, Biff begs his father to release him from this grandiose role, "speak the truth" in the family for the first time, and acknowledge that he is just another regular guy—nothing more, nothing less—and to let that be good enough. However, Willy cannot relinquish his own rising-above defense and, therefore, cannot grant Biff's request to "let me off the hook." Alternately, Willy rejects and condemns Biff and continues to idealize him as magnificent.

Biff finally recognizes the conflict and interpersonal process that he and his father have been enacting all of their lives. By directly confronting his father, Biff is able to change his part of their conflict. Although this confrontation does not lead to an interpersonal resolution with Willy, it does lead to an internal resolution for Biff. Soon after the confrontation Biff decides to leave home. He states that he now knows who he is and what he wants to do with his life. He is going to pursue his own Dream and do what he has always wanted to do: leave the city, move out west, and work outdoors where he can feel the sun on his back and smell the grass. Whereas Biff could relinquish the neurotic strivings to be special and allow his own attainable Dream to emerge, Willy could not.

In one last attempt to change their relationship and have a genuine closeness, Biff reaches out and puts his arms around his father. Horrified, Willy recoils in fear and disgust. Although his lifelong obsession has been to win the approval and respect of others, he must rigidly reject exactly what he has always wanted from his son. To accept the love that Biff was offering, his own unacceptable, generic conflict would emerge. That is, Willy's own unmet needs to be respected and wanted, his profound sense of being unlovable, and his intense feelings of inadequacy and shame would overwhelm him. Thus, Willy is now trapped in his conflict: He is no longer able to maintain his own (or Biff's) defensive strivings to rise above, and he is unable to let his true feelings and concerns emerge. Desperately bound in that unresolvable conflict, Willy's only solution is to end his own life.

As clients' neurotic strivings to be special and rise above their conflicts fail, their generic conflicts are revealed. If the therapist can provide a different and more satisfying response to the conflict than clients have received in the past, however, clients can resolve their conflicts and change maladaptive behavior. As this occurs and clients begin to improve during the working-through phase, the Dream will often emerge.

In order to help clients change, therapists must support and encourage the Dream. They can do this in many ways. First, therapists must listen for what it is that clients really want to do and inquire about what holds a feeling of rightness for them. Therapists can also help clients discover and articulate their Dreams. For some clients, their Dreams are completely unarticulated and undeveloped because their parents never accepted their feelings or responded to their interests. These clients with a less developed sense of self are unaware not only of what they want to do in life but also of what they like or dislike. Therapists can help these clients discover and successively articulate their feelings, preferences, interests, values, and later, their Dreams by repeatedly doing the following:

- Asking clients to attend to what they are experiencing right now
- Orienting clients to listen to themselves and simply be aware of what they want to do in different situations—even if they cannot act on their wishes (for example, "I'm not liking talking to him right now.")
- Being interested in and entering into clients' subjective experience
- Observing aloud what seems to interest or hold meaning for clients
- Acknowledging what clients do well
- Encouraging clients to act on their own internal preferences when possible (for example, "I'm sleepy—I'm going to take a nap.")

Therapists will need to teach some clients to begin attending to their own internal experience in these very basic ways. Although most clients are more developed than this, it is very rewarding for therapists to help clients differentiate a self by responding to their own feelings, perceptions, and interests.

As clients begin to experience their own inner life more fully, and the therapist responds affirmingly, their Dreams will start to emerge. At this more differentiated point, therapists can do several things to help clients bring aspects of their Dreams into their current lives. For example, therapists must provide a safe "practicing" sphere in which clients can discuss and explore various possibilities of their Dream without prematurely having to become committed to any action. Therapists can also help clients tailor their Dreams to reality and find ways that clients can express components of their Dreams in their everyday lives. Still another way to bring aspects of their Dream into their everyday lives is to help clients identify training or education routes that will facilitate realization of their Dreams. Similarly, therapists must also give clients permission to develop close relationships with others who can inform them and act as mentors in their chosen fields and pursuits.

Finally, clients will confront the same generic conflicts in exploring their Dreams that they have experienced in other aspects of their lives. Thus, therapists will also have to help clients work through their old conflicts that are aroused by pursuing their Dreams. For example, therapists will have to help clients differentiate between their Dreams and their interpersonal coping style and defensive strivings to rise above (for example, to be loved by everyone, to be wealthy and powerful, or to be safely aloof and superior). Pursuing what they really want to do will threaten object ties and arouse separation guilt and separation anxiety for many clients. However, as clients successively work through their conflicts and start to follow through on realistic plans for manifesting aspects of their Dreams, therapy will evolve to a natural conclusion.

TERMINATION

Termination is an important and distinct phase of therapy that must be negotiated thoughtfully. Ending the therapeutic relationship will almost always be of great significance to clients. The way in which this separation experience is resolved is so important that it influences how well clients will be able to resolve future conflicts in their lives. More specifically, the way in which the termination is dealt with helps determine whether clients leave therapy with a greater sense of their own personal resources and ability to manage their own lives. Termination is a potent and far-reaching experience for clients. It holds the potential either to undo the growth and resolution that has come before or to confirm and extend the changes that have come about in therapy. Thus, therapists must be prepared to utilize the potential for change that is still available as therapists and clients prepare to end their relationship.

Beginning therapists often ask, "How do you know when it's time to end therapy?" It is time to end when clients no longer have symptoms, can respond more flexibly and adaptively in current situations that arouse their old generic conflicts, and have begun to take steps toward promising new directions in their lives. Therapists are also informed that clients are ready to terminate when they have converging reports of client change from three different sources. First, therapists know that clients are ready to terminate when clients report that they consistently feel better, can respond in more adaptive ways to old conflict situations, and find themselves capable of new responses that were not available to them before. Second, the therapist knows that termination is approaching when clients can consistently respond to the therapist in new and different ways that do not enact their old interpersonal coping styles, defenses, resistances, transference reactions, or eliciting behaviors. Third, termination is approaching when significant others in clients' lives give clients feedback that they are different, or have changed, or make comments such as "you never used to do that before." With this convergence of perceptions that important changes have occurred, it is time for therapy to end. Before going on to discuss issues essential to successful termination, we must distinguish between two types of endings.

The termination sequence just described is a "natural ending" because clients' work is finished. One of the therapist's primary goals in these natural endings is to accept both sides of clients' feelings about ending. That is, the therapist must take pleasure in clients' independence and actively support their movement out on their own. At the same time, clients must also feel that the therapist accepts their continuing need and will not be disappointed or burdened if they want to return later. Because so many clients could only go or only stay in past formative relationships, this resolution of the separateness-relatedness dialectic in the therapist-client relationship is a potent corrective emotional experience. Assured of the therapist's support for both sides of their feelings, clients can internalize the therapist as a good introject, solidify their own sense of self, and successfully end the relationship.

Unfortunately, however, most graduate student therapists do not have the satisfaction of seeing many cases evolve to a natural close. Instead, therapy ends before the client is finished because the graduate student must move on to another placement or because the school year ends. Sometimes the therapist and client have made substantial gains at the point when external constraints demand termination; at other times, the treatment process may be only in midstream. In either case, significant therapeutic gains can still be made despite unnatural endings. To accomplish this more difficult task, however, it is essential that the therapist and client address and work through the conflicts that an unnatural ending arouses. Because graduate student therapists often have to initiate terminations before clients are ready, the discussion that follows emphasizes unnatural endings.

The Ending Must Not Be Avoided

It is usually difficult for both the therapist and the client to end their relationship. In many cases, bringing up the topic of termination will arouse emotional responses that are far more intense and difficult than either the therapist or the client have anticipated. As a result, therapists and clients regularly collude to deny the reality of the impending ending and to avoid the difficult feelings it arouses for both of them. When therapists and clients stumble in this way and do not confront the ending squarely, their interpersonal process will usually recapitulate clients' generic conflicts and prevent clients from fully resolving their conflicts.

The single most important guideline for negotiating a successful termination is to unambiguously acknowledge the reality of the ending. The therapist and client must then discuss all of the client's emotional reactions about the ending, especially the client's reactions toward the therapist. Although the therapist and client may both want to avoid this topic, the therapist cannot let this occur. Once the therapist and client mutually decide that the client is ready to terminate, or that the therapist must terminate because of outside constraints, *they must set a specific date* for the final session. Because the therapist and client need time to work through their ending, the final session must be scheduled several weeks hence.

In order to have a successful ending, the therapist must insist on establishing a final date and then explore the client's reactions to ending their relationship. Clients may angrily disapprove when therapists insist on focusing on the termination date, and some therapists will feel that they are being unnecessarily harsh, mean, or rigid. It is difficult to set a specific termination date and discuss the ending because this will arouse both the therapist's and the client's conflicts over endings. In addition, setting a clear termination date will often bring up the client's generic conflict again. In order to definitively resolve their central conflicts, however, clients must again work through in the termination phase the same issues that have been dealt with before. For these reasons, therapists must count down the final sessions and repeatedly invite clients to discuss their reactions to the termination:

> After today, we will have only three sessions left. How is it for you to hear me say that?
> We have only two sessions left now. It's important that we talk about our ending. What comes up for you when I acknowledge the fact that we will soon stop working together?
> Next week will be our last session. What do you find yourself thinking about our relationship and the work we have done together?
> This is our last session. What are you feeling toward me right now?

This type of countdown precludes any ambiguity that clients may have about the ending (for example, Client at end of last session: "Will I be seeing you next week?"). This approach also keeps the therapist from acting out and avoiding the separation as well (for example, Therapist at end of last session: "Oh, I see our time is up. Well, I guess that's it."). When therapists do not address the termination directly, they are often acting out their own separation anxieties. This commonly occurs, and when it does, therapists need to seek consultation from a supervisor or colleague.

Therapists must address the termination forthrightly and give clients the opportunity to work through their reactions to it. Why is this so important? In most clients' pasts, they have painfully experienced endings with significant others as "just happening to them." In many cases, either they were not prepared in advance for the separation, they did not understand when or why this particular ending was occurring, or they were not able to participate in the leave-taking by discussing it with the departing person. These types of responses have left many clients feeling powerless and out of control in regard to some of the most important experiences in their lives. In contrast, the approach suggested here gives clients a mastery experience by allowing them to be active, informed participants in the ending. In order to achieve a successful leave-taking, the therapist must acknowledge clients' unfinished business and how this termination may evoke certain other endings in their past that were unwanted or premature. However, even though it may seem as if clients' conflicts are being recapitulated by therapist-initiated endings, this does not have to occur. The therapist can make the current therapy termination different from past problematic endings by doing the following:

- Telling the client about the ending in advance
- Inviting the client to communicate angry, disappointed, and sad feelings and accepting these feelings
- Talking with the client about the ending and the meaning it holds for both of them
- Validating the client's experience by acknowledging the ways that the ending evokes other conflicted endings
- Saying good-bye to each other

In most other endings that have been problematic, clients could not do any of these things with the departing person. *Too often, beginning therapists fail to keep in mind the essential differences between this ending and past endings.* As a result, therapists accept the client's anger and blame at face value and feel guilty about "letting the client down." Acting out this inappropriate guilt, therapists often avoid the ending or feel the need to invalidate the client's sad, disappointed, or angry feelings. When therapists do this, then they are actually reenacting the client's past conflicted endings. To keep from doing this, therapists must acknowledge the fact that this ending evokes dynamically related concerns from the client's problematic past endings and differentiate how this termination can be different from other past endings. Although most clients cannot recognize these differences initially, the therapist offers clients an opportunity to resolve long-standing conflicts by helping clients differentiate this type of mutually shared ending from other incomplete or unsatisfying endings with which they have had to cope in the past.

Termination Arouses the Client's Conflicts Again

Once the therapist and client set a termination date, the client's generic conflict may be aroused again. Some clients will begin to feel that they have not changed in therapy after all, and their initial presenting symptoms will return. Therapists must be alert for how the termination may tap into the client's generic conflict and how this may be reenacted in their relationship. Then, therapists must ensure that their interpersonal process enacts a resolution of the client's conflict rather than a recapitulation of it. The best way for therapists to accomplish this is by drawing out and responding to all of the client's emotional reactions to the ending.

During the termination period, clients may have a diverse range of sad, hopeful, angry, excited, disappointed, and grateful feelings toward the therapist. As therapists track the client's reactions to the ending, they will often see how the client's central conflict is simultaneously being aroused in two contexts. First, the client's primary feelings toward the therapist about the ending (anxiety, anger, guilt, helplessness) may match the feelings that existed in relation to the earlier, formative relationship in which the generic conflict originally arose. Second, the client's reaction toward separating from the therapist may also match the feelings that were aroused in the crisis situation that originally brought the client to treatment.

If the therapist can respond to the client's feeling and clarify its connection to these two sources, the therapist is helping the client further resolve the central conflict. In contrast, if the therapist avoids or cannot respond to all of the client's reactions to termination, this will usually recapitulate the client's conflict in some way. When this occurs, it prevents clients from resolving their conflicts. They cannot access their own resources and capacity for autonomous functioning, cannot outgrow their dependency on the therapist, and cannot disengage from therapy as they need to do.

For all of these reasons, the therapist must address and help clients work through their feelings about ending the relationship. This is difficult to do, however, when in part both the therapist and the client wish to avoid the ending. The therapist and client have become close through their work together, and the relationship holds significant meaning for both of them. In order to defend against the conflicts that are aroused by the termination, clients (and therapists too) may try to deny the reality of the ending. Or, some clients may try to devalue the significance of their relationship with the therapist or to diminish the importance of the work that has been accomplished. Still other clients will become symptomatic again and anxiously communicate that they are still too troubled to terminate and make it on their own. A few clients will try to avoid the conflicts aroused by the ending by asking the therapist if they can become friends. All of these responses help clients avoid facing current and past losses, preclude clients from receiving a new and more satisfying response to their concerns about endings, and keep clients from internalizing the therapist and integrating the gains they have made in treatment.

Resolving such conflicts over separation is the prototype for mastering all conflicts. Therapists must not overreact to these defenses against ending, but instead must recognize and respond to the underlying concerns that are aroused by the impending separation. Too often, the client's defensive maneuvers elicit countertransference reactions in therapists that prevent them from responding to the client's real concerns. That is, therapists may "buy" the client's defensive responses and feel guilty, angry, or inadequate because of the client's attempts to undo the importance of their relationship or the work they have accomplished. Whenever therapists are immobilized by such countertransference reactions, they must seek consultation to help manage their emotions more effectively. Only then will therapists be able to effectively return to the task of responding to the client's concerns over ending.

Ending the Relationship

Although some clients will reexperience their central conflicts at the time of termination, others will not. Both clients and therapists still need to talk about the ending, however. For example, therapists can talk with the client about the different ways in which they have seen the client change over the course of therapy. Therapists can also acknowledge the limitations of their relationship and the unfinished issues that the client will need to continue to work with on his or her own. Recollections of close moments, awkward misunderstandings, threatening confrontations, and humorous incidents can all be recounted as well. This is also a time when therapists can share their own feelings about the client: what they have learned about themselves and life from the client, how the client has changed, enriched or influenced them, and ways in which therapists have cared about and will miss the client.

Finally, in natural and unnatural endings, termination brings the therapist and client back to the separateness-relatedness dialectic again. For natural endings, therapists must give clients permission to leave. That is, clients must know that the therapist enjoys their success, is pleased by their independence, and wants them to become committed to other, new relationships. Conversely, just as all clients need permission to emancipate, they also need to be reassured that they can have future contact with the therapist if necessary. Clients will be reassured to know that, whenever possible, the therapist is available to help them with future crises should the need arise. Knowing that the therapist is available if needed, but also supporting the client in leaving, allows the client to internalize the therapist and the help the therapist has provided. This type of natural termination supports the client's own individuation and mastery strivings and helps clients to further claim their own personal power and identity.

However, as noted earlier, graduate student therapists often cannot be available in this way because endings with their clients are of necessity unnatural. In these cases, the finality of the ending must be honestly acknowledged, and the therapist must respond to all of the client's emotional reactions. The unfinished business that remains must also be honestly acknowledged, and the therapist may need to help the client find a new therapist to finish the work that was just begun. If the therapist can do this, most clients can accept the limitations of the relationship without having to reject the therapist or undo the work that was accomplished. Even if incomplete, when clients can keep inside what they have gained with the therapist, a successful and productive relationship has occurred.

TWO CASE SUMMARIES

In Chapter 7, a model for conceptualizing client dynamics was presented and illustrated with the case study of Peter—a moving-toward-others client. Now, further guidelines for conceptualizing clients have been provided, and the entire course of therapy has been detailed. With this conceptual framework and treatment course complete, two case studies illustrate the other interpersonal styles. Below, salient features in the treatment of a moving-against and a moving-away client are summarized.

Chuck—Moving Against Others

Chuck had improved dramatically since he entered therapy a year ago. Chuck had been riding high, on his way to becoming a real estate king, when his business failed. Buoyed by his initial success in a booming real estate market, Chuck had been woefully overextended when interest rates rose unexpectedly. His business went bankrupt, his new home and sports car were repossessed, and friends deserted him as creditors and the IRS aggressively pursued him. Chuck entered therapy when his dreams of wealth and power were dashed, leaving him desperate, frightened, and suicidally depressed.

With the therapist's help, however, his suicidal preoccupation and other concerns had greatly improved. Chuck recognized how helpful the therapist had been to him and had recently told someone that he probably would not be alive today if it were not for the therapist's expertise and genuine concern. On this particular day, however, Chuck was ready to quit therapy. He was frustrated by having to come to therapy for such a long time, and he did not want to need the therapist anymore. In particular, he was fed up with the therapist's fees. Chuck began the session by bitterly taunting the therapist:

> Who do you think you are to charge so much? Do you really think you're worth all that?!

The therapist acknowledged the feeling in Chuck's provocation:

Therapist:
> You're angry about my fees. Let's talk about them.

Chuck:
> [*continuing his assault*] What are you doing, trying to prove that you can gouge as much money as the psychiatrist next door?! Did your mother want you to be a "real" doctor and make a lot of money or what?!

Fortunately, Chuck's therapist was able to stay in relationship with Chuck during this critical incident. The therapist did not retreat or counterattack, which is what Chuck's provocations usually elicited from others. Instead, the therapist mediated his own reflexive response to justify and explain and tried to maintain an effective middle ground of involvement:

> Yes, of course you're angry with me. I do charge you for my time, and it's hard for you. And there are still many problems in your life that haven't changed yet.

The therapist's accepting response only infuriated Chuck further:

Chuck:
> I hate your "understanding," I hate coming here, I don't want to do this anymore! What do you do, be nice to people when they're falling apart so they become dependent on you? Then they can't leave you and you can keep taking all of their money. There's something wrong with you; you're sick!

Therapist:
> It seems like I am trying to make you dependent on me so that I can take advantage of you financially?

Chuck: [*livid*]
> Yes, you idiot, I want to leave and get out of here, but I can't. I know I'll just get depressed again if I leave, and probably go kill myself. I need you and you know it, and you use that to take the little money I have left. I'm trapped by you. You've got me and I hate it, I hate *you!*

The intensity of Chuck's reactions told the therapist that a central conflict was being reenacted in this transference reaction. Based on other hypotheses he had already formulated, the therapist reasoned that for Chuck, having a need of someone automatically meant being used by them. Trying to articulate what Chuck was experiencing in their relationship right then, the therapist responded:

> It's as if you don't experience the decision to remain in therapy as your own choice, Chuck. You feel trapped by your own need to be helped or understood. You have learned that to let yourself need somebody puts them in control of you and leaves you subject to their own selfish needs. Your only choice then is to resist by leaving the help you still want or stay in treatment with me but be exploited. You may have experienced this with others, Chuck, but I want you and I to have a different kind of relationship. I want to respond to your need for help, not use your trust and vulnerability for my own gain.

Over the course of the session, Chuck gradually calmed down and was somewhat able to accept what the therapist was saying. Chuck's transference reaction—that the therapist had manipulated his dependency in order to meet the therapist's own financial need—encapsulated Chuck's generic conflict. Chuck had grown up in an orphanage and had been emotionally deprived throughout his early childhood. When he was placed with foster parents, they took advantage of his intense, unmet dependency needs. They manipulated Chuck to respond to their needs under the guise of their love for him.

By the time he was 9 years old, Chuck had become an exploited laborer on his foster parent's farm. In order to earn their approval and affection, he worked sunup to sundown on the days he wasn't in school. By the time he was 18 and ready to leave home, Chuck had long since realized that his foster parents were taking advantage of him and were not to be trusted. At some point during his early adolescence, Chuck's anxious efforts to please his foster parents had evolved into an angry defiance toward them and others. He had vowed to himself that he was never going to be dependent on or one down to anybody again. Chuck decided that he was going to be rich and powerful—strong enough that no one would ever be able to take advantage of him again.

The dramatic confrontation described above was a critical incident in therapy that proved to be a corrective emotional experience for Chuck. Chuck's old fear of being used was aroused in relation to the therapist, just as it was aroused whenever Chuck began to trust or get close to anyone. This angry encounter was a corrective experience for Chuck because his old conflict was intensely aroused but his defensive eliciting behavior did not push the therapist away. The therapist was able to tolerate Chuck's provocative attacks and continue to remain engaged with him and responsive to his concerns.

As the therapist remained available to him—and provided a different response to his conflict than Chuck had received in the past—the next feeling in his affective constellation emerged. That is, once Chuck's reactive feeling of anger was responded to, his primary feelings of hurt and deprivation emerged as the predominant issue in therapy. The therapist responded to these primary feelings effectively, and they soon began to diminish. Chuck's accompanying shame about not being "strong," however, and his recurring fear of being used by the therapist continued to be acted out in the therapeutic relationship. Thus, Chuck reexperienced over and over again with the therapist his same conflicts and fears. Each time these concerns were manifested in a conflict between them, however, Chuck received a genuinely empathic and understanding response from the therapist that was different from what he had experienced in the past.

In addition, the therapist validated Chuck's perception that he had indeed been taken advantage of as a child, but stressed that others were not always trying to do this to him now in his current relationships. The therapist also observed that as a child, Chuck had made the best and only adaption that he could have made to his unsolvable childhood predicament. Emphasizing the health component, the therapist pointed out that there was courage and strength in Chuck's defensive attempt to rise above his conflict by adopting an aggressive and defiant interpersonal style. Although this defensive attempt to rise above his conflict was no longer necessary or effective, it had served to protect him from his old feelings of vulnerability that he was determined never to expose again. Eventually, Chuck understood what the therapist meant when he said that it took just as much strength to confront his old conflicts and "weak" feelings now as an adult as it originally did to defend against them as a child by compulsively striving to achieve success and power.

With the therapist's consistent support, Chuck was gradually able to reexperience his old feelings of desperate need and simultaneous outrage at being used by his foster parents. As he gradually let go of his strong combative and competitive stance with the therapist, and let himself undergo those painful feelings of his childhood that had always seemed "disgusting and weak," Chuck began to change. First, his combative, argumentative style gave way to a friendlier comradery with the therapist. Chuck began to disclose more easily and felt less competitive with the therapist. In particular, Chuck's heightened sensitivity to needing the therapist and being taken advantage of by him diminished.

In turn, these changes with the therapist began to carry over to other relationships as well. Chuck began to establish male friendships for the first time, which his competitiveness had always precluded in the past. Previously, Chuck's relationships with women had been short-lived, superficial sexual contacts that, at times, were exploitative. As Chuck stopped defending against and came to terms with how he had been used in his childhood, he no longer continued to use women as well. This symptom abated, but Chuck was still unable to establish an intimate, egalitarian love relationship at this time in his life.

Other evidence of change came from business associates, who remarked that Chuck seemed less driven and less pressured than he used to be. Chuck's compensatory attempts to rise above his conflicts through achieving wealth and power were modulated and gave way to merely an ambitious, achieving work ethic. When an established banker in town offered Chuck a good job as a loan officer/appraiser in his real estate division, Chuck felt ready to terminate therapy. All of his problems were certainly not solved, but Chuck now felt capable of successfully moving on in life on his own. Chuck did not recapitulate his conflicts as therapy ended, but it was important to him that the therapist remain available should future crises arise. Assured of the therapist's continuing availability, Chuck terminated and did not recontact the therapist.

Pamela—Moving Away from Others

Four months after her adolescent daughter had been raped, Pamela was still in crisis. Nightmares stole her sleep, tension headaches persecuted her days. Helpless to comfort her daughter, enraged at the casual indifference of the police and courts, Pamela was afraid she was going out of control. At work, her supervisor evaluated her as irritable, sullen, and withdrawn and suggested that she seek counseling. Although she had always been reluctant to ask for help with anything, Pamela contacted a therapist when she realized that her job was in jeopardy.

The therapist was empathic to all of the different feelings and concerns that her daughter's tragedy had aroused for Pamela. To her surprise, Pamela felt understood by the therapist and soon began looking forward to their meetings. Over a slow period of months, Pamela gradually came to trust the therapist and increasingly invested herself in their relationship. After several months in treatment, Pamela reported a dream from the previous night—a recurrent dream that she had dreamt throughout her life. In the dream, Pamela was alone in a vast desert night. No other people existed in this great, silent space. The desert night was black, no light shone from stars or moon. As she walked across the endless sand, a cool, dry wind began to move lightly across her face. Pamela laid down on the sand, closed her eyes, and silently slipped away into the darkness.

Because variations of this dream had recurred throughout her life, the therapist knew that the dream expressed a lifelong generic conflict. Hoping that the dream could also provide an avenue to reach her central feeling of aloneness, the therapist tried to bridge her moving-away orientation:

Therapist:
Can you close your eyes and see the dream again?

Pamela:
Yes. *[settles back and closes her eyes]*
Therapist:
Describe what you see to me.
Pamela:
I'm walking; it's quiet and dark. I'm alone. I can feel the breeze. Now I'm lying down on the sand and I close my eyes, like going to sleep.
Therapist:
I don't want you to be there alone. Will you let me join you?
Pamela:
[pause, then slowly] Yes, you can.
Therapist:
Keep your eyes closed, and hold that same, familiar image. But you're not alone this time. I am walking toward you, and I reach my right hand out toward yours. Will you take it?
Pamela:
Mm hmm.
Therapist:
I'm now in the dream with you. We're holding hands, and walking together through the desert night. Can you see that?
Pamela:
Yes, we're walking toward the lights of a distant city. *[opens her eyes, and looks kindly at the therapist]* I'm not alone. It's good to have you with me.

This *joining* experience was a turning point in therapy. Pamela had grown up in a silent void—much like the setting in her dream. She had never known her father, and her mother was usually "away." By 10 years of age, Pamela was regularly spending entire weekends alone, fixing her own meals, and putting herself to bed while her mother was out. The dream reflected both the aloneness and emptiness of her childhood and her lifestyle adaptation of moving away from others. However, the crisis with her daughter overwhelmed her lifelong coping strategy to withdraw and be self-sufficient and aloof. In letting the therapist join her in her dark, empty space, Pamela was accepting the human contact that she longed for but had long since learned to defend against. This single experience did not resolve her conflict, but as other incidents of shared mutuality continued to occur in their relationship, Pamela began to change in three ways.

First, Pamela's conflicted affective constellation emerged. The emptiness and longing of her childhood abandonment became accessible and was shared with the therapist. To ensure that the lack of response that Pamela had experienced as a child was not recapitulated, the therapist was careful to let Pamela know that her feelings were being listened to this time. The therapist was skilled in communicating to Pamela that she was not in a dark, silent void anymore, but in a caring and concerned relationship. Pamela became more comfortable sharing her deprivation and longing with the therapist. However, the intense anger at her mother for abandoning her, and the frightening separation anxieties aroused by her rage at her mother to whom she was so insecurely attached, were worked through much more slowly. As the therapist continued to provide a corrective emotional experience in which all of these difficult feelings were supported and understood, Pamela began to change in her relationship with the therapist.

Although Pamela had become attached to the therapist because of her crisis state, she still hated needing help from anyone and still kept part of herself held away from the therapist. Only at this later point in treatment was Pamela able to further let go of her coping style, give herself up to her need of the therapist, and allow the therapist to help her. As a result, Pamela began to act less reserved toward the therapist and became more expressive than she had ever been with anyone else. She talked freely about herself with the therapist and found herself being curious and interested in the therapist's own life. Her nightmares and headaches had been alleviated several months ago, but now a sense of humor, interpersonal warmth, and graciousness were flowering as well. As Pamela talked about feeling "fuller" inside, the therapist observed that changes were occurring in her other relationships as well.

At work, her supervisor was pleased to observe that Pamela was more involved and available that she had been, which made it easier for others in the office to work with her. Whenever interpersonal conflicts surfaced at work, Pamela's initial reaction was still to withdraw and "go away." Now, however, she was better able to discuss the problems and her reactions to them with the therapist. Together, they would find new ways for her to remain involved in the situation rather than to withdraw or remain aloof as she had always done in the past. Pamela also became more accessible to her two adolescent children. For the first time, she talked more about her own feelings, interests, and personal history with them. The nearly grown children welcomed this contact and, in turn, they began to disclose more to her as well. In general, Pamela felt closer to her children than she had ever been before and even felt somewhat more capable of helping her daughter cope with the painful aftereffects of her assault.

Finally, Pamela also began to change how she responded to her long-term boyfriend. Pamela asked for more personal sharing and for more commitment from him. She asked him to talk about his feelings more and to spend more time with her. She initiated an agreement that they not date other people. It was exciting but anxiety arousing to take each of these steps forward. Her old coping style of moving away was activated each time she took a step toward others, as she still reflexively defended against the hurt that relationships had originally held for her. As the therapist repeatedly helped her work through her concerns in each of these arenas, Pamela tentatively suggested that it may be approaching time to end.

Although things had been going well for the past few months, Pamela became depressed as soon as they talked about ending. She "forgot" the next appointment and arrived late to another session. As before, the therapist continued to focus Pamela inward, and her old feelings of emptiness and abandonment emerged again. The therapist suggested that they put off setting a termination date for awhile and work further with these conflicted emotions. With more vividness and detail than before, Pamela recalled her childhood abandonment depression. Painful memories returned, such as being 8 years old, sitting alone on the living room couch, and listening to the clock tick the empty afternoon away. Pamela sobbed as she recalled her desperate childhood wish for someone to come home to. Touching the original pain so directly relieved the depression that the suggestion of terminating had precipitated. Before long, Pamela again felt ready to terminate. This time, with the therapist's reassurance that she could recontact her if necessary, Pamela successfully terminated.

CLOSING

This book has paralleled the course of therapy from beginning to end. Just as clients still have some unresolved conflicts when treatment ends, many questions and concerns about therapy remain unanswered for therapists in training. Complex psychological issues and interpersonal processes have been introduced here, but further reading and supervision is needed to help with the myriad exceptions, nuances, and complications that occur in every therapeutic relationship. Despite these limitations, essential guidelines for working with process and relationship in psychotherapy have been provided. The conceptual and intervention framework presented here should enable beginning therapists to function more effectively and autonomously as professionals and to better assimilate further training experiences. In closing, therapists have been encouraged to utilize themselves and the relationships they provide their clients as the most effective way to help clients change.

SUGGESTIONS FOR FURTHER READING

1. "The Dream" is an important psychological dimension in people's lives that has received too little attention. The reader is encouraged to read Daniel Levinson's groundbreaking work in this area, *The Seasons of a Man's Life* (New York: Ballantine, 1978). See especially pp. 91–109.

2. A dramatic illustration of Horney's concepts of rising above and interpersonal coping styles can be found in Arthur Miller's play, *Death of a Salesman* (New York: Penguin, 1949).

3. Useful information about identifying clients' generic conflicts and about negotiating successful terminations can be found in J. Mann, *Time-Limited Psychotherapy* (Cambridge: Harvard University Press, 1973).

4. Readers who have found the ideas presented here to be helpful are likely to enjoy Irving Yalom's modern classic, *Existential Psychotherapy* (New York: Basic Books, 1980), and *Love's Executioner* (New York: Basic Books, 1989).

5. For more experienced therapists, Stephen Mitchell's book, *Relational Concepts in Psychoanalysis* (Cambridge: Harvard University Press, 1988) provides an excellent theoretical statement of interpersonal psychotherapy. See especially Chapters 9 and 10.

BIBLIOGRAPHY

Alexander, F., & French, T. M. (1946). *Psychoanalytic therapy: Principles and applications.* University of Nebraska Press, 1980.

Anchin, J., & Kiesler, D. (1982). *Handbook of interpersonal psychotherapy.* New York: Pergamon.

Anderson, C. M., & Steward, S. (1983). *Mastering resistance: A practical guide to family therapy.* New York: Guilford Press.

Bandura, A. (1977). Self efficacy: Toward a unifying theory of behavioral change. *Psychological Review, 84*(2), 191–215.

Baumrind, D. (1967). Child care practices anteceding three patterns of preschool behavior. *Genetic Psychology Monographs, 75*, 43–88.

Baumrind, D. (1971). Current patterns of parental authority. *Developmental Psychology Monograph, 4* (1, Pt. 2).

Boszormeni-Nagy, I., & Spark, G. (1973). *Invisible loyalties: Reciprocity in inter-generational family therapy.* New York: Harper & Row.

Bowen, M. (1966). The use of family theory in clinical practice. *Comprehensive Psychiatry, 7*, 345–376.

Bowlby, J. (1988). *A secure base.* New York: Basic Books.

Bugental, J. (1965). *The search for authenticity: An existential-analytic approach to psychotherapy.* New York: Holt, Rinehart & Winston.

Cashdan, S. (1988). *Object relations therapy.* New York: Norton.

Davanloo, H. (Ed.). *Short-term dynamic psychotherapy.* New York: Aronson.

Engle, L., & Ferguson, T. 1990. *Imaginary Crimes.* Boston: Houghton Mifflin.

Erikson, E. (1986). *Childhood and society* (2nd ed.). New York: Norton.

Farley, J. (1979, January). Family separation-individuation tolerance: A developmental conceptualization of the nuclear family. *Journal of Marital and Family Therapy*, 61–67.

Fraiberg, S., Adelson, E., & Shaprio, V. (1975). Ghosts in the nursery: A psychoanalytical approach to the problems of impaired mother-infant relationships. *Journal of the American Academy of Child Psychiatry, 14*, 387–421.

Fromm, E. (1982). *Escape from freedom.* New York: Avon Books.

Fromm-Reichmann, F. (1960). *Principles of intensive psychotherapy.* Chicago: University of Chicago Press.

Gilligan, C. (1982). *In a different voice: Psychological theory and women's development.* Cambridge: Harvard University Press.

Goldenberg, I., & Goldenberg, H. (1991). *Family therapy: An overview* (3rd ed.). Pacific Grove, CA: Brooks/Cole.

Greenberg, J., & Mitchell, S. (1983). *Object relations in psychoanalytic theory*. Cambridge: Harvard University Press.

Greenson, R. (1967). *The technique and practice of psychoanalysis* (Vol. 1). New York: International Universities Press.

Guest, J. (1980). *Ordinary people*. (Film directed by R. Redford.)

Guggenbuhl-Crain, A. (1971). *Power in the helping professions*. New York: Springer.

Haley, J. (1967). Toward a theory of pathological systems. In G. H. Zuk & I. Boszormenyi-Nagy (Eds.), *Family therapy and disturbed families*. Palo Alto, CA: Science and Behavior Books.

Haley, J. (1980). *Leaving home: The therapy of disturbed young people*. New York: McGraw-Hill.

Hartman, E. (1978, October). Using eco-maps and genograms in family therapy. *Social Casework*, 464–476.

Horney, K. (1966). *Our inner conflicts*. New York: Norton.

Horney, K. (1970). *Neurosis and human growth*. New York: Norton.

Horowitz, M., Marmar, C., Krupnick, J., Wilner, N., Kaltreider, N., & Wallerstein, R. (1984). *Personality styles and brief psychotherapy*. New York: Basic Books.

Kafka, F. (1966). *Letter to his father*. New York: Schocken.

Kelly, G. (1963). *The psychology of personal constructs*. New York: Norton.

Kohut, H. (1977). *The restoration of the self*. New York: International Universities Press.

Klerman, G. L., Rounsaville, B., Chevron, E., & Weissman, M. (1984). *Interpersonal psychotherapy of depression*. New York: Basic Books.

Laing, R. D., & Esterson, A. (1970). *Sanity, madness and the family*. Middlesex, England: Penguin.

Levinson, D. (1978). *The seasons of a man's life*. New York: Ballantine Books.

Mahler, M., Pine, F., & Bergman, A. (1975). *The psychological birth of the human infant*. New York: Basic Books.

Malan, D. H. (1976). *The frontier of brief psychotherapy: An example of the convergence of research and clinical practice*. New York: Plenum.

Mann, J. (1973). *Time-limited psychotherapy*. Cambridge: Harvard University Press.

Mann, J., & Goldman, R. (1982). *A casebook in time-limited psychotherapy*. New York: McGraw-Hill.

Masterson, J. (1972). *Treatment of the borderline adolescent: A developmental approach*. New York: Wiley.

Masterson, J. (1976). *Psychotherapy of the borderline adult: A developmental approach*. New York: Brunner/Mazel.

Miller, A. (1949). *Death of a salesman*. New York: Penguin.

Miller, A. (1981). *Prisoners of childhood*. New York: Basic Books.

Miller, A. (1984). *For your own good*. New York: Farrar, Straus & Giroux.

Minuchin, S. (1974). *Families and family therapy*. Cambridge: Harvard University Press.

Mitchell, S. (1988). *Relational concepts in psychoanalysis*. Cambridge: Harvard University Press.

Mueller, W., & Kell, B. (1966). *Impact and change: A study of counseling relationships*. Englewood Cliffs, NJ: Prentice-Hall.

Olson, D. H., McCubbin, H. I., Barnes, H., Larsen, A., Muxen, M., & Wilson, M. *Families: What makes them work*. Newbury Park, CA: Sage.

Passons, W. (1975). *Gestalt approaches in counseling*. New York: Holt, Rinehart & Winston.

Pinderhughes, H. (1989). *Understanding race, ethnicity and power*. New York: Free Press.

Rogers, C. (1951). *Client-centered therapy*. Boston: Houghton Mifflin.

Rogers, C. (1959). A theory of therapy, personality and interpersonal relationships as developed in the client-centered framework. In S. Koch (Ed.), *Psychology: A study of science* (Vol. 3), *Formulations of the person and the social context*. New York: McGraw-Hill.

Satir, V. (1967). *Conjoint family therapy*. Palo Alto, CA: Science and Behavior Books.

Schatzman, M. (1973). *Soul murder: Persecution in the family*. New York: Random House.

Seligman, M. (1975). *Helplessness*. New York: W. H. Freeman.

Shapiro, D. (1965). *Neurotic styles*. New York: Basic Books.

Sifneos, P. (1979). *Short-term dynamic psychotherapy: Evaluation and technique*. New York: Plenum.

Solomon, M. (1973). A developmental, conceptual premise for family therapy. *Family Process, 12*(2), 179–188.

Steinbeck, J. (1952). *East of eden*. New York: Viking.

Stierlin, H. (1972). *Separating parents and adolescents*. New York: Quadrangle.

Strupp, H., & Binder, J. (1984). *Psychotherapy in a new key: A guide to time-limited dynamic psychotherapy*. New York: Basic Books.

Sullivan, H. S. (1968). *The interpersonal theory of psychiatry*. New York: Norton.

Sullivan, H. S. (1970). *The psychiatric interview*. New York: Norton.

Teyber, E. (1981). Structural family relations: A review. *Family Therapy, 1*, 39–48.

Teyber, E. (1983). Effects of the parental coalition on adolescent emancipation from the family. *Journal of Marital and Family Therapy, 9*, 89–99.

Teyber, E. (1992) *Children and divorce: A practical guide for parents*. New York: Lexington Books/ MacMillan.

Wachtel, P. (1982). *Psychoanalysis and behavior therapy: Toward an integration*. New York: Basic Books.

Weiss, J., & Sampson, H. (1986). *The psychoanalytic process: Theory, clinical observation and empirical research*. New York: Guilford.

Wenar, C. (1990). *Psychopathology from infancy through adolescence* (2nd ed.). New York: Random House.

Wheelis, A. (1974). *How people change*. New York: Harper & Row.

White, R. (1959). Motivation reconsidered: The concept of competence. *Psychology Review, 66*, 297–333.

Winnicott, D. W. (1965). Ego distortion in terms of true and false self, 1960b. In *The maturational process and the facilitating environment*. New York: International Universities Press.

Woodward, B. (1984). *Wired*. New York: Simon & Schuster.

Yalom, I. (1980). *Existential psychotherapy*. New York: Basic Books.

Yalom, I. (1989). *Love's executioner*. New York: Basic Books.

NAME INDEX

SUBJECT INDEX